A City in War:
American Views
On Barcelona and the
Spanish Civil War, 1936-39

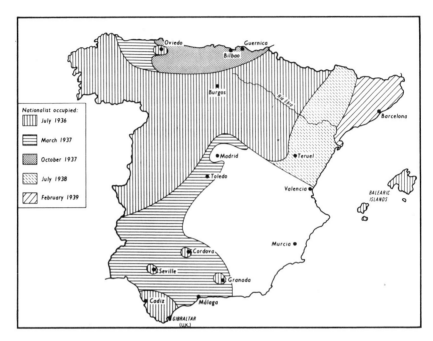

Nationalist occupied:

|||| July 1936

≡ March 1937

▦ October 1937

▨ July 1938

▧ February 1939

Oviedo Guernica
Bilbao
Burgos
Barcelona
Madrid Teruel
Toledo
Valencia
BALEARIC ISLANDS
Murcia
Cordova
Seville Granada
Cadiz Málaga
GIBRALTAR (U.K.)

Spain, Spanish Civil War, 1936–39

Source: Eugene K. Keefe, et al., AREA HANDBOOK FOR SPAIN (Washington, D.C.: U.S. Government Printing Office, 1976).

A City in War:
American Views
On Barcelona and the
Spanish Civil War, 1936-39

Edited by

James W. Cortada

SR Scholarly Resources Inc.
Wilmington, Delaware

Scholarly Resources Inc.
104 Greenhill Avenue
Wilmington, Delaware 19805

Library of Congress Cataloging in Publication Data
Main entry under title:

A City in war.

Bibliography: p.
Includes index.
1. Spain—History—Civil War, 1936–1939—Sources.
2. Barcelona (Spain)—History—Sources. 3. Spain—
History—Civil War, 1936–1939—Foreign public opinion,
American—Sources. 4. Spain—History—Civil War,
1936–1939—Diplomatic history—Sources. 5. Public
opinion—United States—History—20th century—
Sources. I. Cortada, James W.
DP269.27.B3C57 1985   946.081   84-20302
ISBN 0-8420-2229-5

To
Dora

CONTENTS

INTRODUCTION

I

IN EXAMINING THE bibliography on the Spanish Civil War, one is struck by the paucity of material dealing with the role of all urban centers except Madrid.[1] The capital city of the Second Republic was the most important center of military activity throughout the Civil War because it was the primary target of Nationalist military campaigns. General Francisco Franco and the other rebels reasoned that if they could seize Madrid, they would have control over the government, thereby bringing to a close the Civil War.[2] Little work has been done by historians on life and affairs in Barcelona during the Civil War, even though it was Spain's second largest city, with a population of over one million during the 1930s, and was for a time the capital of the Republic.[3]

Barcelona is especially useful to historians of modern European history. Many of the events that took place in this Spanish community presaged similar trauma throughout Europe during World War II. Its political life was frenetic; its economic condition changed radically; and it was bombed, crowded with refugees, attacked, and occupied. Bombing of major urban centers was perfected by Italian and German air units during the Civil War, and one of their major targets was Barcelona. The use of combat troop transportation and the implementation of improved technologies in weaponry and logistical support

---

[1]For a discussion of this effort see James W. Cortada, ed., *An Historical Dictionary of the Spanish Civil War, 1936–1939* (Westport, Conn., 1982), in which over forty specialists discuss the topic.

[2]Some of the more important recent work on Madrid and consequently on modern European cities at war include Robert Colodny, *The Struggle for Madrid* (New York, 1958); George Hills, *The Battle for Madrid* (New York, 1977); Vincente Rojo, *Asi fue la defensa de Madrid* (Madrid, 1967); and most recently, Dan Kurzman, *Miracle of November: Madrid's Epic Stand, 1936* (New York, 1980).

[3]Some of the more recent important monographic work include Manuel Cruells, two books, *Els fets de maig. Barcelona, 1937* (Barcelona, 1970) and *El separatisme català durant la guerra civil* (Barcelona, 1975); José Antonio González Casanova, *Elecciones en Barcelona, 1931–1936* (Madrid, 1969); J. Arias Velasco, *La Hacienda de la Generalitat, 1931–1938* (Barcelona, 1977); Luis Romero, "La sublevación en Barcelona," *Tiempo Histórico* 7 (1978): 94–118.

that were common to World War II were first exercised in and around Barcelona and central Spain. The effects of campaigning and bombing on urban centers—the need for air raid shelters and the special use of medicine, food supplies, and municipal services—were noticed by military planners all over Europe as they watched closely events in Spain, especially in Barcelona. Diplomatic personnel in the city were careful to comment on such topics for officials back home. For this reason it was possible to prepare a volume of collected papers drawn from diplomatic sources that describe a modern city at war.

The material available to historians on Barcelona is massive and yet hardly touched for the modern period. City records were not badly damaged during this and earlier civil wars, and military records of the various armies operating in Catalonia exist.[4] While memoirs and diaries are not as extensive for the Spanish Civil War as, for instance, for the civil wars of Great Britain, France, and the United States, passing comments giving us a perspective on life in Barcelona do exist. In the pages that follow, these will be used to enhance the material presented within the body of the book. Yet by far the most consistently valuable sources of information on Barcelona available outside of Spain are consular papers. Each major European and American government maintained consular offices in Barcelona, since it was and is one of the most important port cities of the Mediterranean. The most useful consular files for nineteenth and twentieth-century Barcelona are those of Great Britain, France, and the United States—almost none of which have been studied by historians.[5]

In the pages that follow, American diplomatic papers bearing on the city of Barcelona during the Civil War have been brought together in an attempt to shed light on what happened there from 1936 to 1939. Naval, consular, ambassadorial, and military files were brought together in a chronological fashion to recreate events in Barcelona. (Because the American embassy moved to Barcelona as Republican-held territory shrank in size, files dealing with the city have been pulled out of embassy records as well.) As a collection they provide a view of Barcelona written by competent observers who were trained to record key events and who had working relationships with important city officials. Much memoir documentation drawn from British and American visitors and residents is also presented in the introductory sections to each chapter in order to enhance our understanding of issues and feelings. In addition, enclosures consular writers included with their telegrams and dispatches have been reproduced when they have historical value. The blend of

---

[4]James W. Cortada, "Libraries and Archives of Barcelona," *The Library Chronicle*, 42 (Winter 1978): 98–112.

[5]I have been able to use to advantage this material in the past, see "British Consular Reports on Economic and Political Developments in Cataluña, 1842–1875," *Cuadernos de Historia Económica*, 10 (December 1973): 149–98; "Catalan Politics and Economics, 1906–1911: The View From the American Consulate at Barcelona," *Cuadernos de Historia Económica*, 13 (May 1975): 129–81.

available contemporary materials allows a statement to be made about what happened at the time and, equally important, gives a sense of life in wartime Barcelona. In short, this collection of material contributes to a historical appreciation of the political, economic, military, and social life of Spain's second largest city during one of its most critical moments.

II

Neither participants nor historians have agreed about the origins of the Spanish Civil War. Some, like Ricardo de la Cierva and Raymond Carr, have seen this conflict as a continuation of a long-standing battle between liberals and conservatives for political dominance in Spain during an era of significant economic and social change, a battle that goes as far back as the eighteenth century. Others, such as a host of Nationalist historians or even Gabriel Jackson, who has argued the cause of the Republic favorably, have cast the Civil War in a different light by suggesting that it was a prelude to World War II, a struggle between the forces of light and modernity (democracy) and those of darkness and dictatorship (fascism). Each camp confused the terms. Thus Nationalist supporters argued that they supported democracy and were the modern view while pro-Republican historians felt the opposite. A more recent set of interpretations is thematic in nature; for example, it has been posited that the economic malfunctions in Spain in our century caused the Civil War. Edward Malefakis has clearly identified the significance of agriculture. The anticlerical policies of the Republic brought on the Civil War according to some scholars (especially by José M. Sánchez), while many subscribe to the thesis that the army thought the government too liberal and therefore sought to destroy it.[6] While it is not the intention of this book to review in detail the causes or consequences of the Civil War, it is important to have at least a brief understanding of the problems Spain faced as they affected Barcelona.

Throughout the nineteenth century, Spain struggled within itself politically as it worked its way out of the disasters of the Napoleonic wars (1808–14), two civil wars (1833–40 and 1868–74), and the loss of all of its American colonies (1808–20 in South America; 1898, Cuba and Puerto Rico). Spain

---

[6]On the social origins and causes of the Spanish Civil War see Gerald Brenan, *The Spanish Labyrinth* (Cambridge, 1943): Pierre Broué and Emile Témime, *La révolution et la guerre d'Espagne* (Paris, 1970); Raymond Carr, *The Republic and the Civil War in Spain* (London, 1971); Edward Malefakis, *Agrarian Reform and Peasant Revolution in Spain* (New Haven, 1970). For the military aspects see Stanley G. Payne, *Politics and the Military in Modern Spain* (Stanford, 1967); for a political view of the Republic an important work is by Paul Preston, *The Coming of the Spanish Civil War* (London, 1978) but do not overlook an earlier work on the political right by Richard Robinson, *The Origins of Franco Spain* (Newton Abbot, 1970). For a recent general overview see Hugh Thomas, *The Spanish Civil War* (New York, 1977); for a specific discussion on the origins and its various interpretations see Gerald Meaker, "Origins," in Cortada, *An Historical Dictionary of the Spanish Civil War*, pp. 371–77.

remained a monarchy until 1931, but for a brief interval between 1868 and 1874. As time passed, however, the power of the throne diminished while that of ministerial governments grew. Liberals and conservatives alternated in office in the second half of the nineteenth century and through the early decades of the twentieth. The Spanish economy was dominated by agriculture, but it also saw the birth of an industrial and banking revolution that, by the end of the 1800s, had marked the land with major industrial, banking, and transportation centers, centers still developing in the present century. Oligarchic, land-based political control in many parts of Spain remained despite a growing shift of population from the agricultural to the industrial and urban centers.

It was during this period that a middle class became active in politics and in the economy and that labor movements (especially anarchist) emerged, particularly in Barcelona. Strikes, economic crisis, political rivalries and a sense of change created tensions seriously threatening the fabric of Spanish society by the early 1900s. The process of change was slow in Spain owing primarily to poor communications, under-capitalized industries that were slow to develop, and widespread illiteracy. Traditional sources of power—monarchy, army, landed aristocracy, the Church—felt threatened by the change to more modern economic, political, and social structures and consequently blocked the metamorphosis that Spain was experiencing. What happened in Barcelona clearly illustrated the processes at work.

Barcelona played a central role in the development of an industrial economy because it served as a major port on the Mediterranean. This city was a major textile manufacturing center whose cotton products were sold all over Spain, in Europe, and in Latin America. Some of the most important banking enterprises in Spain were also centered in Barcelona as were rail lines to France and to the inner provinces of the Iberian peninsula. More European than Spanish in its ambiance, Barcelona was frequently likened to a miniature Paris by many visitors before the Civil War. Its energetic citizens were far less introspective than their counterparts in other Iberian urban centers, who rarely felt influences from other countries. As a large industrial center, it had commercial ties to other cities throughout Europe and Latin America. Its growing number of factories and mills attracted jobless peasants from southern Spain and also led to the birth of a significant labor movement. Barcelona was a home to anarchism, the *Confederación Nacional de Trabajo* (CNT) and the *Unión General de Trabajadores* (UGT) similar to the French socialist organization, and to a patchwork of unions and labor associations. By the time that the Second Spanish Republic was established in April 1931, Barcelona had become a major source of support for a republic with an active political life equal to any found in Madrid, London, or Paris.[7]

---

[7]For Barcelona over the past century and a half see R. Alberich Roselló, *Un siglo de Barcelona* (Barcelona, 1944); F. Curet, *Visions barcelonines, 1760–1860*, 3 vols. (Barcelona,

No understanding of life in Barcelona is possible without an appreciation for the volatile anarchist activities of the Catalan region. Barcelona was the only major urban center in Europe ever to be controlled by anarchist leadership. In addition, the anarchists represented a considerable percentage of the city's population. The role of the anarchists during the 1930s in Barcelona and throughout Catalonia is central to any understanding of Spanish political life during the Second Republic. While the diplomats reporting on political life in Catalonia frequently underestimated the significance of anarchism, the citizens of Barcelona did not.

Spanish anarchism first appeared in Spain during the 1860s. As the conditions of workers throughout the country deteriorated in the second half of the nineteenth century, workers were drawn to the anarchist politics and philosophies of Bakunin. This was particularly true in Andalusia, where the number of landless peasants was often a half million, not a small community when one considers that the total population of Spain at the time was less than sixteen million. Anarchism also appealed to the large proletariat in Catalonia, many of whom were recent arrivals from Andalusia.

The CNT was formed in 1911 in an effort to organize anarchist activities. A trade union heavily influenced by anarchist thought, it quickly developed a powerful base in Barcelona, home of thousands of textile workers, machinists, construction laborers, and peasants. By 1917 the CNT had become the largest labor union in Spain and dominated labor activities in Catalonia. By August 1931, the CNT claimed 400 thousand members in Catalonia alone. Of these, 58 percent of all workers in Barcelona were members. Despite erosion in membership during the Second Republic, in large part caused by the growth of other unions and political parties, 30 percent of Barcelona's workers were still members of the CNT at the start of the Civil War. In 1927 a more militant anarchist movement called the *Federación Anarquista Ibérica* (FAI) was formed. During the Civil War, it would profoundly influence politics and life in Barcelona and even affect republican affairs in general. We do not know how large an organization it was, but its leadership was relatively efficient and frequently worked closely with the CNT, thereby increasing the group's significance in Barcelona.

In July 1936, the second largest group was the *Partido Obrero de Unificación Marxista* (POUM). It, too, was militant and had ties to the anarchists, often practicing the strident policies of the FAI. After the rebellion by army officers was suppressed in Barcelona, this party struggled with others for political control of the city. The contest was quickly resolved as the much larger CNT dominated the government of the city. As the documents below

---

1952–1953); F. Soldevila Zubiburu, *Història de Catalunya* (Barcelona, 1963); Alberto Balcells, *Crisis económica y agitación social en Cataluña de 1930 a 1936* (Barcelona, 1971); J. Carrera Pujal, *Historia política de Cataluña en el siglo XIX*, 7 vols. (Barcelona, 1957–1958); Jaime Vicens Vives, *Cataluña en el siglo XIX* (Madrid, 1961).

suggest, committees formed by the CNT executed municipal policies and programs. Indeed, by decree of 24 October 1936, the regional government officially acknowledged this fact, thereby giving quasi-official status to many of the CNT's efforts.

As the war continued during the summer months of 1936, the role of the more militant FAI became increasingly significant. The CNT worked with existing institutions to improve the lot of its members. The FAI, on the other hand, advocated immediate revolution as the method for helping its members. It did not hesitate to kill opponents or to use propaganda extensively to articulate its views. It conducted strikes in Barcelona and formed armed bands. Led by Buenaventura Durruti, anarchist brigades were some of the first to do battle with the rebels in western Catalonia and in Huesca, thus garnering much publicity favorable to anarchism within Barcelona. In short, the FAI increased political and economic tensions in Barcelona.

As the CNT and FAI competed with each other for political power in Barcelona and throughout Catalonia, poorly organized anarchist units could hardly sustain a long-term military campaign on the western front, particularly in Huesca. Thus tensions on the battle front, coupled with political and philosophical differences within the anarchist movement, ensured a lively political life in Barcelona. The documents below and the work of many historians offer considerable evidence, for example, that the events of May 1937 grew out of these political rivalries.

To complicate Catalan political life even further, there were a variety of liberal, conservative, socialist, and Marxist parties within the labor community, all competing with the anarchists. A similar matrix of parties attracted the loyalties of the middle class and even of the local upper classes and aristocracy. The most significant of these other parties for any understanding of labor politics was the POUM. This party advocated collectivization and reflected Leon Trotsky's ideas about permanent revolution. Although small, its influence on Catalan politics should not be minimized because it had good links to the larger anarchist movement and was able to express its views effectively with aggressive propaganda campaigns. It, too, supported militarized bands and fielded fighting units. The POUM also had a romantic utopian aura that attracted educated members of the middle class, some of whom sat in various Catalan and municipal governments during the Civil War. Some foreign visitors to Spain, including George Orwell, aligned with the POUM.

The POUM also had links to the communist movement, a political faction that grew in enormous proportions during the Civil War. The Spanish Communist Party, with the help of the Soviet Union, sought to gain control of the Republican government and dominate all the affairs of the Republic. POUM was a rival since it did not submit to the dictates of the national party. By the summer of 1937, the Communist Party had effectively taken control of the Republican government and in the process destroyed the POUM. The influence of anarchist parties also diminished sharply throughout the Republican zone as a direct consequence of the May events. The death of the POUM is a major aspect of those May events.

Thus, whether looking at life in Barcelona before or after the start of the Civil War, politics represented a sophisticated, extensive, and often dangerous configuration of activities involving all social classes. The statistics on memberships suggest that a high percentage of Barcelona's working classes and of the middle class were politically active. In addition to these parties and quarrels, socialists in Republican Spain competed among themselves for political power in Madrid and in Barcelona. While the majority of their activities lie outside the scope of this book, it is important to keep in mind that factions existed within the Socialist Party that were as strident and divisive as those within the anarchist movement. The factionalism among the socialists is important because it was this party that dominated national politics at the start of the Civil War and provided the majority of the political leadership of the Catalan governments during the Second Republic.

These same leaders were also regional nationalists. In general, their links to the much larger and important anarchist movement in Barcelona were limited. They believed that the anarchists threatened the regionalist aspirations of the Catalans. In fact, a large number of the workers in Barcelona were not native Catalans but Andalusians who had moved north to find work in Catalan factories. The regionalists, all local and generally from the middle and upper classes, added yet another layer of complexity to the political life of Barcelona.

Barcelona was the capital of Catalan cultural and political aspirations. Surrounded by four Catalan-dominated provinces (Lérida, Gerona, Tarragona, Barcelona), the city had a cultural and political base that enhanced its already important economic position within Spain. This circumstance added to its differentiation from the Castilian, Andalusian, and Basque urban centers, which did not prosper economically and which had cultural and linguistic traditions unique unto themselves. By the time the Republic came into being, Barcelona was a distinct urban center with its own political, social, and economic concerns buttressed by a healthy local language and culture.[8]

During the days of the Second Republic (1931–36), leaders of the Catalan political community argued the case for an autonomous government within Spain. The Cortes finally authorized the establishment of a regional government on 9 September 1932. The Generalidad (known as the *Generalitat* in Catalan), named after the previous independent Catalan parliament and government of the Middle Ages, had its own president, Francisco Macìa and

---

[8]Regionalism in Spain has been the subject of much recent writing. In English the most useful introduction to this problem is by Stanley G. Payne, *Basque Nationalism* (Reno, Nevada, 1975), which has considerable material on Catalonia; see also Victor Alba, *Catalunya sense cap ni peus* (Barcelona, 1971); Fèlix Cucurull, *Orígens i evolució del federalisme català* (Barcelona, 1970); Maximiano Garcia Vero, *Historia del nacionalismo catalán*, 2 vols. (Madrid, 1967); Pierre Vilar, *La Catalogne dans l'Espagne moderne*, 3 vols. (Paris, 1963).

then Luis Companys upon the former's death in 1933. It also had a cabinet and a legislative body. These institutions were in Barcelona, where they tackled municipal and regional problems with the aim of improving education, road and rail communications, and telegraph and telephone service. They established new agencies and commercial codes and encouraged new building construction, expansion of local cultural events, and economic life. This active political environment also provided a number of members to the Second Republic's government. The political mood of both the local government and the principal leaders of Barcelona was liberal, republican, and regionalist. While friction between the central government in Madrid and that of Barcelona remained, it seemed that a middle-class Catalan society was flowering concurrently; and Barcelona had a growing proletarian political movement reflecting both the economic importance of the community and its ever-expanding urban work force.[9]

Other problems and frictions existed at the national level that would ultimately affect Barcelona. The Republic launched a major agricultural reform program designed to break up large landed estates (although in Catalonia small farms dominated) in order to distribute land ownership among a large, landless agricultural work force. The landed politicos saw this reform as a threat to their existence both politically and economically. The departure of King Alfonso XIII in April 1931, which made possible the establishment of a republic, had already signaled to conservatives and especially monarchists that the "other" Spain was rising to power, composed of left-wing political movements, workers, and urban and anticlerical constituencies. Further, reforms intended by the Republic to modernize and reorganize the army led to rising discontent within the armed forces and by 1936 had created what Stanley G. Payne termed an impasse which "triggered a reaction more violent than anything the army or the country had previously experienced."[10]

The Republic faced other problems. For example, it sought to separate church and state, an action which offended supporters of the old order. The constitution separated the two institutions; the Republic next cut salaries of clerics and reduced Catholic influence in public schools. The Republic also faced an economic crisis, brought on as much by the world depression as by the inability of the central government to improve conditions. The scene was set for a major confrontation between two Spains: one liberal; the other conservative, pro-Catholic, landed and noble, and fearful of a "communist" or "red" state usurping traditional sources of power within Spain. The former

---

[9]For the specific period of 1931–36, some of the more useful monographs include Isidre Molas, *Lliga Catalana*, 2 vols. (Barcelona, 1972) and his *El sistema de partits polítics a Catalunya (1931–1936)* (Barcelona, 1972) for political activities; for economic issues see Albert Balcells, *El problema agrari a Catalunya, 1890–1936* (Barcelona, 1968) and Josep Maria Bricall, *Política económica de la Generalitat (1936–1939)* (Barcelona, 1970); Monserrat Duch et al., "La autonomiá catalane durante la Segunda República (1931–1939)," *ARBOR*, 109 (1981): 95–109.

[10]Payne, *Politics and the Military in Modern Spain*, p. 453.

included such groups as intellectuals and much of the middle class and large urban work forces. The latter counted among its supporters such elements as the church, some peasants, most of the upper ranks of the armed services, the wealthy and titled, and monarchists.[11]

Throughout the 1930s, Barcelona supported the Republic and when the army finally revolted on 19 July 1936, it again displayed its loyalty to the Republic by suppressing attempts by local rebels to seize power in the city. Barcelona's ability to suppress the Nationalists during the first several days of the Civil War was significant because it saved all of Catalonia and much of east-central Spain (Aragon) for the Republic. From the very first day of the conflict, then, Barcelona played a major role in both political and military affairs.[12]

In the three years that followed, Barcelona was a funnel through which members of the International Brigades came to fight in the Republic's armies. Supplies for the Loyalists from the Soviet Union, France, and other countries also passed through its harbors. Troops, and later refugees, were quartered here. In May 1937, Barcelona was the scene of a mini-civil war between those Republicans supporting the anarchists, on the one hand, and, on the other, those siding with the Communist Party and its allies in a struggle for control over Republican political affairs. Of considerable importance to both camps was the dominance of Barcelona and Catalonia's contribution to the war effort. The anarchists were defeated and persecuted. The resulting split of loyalties within the Republican zone was somewhat minimized by having the Republican government take increasing charge of the affairs of Catalonia and Barcelona.[13] Finally, in late 1938, Nationalist forces turned their attention toward Catalonia and Barcelona; a major campaign that proved to be the last significant one of the Civil War was begun by launching a drive at Christmas for the conquest of northeast Spain to the French frontier. The Second Republic moved to Barcelona on 31 November 1938, making that city capital of the national government before it fled during the final weeks of the war through northern Catalonia and ultimately into exile. In the final several months of the Civil War, the Nationalists conquered one Catalan community after another and occupied Barcelona on 26 January 1939. The Civil War ended in Spain in late March and on 1 April 1939, General Franco proclaimed an end to hostilities.

---

[11]Recent research on the Republic is reflected in Thomas, *The Spanish Civil War*; Burnett Bolloten, *The Spanish Revolution* (Chapel Hill, 1979), which discusses politics; Ramón Tamames, *La República La era de Franco* (Madrid, 1973) for a Marxian view heavy with economic analysis; Ronald Fraser, *Blood of Spain: An Oral History of the Spanish Civil War* (New York, 1979).

[12]On Barcelona in July 1936, see Thomas, *The Spanish Civil War*, pp. 232–36; Frederic Escofet, *Al servei de Catalunya i de la república* (Paris, 1973), 2, passim; Francisco Lacruz, *El alzamiento, la revolución y el terror en Barcelona* (Barcelona, 1943).

[13]Bolloten provides an excellent review of the May Days in *The Spanish Revolution*, pp. 368–430; and on the military campaigns in Catalonia see Col. José Manuel Martínez Bande, *La campaña en Cataluña* (Barcelona, 1979).

III

With the retirement of Claude I. Dawson as Consul General on 6 March 1936, the post of United States Consulate General in Barcelona remained in the hands of Consul Lynn W. Franklin. This diplomat was the author of the numerous telegrams and dispatches, collected below, dealing with the complicated early stages of the Civil War in Barcelona. The conflict brought its own problems and excitement for the consulate. Of primary importance was concern for the lives and properties of American citizens; secondarily, there was the reporting of local conditions to the Department of State. It should be noted that the policy of the American government was one of neutrality. Officially, it favored neither side and attempted to keep the American public uninterested in the war. While few telegrams and dispatches that deal with the implementation of American foreign policy were selected for this book, suffice it to note that diplomats in Barcelona expended considerable energy in this direction.[14]

Franklin was born in Ocean Grove, New Jersey, on 11 June 1888. He went to work for the State Department in 1912 in Tegucigalpa and went on to serve as a vice consul in San Salvador, later at Callao-Lima (1916) and at Guayaquil in 1918. He subsequently worked in Washington, D.C., served as a delegate to the Pan American Commercial Conference in 1919, went back to San Salvador, and later moved on to Hong Kong (1924). He then served in various posts in the Orient. The department assigned him to Barcelona on 25 October 1933. Thus he had become familiar with Catalan affairs long before the start of the Civil War, and after having served in Spanish-speaking countries, he had acquired command of the language and understood Hispanic culture.[15] On 2 June 1937, soon after receiving another promotion within the Foreign Service, he was sent as consul to Stockholm and eventually ended his career with service in the United States.[16]

Franklin spent the early months of the Civil War working to ensure the lives of Americans living in his consular district (which included all of Catalonia), advising local residents and consulting with the Catalan government regarding concerns over American properties. During the summer months, his office managed to help some three hundred Americans evacuate Barcelona. Franklin was convinced that the local situation was far too dangerous for Americans and thus urged their removal, requested gas masks for his staff,

---

[14]The general theme of U.S.–Spanish relations during this period is well served with several monographs: Allen Guttmann, *American Neutrality and the Spanish Civil War* (Boston, 1963) and his *The Wound in The Heart: America and the Spanish Civil War* (New York, 1962); Foster Jay Taylor, *The United States and the Spanish Civil War* (New York, 1956); Richard P. Traina, *American Diplomacy and the Spanish Civil War* (Bloomington, 1968).

[15]Department of State, *Register of the Department of State, July 1, 1936* (Washington, D.C., 1936), pp. 174–75.

[16]For additional details see Department of State, *Biographical Register of the Department of State, September 1, 1944* (Washington, D.C., 1944), p. 77.

and obtained permission from Washington to close the consulate should it prove too dangerous to remain. Since his office was located on the Plaza de Cataluña, in the heart of the city and traditionally either a rallying point for demonstrations or the locale for street fighting, his concerns were justified.[17]

On 24 July 1936, Mahlon F. Perkins was named Consul General in Barcelona, where he served until May 1937. Perkins was born in North Adams, Massachusetts, on 23 November 1882. In 1911 he became a vice consul and subsequently held a number of posts in the Far East until 1934 when he came back to the Department of State as an historical advisor. His next post was Barcelona. He brought to his new job in Spain little or no knowledge of the language or Spanish culture. However, in his new assignment he quickly took advantage of the skills evident in the consular staff to make up for his personal lack of understanding of Spanish affairs. As the reader will note, his dispatches and telegrams reported accurately on current events, which is remarkable considering that he came to Barcelona at a particularly critical period during the Civil War. After his tour of duty in Spain he held various other posts in Europe and in Washington, D.C.[18]

As his telegrams and dispatches suggest, Perkins paid particularly close attention to domestic developments in Barcelona and in Catalonia, while carrying out the normal functions of a consular official as best he could under the difficult circumstances of war. He believed that the radical and multiple political groups in Barcelona had virtually unlimited freedom to act and that the Republican government had little or no control over them, thus making the possibility of American casualties likely. He had to worry about the security of Americans and the protection of their properties. He also had to track American volunteers coming into Spain to fight for the Republic within the International Brigades.[19]

When Perkins left Barcelona on 12 June 1937, Vice Consul Douglas Flood assumed responsibilities for the consulate. Flood was born in Macon, Missouri on 11 February 1902, practiced law between 1928 and 1931, then became a diplomat. He served as vice consul in Ottawa and, in 1933, in the same capacity in Buenos Aires. The following year he transferred to Asunción, finally arriving in Barcelona as vice consul in September 1936. He remained in Spain until the end of the Civil War, then moved first to Naples and afterwards to Rome during the early years of World War II, and came back into the Iberian peninsula as third secretary at the embassy in Lisbon, Portugal, in 1942. Flood brought to his job in Barcelona some knowledge of Spanish and Hispanic culture, not to mention a clear experience in legal matters, all of which proved useful in his service in Spain.[20]

---

[17]Eula McDonald, "Highlights in the History of the United States Post at Barcelona, Spain, 1797–1959," *Cuadernos de Historia Económica de Cataluña,* 1 (1969–1970), 44–50.

[18]Department of State, *Biographical Register, 1944,* p. 171.

[19]For details see McDonald, "Highlights in the History of the United States Post at Barcelona," pp. 50–53.

[20]Department of State, *Biographical Register, 1944,* p. 74.

In November 1937, the government of the Second Republic moved from Valencia to Barcelona, causing the U.S. government to authorize within days the movement of its embassy to the Catalan capital.[21] The staff at the embassy was led by Councilor of Embassy Walter Thurston, also the author of some telegrams and other correspondence below. Ambassador Claude G. Bowers, a noted historian and later the author of an important memoir on the Spanish Civil War,[22] resided in France in order to stay close to other diplomats assigned to Spain and because he preferred the safety of being outside Spain. Thurston, like Flood, reported on local events in Barcelona as part of his broader responsibility for dealing with the Spanish Republican government. Of Flood and Thurston, the more valuable reporting was done by the latter. Thurston was born near Denver, Colorado, on 5 December 1895 and first worked for the Department of State in Mexico from 1914 to 1916. He next served in Guatemala until 1920 and, after a tour in Washington, went to Managua in 1923, then to São Paulo in 1925. He subsequently became sec- retary of the embassy in Lisbon in 1927 and was a delegate to various Latin American conferences. In 1930 he became the chief of the Division of Latin American Affairs in the Department of State. He continued his distinguished career by becoming counselor of legation at Asunción in 1934, then holding the same position in Spain effective 1 October 1936. He served in Spain until the end of the Civil War, when he was transferred to Moscow. During most of World War II, he was ambassador to El Salvador and then later to Mexico.[23]

Thurston's reporting on Barcelona, while limited, complemented and expanded upon those comments made by consular officials, particularly with his telegrams and dispatches dealing with Franco's advance into Republican Catalonia and finally its fall. On 18 March 1939, he received instructions from the Department of State to move the embassy out of Barcelona and in early April he did.[24] On 1 April 1939, the United States made public its desire to establish formal diplomatic relations with the new regime of General Franco. The consulate then was moved back to Barcelona and once again was housed in its old quarters on the Plaza de Cataluña.[25]

IV

In the course of putting this book together, I have been helped by a number of people and institutions. The staff responsible for maintaining dip- lomatic papers at the National Archives were extremely helpful in pulling

[21]Department of State, *Foreign Relations of the United States, 1937* (Washington, D.C., 1939), 1, p. 446.
[22]Claude G. Bowers, *My Mission to Spain: Watching the Rehearsal for World War II* (New York, 1954).
[23]Department of State, *Biographical Register, 1944*, pp. 215–16.
[24]Department of State, *Foreign Relations of the United States 1938*, 1, pp. 166–70.
[25]McDonald, "Highlights in the History of the United States Post at Barcelona," pp. 52–56.

various files together for me. This voluminous material was scattered across embassy and consular files, while other files dealing with such topics as refugees, the Civil War, relations with France, and military themes were not as convenient. These would have been overlooked without the help of these archivists. The general topic of consular files as a source for historians working on Barcelona was the brainchild of Dr. Pedro Voltes Bou, director of the Municipal Institute of History for the City of Barcelona and professor of history at the University of Barcelona. Over the years he has encouraged the publication of such material from various consular collections through the *Cuadernos de Historia Económica de Cataluña*, of which he was editor. Robert Kern, of the University of New Mexico, rigorously criticized the manuscript, for which I am grateful. My wife was particularly understanding, silently doing chores that I should have done so that I could finish this book. It is for her constant help in this and in my other books on Spanish affairs that I have dedicated this volume to her. My publisher has been efficient and attentive to the many details of publishing a book, often beyond the normal bounds of patience. In addition, I would like to thank the National Archives and Records Service for their cooperation in providing the photographs and the Institute for the Study of Human Issues (ISHI), the Government Printing Office, and Greenwood Press for use of the maps reproduced in this volume. Any errors, weaknesses or omissions are justifiably my sins.

James W. Cortada

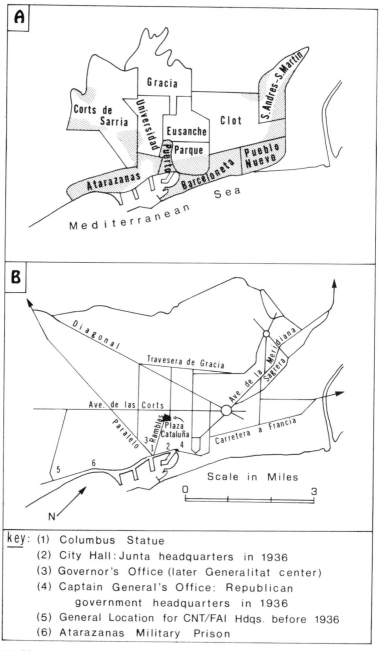

key: (1) Columbus Statue
(2) City Hall: Junta headquarters in 1936
(3) Governor's Office (later Generalitat center)
(4) Captain General's Office: Republican
government headquarters in 1936
(5) General Location for CNT/FAI Hdqs. before 1936
(6) Atarazanas Military Prison

(A) Districts of the town, with workers' neighborhoods marked by dotted
pattern. (B) General street plan, with some important locations.

Barcelona during the Civil War

Source: This map appeared in RED YEARS/BLACK YEARS: A POLITICAL HISTORY OF SPANISH ANARCHISM,
1911–1938 by R.W. Kern, Philadelphia, © Institute for the Study of Human Issues (ISHI) Publications, 1978.

1

A CIVIL WAR BEGINS
(JULY–OCTOBER 1936)

TENSION HAD BEEN mounting all over Spain since the national elections in February 1936 brought the left more political power. Rumors spread of suspected conspiracies, revolts, and plots. Officials either denied or ignored the possibilities or refused to accept the idea that this time they were real. Barcelona, like other cities at the time, was a rumor mill. Its leaders worried about the impact of these rumors on local affairs; workers, about their salaries and political aspirations. Every class consulted itself on the eventuality of another coup or series of attempts to overthrow or modify the nature of the national government, a common concern throughout the years of the Second Republic. Uncertainty accumulated to the point that by the spring of 1936, too many murderous and uncompromising political events had taken place to permit any further compromises. The nation was rapidly polarizing into the two camps that would fight a civil war. In short, time had run out on peaceful solutions. Yet nobody expected the kind of bloody, lengthy civil war that came.

The tension in Barcelona in the early months of 1936 stood in sharp contrast to the common prewar image of the city. A visitor to the city a few years earlier, for example, sensed an introspective quality about Barcelona that would stand in sharp contrast to conditions during the war. He noted that the city was a place filled with "progressive, commercial people," graced with "broad, tree-planted boulevards" and "fringed by handsome buildings." Robert McBride found the city "animated with a multitudinous life" similar to that of Paris. The docks were cluttered with shipping and its warehouses bulged with goods that served as visible symbols of Barcelona's prosperity. Indeed, 25 percent of the nation's commerce passed through. Its industrial strength lay in the textile and chemical factories constructed along the outskirts of the city.[1]

Barcelona was the headquarters for Catalan regionalism and a significant base for the Spanish labor movement, as well as a cultural and economic center. The Liceo ended another brilliant season of opera and ballet while

---

[1] Robert M. McBride, *Spanish Towns and People* (New York, 1931), pp. 223–24.

the CNT and UGT grew in strength and noise. Thus by the spring and early summer of 1936, Spaniards in other parts of Spain thought of Barcelona as the source of many labor problems and of unrest. They also knew it was the main center of Catalan autonomist activity. That portion of the Catalan regionalist movement functioning in an organized fashion operated in large part out of the city—its leaders lived and worked there. They relied on the city's wealth and media as a means of carrying their message to Madrid. Moreover, along with the republicans, Catalan regionalist leaders had turned to Barcelona's working class for support and to the intellectuals for expression of their views. The Catalans also depended on the wealthy families of the city for necessary financial support.

During the 1920s and 1930s, the labor movement, radical political groups, regionalist proponents, and ambitious men produced a political life in the city that was extremely active and, on numerous occasions, violent. The drive and initiative of the residents of Barcelona went far to explain why it was possible for an aging Catalanist, Francisco Macìa, to declare the establishment of the "Catalan Republic of the Iberian Federation" in the city even before the Spanish Republic could be created in Madrid during April 1931. After Macìa's death in 1933, his successor as president of the Generalitat, Luis Companys, learned to control the *Esquerra* (Catalan Republican Left Party) in Barcelona and to be an important spokesman for the city's working classes.[2]

Anarchist violence had become an important feature of Barcelona's political life by 1936 and seemed to be the one characteristic of the city most remembered by foreign newspaper reporters and tourists. With the establishment of the Second Spanish Republic in April 1931, political violence increased in Barcelona as various factions vied for power. Police vigilance against anarchist hostilities weakened on orders from Companys, then the local civil governor. Stanley Payne aptly described the policy of the local government during 1931 as Jacobin, reflecting both political concessions to the strong CNT "but also a genuine expression of the ideological" mood of the Republican left. Thus political murders (nineteen in one month alone) continued with little official censure.[3]

During the early 1930s, the world depression and varying economic policies of the Republic soon took their toll on the commercial life of Barcelona. Restrictive banking policies limiting international financial transactions, for example, and protectionist policies and legislation particularly hurt Barcelona, which so heavily depended on foreign trade. Unemployment rose, the standard of living fell as inflation heated, and production declined in many industries. The only large sector of the local economy that thrived was the all important textile industry, which continued to sell its production to the rest of Spain. In fact, textile companies nearly doubled employment between

---

[2]Stanley G. Payne, *The Spanish Revolution* (New York, 1970), pp. 114–16.
[3]*The Spanish Revolution*, p. 117.

the late 1920s and the Civil War to over 200 thousand workers. Automation in the textile plants, however, did prevent further growth in the number of workers in that industry. As a result of the textiles' economic strength, some foreign visitors to Barcelona concluded that the city was financially sound. Despite the comparatively high level of employment, social tensions grew in an already highly politicized city, where a tradition of activist politics and strongly felt ideological positions existed.

The revolt in 1934 by radical Catalans demanding more reforms in the government threatened to break open even further the cracks in the Catalanist movement, hinting that all was not well in Barcelona. The revolt of October 1934 grew out of Socialist Party demands that political rivals in the Cortes be kept out of the cabinet. This action threatened the interests of Catalan separatists, who were in the process of convincing the government in Madrid to grant the Catalans autonomy to run their own domestic affairs. The government in Madrid was reluctant to do this, concerned as it was over conflicts of the Catalan Statute and the Spanish constitution. Debate with Madrid over taxation and local rights in the Basque country created additional tensions. The denial of positions in the republican cabinet to leftist politicians that fall— although not the cause of the revolt—was clearly the event that finally led leftist political groups to attempt a revolution to create a proletariat republic in Spain. The revolt spread to the Basque provinces and to Cataluña. The efforts were poorly organized and soon failed. In the revolt of 1934, forty-six individuals in Cataluña died. This rebellious spirit was kept alive by regionalist aspirations that clearly indicated Barcelona would not support any group wishing to deny the city its rights.

It becomes quite clear, then, why Barcelona supported the Republic when Franco's forces revolted against the authority of the regime in Madrid. The city served as a major communication link to the outside world at the start of the war and was always for Spain a source of industrial and military supplies (along with thousands of soldiers, bureaucrats, and leaders for the Republican cause). Since the entire population of the Republic at the start of the Civil War amounted to about 12,700,000, Barcelona's participation in the conflict proved critical. Events in the city during the early days of the war were important because it was here that Franco suffered a significant defeat, one that ensured most of Cataluña would remain in Republican hands almost until the end of the Civil War.

Tension had been mounting in the city for days before the revolt that broke out on 18 July due to numerous rumors of revolution. Workers attempted to seize arms while political leaders sought to remain unified in the face of anticipated violence. Falangist youths had also been organizing and eagerly waited for military confrontation. Much of the early fighting focused on the Plaza de Cataluña, where workers battled Falangists and the army. A siege of the plaza took place on the first day; workers destroyed the strength of their enemies within hours. Fighting in the nearby streets led to many deaths as well. In fact, several dozen bodies of the slain lay uncared for on the plaza and surrounding streets. Early on the afternoon of 19 July, workers stormed the Hotel Colon and Hotel Ritz, an action soon followed by their seizure of the large Telefónica building in the Plaza de Cataluña. The tide turned in favor of the Republic by late afternoon, and on the following day the soldiers supporting the rebellion surrendered. Others at Fort Montjuich executed many of their officers and joined the side of the Republic. The final episode was the surrender of the Ataranzanas barracks to the workers. Through either surrendering or joining the loyalists, some five thousand soldiers were denied to the rebellion. The hostility of the victorious worker militias toward the Francoists resulted in further deaths. Although reliable figures are not yet available, a reasonable guess would be several dozen immediate deaths, and hundreds more in subsequent weeks. One could comment that the rebellion came and went quickly in Barcelona and that the mess caused by the fighting was soon cleaned up.[4]

Why the struggle centered on the Plaza de Cataluña becomes clear after reading the comments of F. Theo Rogers, a British reporter in Barcelona at the time who discussed the tactical importance of the plaza. He reported that the plaza with its tall buildings dominated old Barcelona and stood on the edge of the newer part of the city; therefore, whoever monopolized the square controlled the entire community. He witnessed the fighting there when workers charged army emplacements and saw proof of the plaza's military value. He remembered that for days afterwards sporadic shots could be heard all through the city as various small factions clashed for control of street corners and tall buildings. Yet once the issue of the Plaza de Cataluña had been resolved, no significant fighting could continue.[5]

Cedric Salter's memoirs also contain a great deal of material on these critical days and what it was like in the streets. He recalled that the Ramblas, one of Barcelona's most fashionable avenues, was noisy and crowded as usual on the evening of 18 July, but Salter suspected that something was not quite right because all the nightclubs remained "unusually empty." That night he witnessed some arrests that seemed to be equally abnormal. By the morning of 19 July, he saw police checking papers and searching for arms. An armed band on the edge of Barcelona took Salter's car, and as he complained to the police, another group opened fire on the station. After finishing with the authorities, Salter walked the streets; he saw churches on fire, heard gunfire in the Plaza de Cataluña, viewed desecrated coffins at a convent, and dodged snipers' sporadic firing. He saw a monastery on the Diagonal attacked by Anarchists in search of some entrenched Fascists. At the end of the day the

---

[4]Broué and Témime, *La révolution et la guerre d'Espagne*, describes the fighting in Barcelona, pp. 112–68; for further details see Vicente Guarner, *Cataluña en la guerra de España* (Madrid, 1975), pp. 103–33.
[5]F. Theo Rogers, *Spain: A Tragic Journey* (New York, 1937), pp. 33–38.

reporter escorted some very scared British citizens to the docks where the H.M.S. *London* conveniently evacuated them back home.[6]

Observers in the city quickly perceived the transformation that came about as a result of Franco's forces being defeated. The workers now dominated Barcelona with their guns, rhetoric, and ideologies. Franz Borkenau called the city the "bastion of Soviet Spain." Workers were seen everywhere, confident that they now had the power to control Barcelona. Many visitors commented on how the armed workers walked along the Ramblas, stood in front of buildings, and gave the city a look of armed casualness. Ties and hats proved too bourgeois and soon disappeared. Uniforms almost vanished. Nightclubs closed and accordingly the city gained a more serious tone. Workers plastered revolutionary labels and signs on buildings, cars, and buses. New radio stations and newspapers appeared to represent various labor factions—all proclaiming the day of the people. Churches, burned during the fighting, stood silent and dark; the main cathedral was closed. Jean Richard Bloch, a communist writer, noted:

> the Ramblas have gone on living at a twofold rhythm. The Ramblas by day are full of flowers, birds, strollers, cafes, automobiles, and streetcars. By dusk, the flower stalls have vanished, the bird sellers are far away, the cafes are shut. The Ramblas by night means the reign of silence and fear and a few furtive shadows along walls.[7]

---

[6]Cedric Salter, *Try-Out in Spain* (New York, 1943), pp. 2–27. Salter also told a good story: "A very English couple arrived at Barcelona by air on the first stage of their honeymoon on the previous evening (18th), and had repaired to the Hotel Colon for the bridal night. They had been out dancing with friends until very late, and no sooner had they retired than the door burst open, and a group of soldiers thrust their way to the windows and began firing across the Plaza Cataluña. The gentleman expostulated in precise but controlled English without producing any results. Further representations being equally ineffective he decided that the well-bred thing to do was to ignore the whole ill-mannered crowd of them, and returned with dignity to the marital bed.

"But as the bullets continued to whistle about the place and troops marched and countermarched about his room, a great and just indignation was born in his bosom. This was emphatically not cricket, and, by God, sir, the consul should know of it.

"During the early morning the hotel which had been a center of Franco resistance was, apart from a few snipers on the roof, captured by the Anarchist mob which had been armed by the Catalan government, known as the Generalidad, in order to destroy all such centers of Fascist resistance.

"When the outraged husband and his haughty spouse, their marriage still unconsummated, swept down to the hotel lobby they were met by a ragged, bloodstained Anarchist, armed with a sub-machine gun. Nothing daunted they descended upon him, and pressing into his hand a twenty-five peseta note in full settlement they informed him, in English of course, but spoken slightly louder than usual in order to ensure comprehension, that they considered his hotel a disgrace and proposed making the strongest possible recommendation to the British consul that he advise the competent authorities that the hotel was unfit for British patronage.

"With that they made their way with dignity and without haste into the bullet-swept streets to make good their threat with the consular representative of his Britannic Majesty," pp. 15–17.

[7]Jean Richard Bloch, *Espagne, Espagne* (Paris, 1936), p. 45.

The nature of the municipal government and the bounds of its authority also changed rapidly. The anarchist leader, Diego Abad de Santillan, best described the situation when he recorded how his group met with the cabinet of the Generalitat on 21 July:

> We went to the seat of the Catalan government, clutching our weapons, not having slept for several days, unshaven, confirming by our appearance the legend that had formed about us. Some members of the autonomous regional government were trembling, whitefaced, at this interview from which Ascaso was missing. The government palace was invaded by the escort of combatants who had accompanied us.

Companys, realizing that he would have to cooperate with the workers or see his government destroyed, welcomed them. His deputy, Jaime Miravittles, commented later that the "Antifascist Militias Committee came into existence two or three days after the fighting in the absence of any regular public force and because there was no army in Barcelona."[8]

The realities of the situation during July could not have been altered by Companys through any strength of personality, let alone political power. Cedric Salter called him "a slick little lawyer" who was "uneasy riding the trade-unionist whirlwind." He added that Companys had "no qualities beyond opportunism, unscrupulousness, and a capacity for appealing to the Catalan mob in its own tongue." In other words, he was a man unable "to arrest the rising tide of anarchy" that swept over Barcelona that summer. Companys remained in power because the CNT felt it needed his support. Stanley Payne agreed with this viewpoint and suggested that a confrontation would have hurt the war effort: "In view of the renewed leftward tendencies in the Esquerra and many years association with the revolutionaries, Companys preferred a compromise in the hope of defeating the right and then of domesticating the CNT without bloodshed." Raymond Carr saw that the city of Barcelona took on a true proletarian flavor, in which a government composed of representatives from various labor groups operated parallel to the regular authorities. On the surface, this dualism did not end until 27 September, when members of the CNT joined the Catalan government, and 4 November, when the CNT contributed members to Largo Caballero's national cabinet.[9] In all probability what happened was that the Republican government could no longer ignore the fact that if it wanted support from Barcelona, the city's major party had to be represented in the cabinet.

Thus Barcelona, in the clutches of a revolutionary spirit that refused to subside, became the battleground in the fall where various elements from the

---

[8]Diego Abad de Santillan, *Por Qué Perdimos la Guerra* (Buenos Aires, 1940), p. 168; Miravittles quoted in *Heraldo de Madrid*, 4 September 1936.

[9]Salter, *Try-Out in Spain*, pp. 87–88; Broué and Témime, *La révolution et la guerre d'Espagne*, pp. 130–31; Payne, *The Spanish Revolution*, p. 223; Raymond Carr, *Spain, 1808–1939* (Oxford, 1966), pp. 664–65.

PSUC, POUM, CNT, UGT, Esquerra (the Catalan leftist republican party), Rabassaires (farmers' union party), Acción Catalan (Catalan republican party and also known as the Accío Catalana), and other groups mixed and competed for political control of the city. Those working within the official government or parallel to it, through parties and labor organizations, established various committees to provide quasi-official direction for the city, depending on their political and military strength. One such committee was established for transportation, another became the War Industries Commission, and a third was created for education. Foreign reporters and diplomats found the proliferation of committees confusing, especially since each commission had to have representatives from multiple political factions. Yet some positive results could be recorded. Most notably, the number of students regularly attending classes rose 10 percent between July and October as a direct result of the workers' government policy to expand enrollments.[10]

Economic changes came to the city almost as quickly as political ones. Seizure of many companies and shops in the city occurred from the start. In most cases, workers simply seized an establishment (the process known as *incautación*), while others established more formal control over an enterprise (*intervención*). Approximately 70 percent of all *incautaciones* came as a direct result of orders issued by the CNT. Gas and electricity were quickly collectivized, as were telephone service, entertainment, restaurants, transportation, hotels, and most large factories. Foreign companies were also seized; workers took over the Ford Iberia Motor Company, Hispano-Suiza, and Ashland Cement. In the Ford plant, a committee of workers soon operated the facilities for their approximately five hundred colleagues. Disruption of the normal management of small and large commercial enterprises inevitably affected adversely Barcelona's economy; business activity dropped due to the lack of raw materials and reduced availability of experienced management. Money and credit were also in short supply as a consequence of declining economic activity and the flight of capital out of the country.[11]

During the fall and winter, Barcelona continued to be the scene of violence as various political factions struggled for control of local affairs. It was a time known as the Red Terror throughout Cataluña. By the spring of 1937, a casualty of the violence of the preceding nine months was Barcelona's healthy and active bourgeoisie, managers and merchants, intellectuals and teachers—all of whom either were killed or left Cataluña in fear of their lives.

Law and order thus became a key issue for all citizens of Barcelona almost from the beginning of the war in July. F. Theo Rogers, then in Barcelona, described the situation as the traditional sources of power and law in the city were overturned:

---

[10]Broué and Témime, *La révolution et la guerre d'Espagne*, pp. 164–65; Pedro Voltes Bou, *Historia de la economía española en los siglos XIX y XX* (Madrid, 1974), 2, pp. 725–803, for more details.

[11]Payne, *The Spanish Revolution*, pp. 225–31; for further details see David T. Cattell, *Communism and the Spanish Civil War* (Berkeley, 1955), pp. 93–94.

My six months' stay in Barcelona showed me that there could be little semblance of law and order in that city and state. There was a true reign of terror with armed bands parading the streets, taking what they wanted and shooting down whom they willed. If the supposedly legal authorities made any effort to intervene, they became marked men, targets for the gangsters dominated by the Federación Anarquista Iberica, known as the FAI, the most dreaded organization in all Spain.

Rogers remembered that executions took place each night from 11:00 P.M. to 4:00 A.M. as a rule. FAI members condemned people, went after them and their families, and seized or destroyed their properties on the least amount of evidence. He noted the police never attempted to prevent such behavior, allowing conditions to exist that resulted in an average of one hundred twenty-five murders per day. "Normalcy ceased to exist. The clock of civilization was turned back to prehistoric times."[12] Cedric Salter made similar observations about actions occurring in July and August. He believed that during the first month of the Civil War alone, twenty thousand individuals died violently in Barcelona. While the number of casualties remained the subject of controversy, the obvious impression he had about the lack of law and order seemed clear. He thought the majority of all executions were directed against the middle and upper classes and especially against suspected or known sympathizers of Franco. However, he, too, mentioned that the settlement of personal grudges accounted for many deaths.[13]

The confusion that grew out of the violence of those early days was set against the clutter and ruin of burned out churches and trash along contested streets and plazas, and it spilled over into other sectors of life in the city. Salvador de Madariaga, passing through Barcelona either at the end of July or during the first few days of August 1936, discussed the problem:

> In Valencia we caught a train for Barcelona and there I found chaos. No one knew anything about anything, particularly as to who was in command. Power. Power was the thing. The official authorities and the "popular" were treading then on each others' toes. So did, physically, the thousands who crowded their offices in the hope of being able to travel.[14]

John Cornford, a Communist killed during the Civil War, lived in Barcelona at the same time, and although he left a more positive description of the period, he still could not help but sense the uncontrolled change:

> In Barcelona one can understand physically what the dictatorship of the proletariat means. All the Fascist press has been taken over. The real

[12]Rogers, *Spain*, p. 52.
[13]Rogers, *Spain*, p. 61; Salter, *Try-Out in Spain*, pp. 28–35.
[14]Salvador de Madariaga, *Morning without Noon: Memoirs* (Farnborough, 1974), p. 422.

rule is in the hands of the militia committees. There is a real terror against the Fascists. But that doesn't alter the fact that the place is free—and conscious all the time of its freedom. Everywhere in the streets are armed workers and militiamen, and sitting in the cafes which used to belong to the bourgeoisie. The huge Hotel Colon overlooking the main square is occupied by the United Socialist Party of Catalonia. Farther down, in a huge block opposite the Bank of Spain, is the Anarchist headquarters. The palace of a marquis in the Rambla is a Communist Party headquarters. But one does not feel the tension. The mass of the people are oblivious to the Anarchist-Government trouble brewing, and simply are enjoying their freedom. The streets are crowded all day, and there are big crowds round the radio palaces. But there is nothing at all like tension or hysteria. It's as if in London the armed workers were dominating the streets—it's obvious that they wouldn't tolerate Mosley or people selling *Action* in the streets. And that wouldn't mean that the town wasn't free in the real sense. It is genuinely a dictatorship of the majority, supported by the overwhelming majority. Not yet in Soviet form—the elections to the committees aren't on the basis of localities or factories but representatives of organizations. That narrows the basis a bit, but not much, as a huge majority of the people are organized.[15]

A French reporter's comments perhaps struck closer to the truth when he said, "I left Barcelona with the sensation that I was leaving Hell." He referred to the constant danger on the streets and the fear everyone had of being picked up by one militia group or another. "In order to avoid suspicion I had to wear old clothes and dirty shirts. Even two months after the outbreak in Catalonia, no woman dares wear a hat in the streets." Because everyone knew that several dozen people died violently each day on the slightest provocation, he could only fear for his life.[16]

---

[15]Quoted in Murray A. Sperber, ed., *And I Remember Spain: A Spanish Civil War Anthology* (New York, 1974), pp. 25–26.
[16]Quoted by Rogers, *Spain*, p. 217.

Barcelona, July 19, 1936

Subject: Fascist Uprising in Barcelona

Sir:

This morning July 19th, 1936, shortly before five o'clock heavy rifle and machine gun firing were heard from the business part of the city. Upon investigation it was ascertained from various sources considered reliable that an uprising had taken place on the part of the fascist element of the army stationed in Barcelona. Firing continued throughout the city until seven P.M.

During the day at various sections of the city loyal troops belonging to the army, as well as *Guardia Civil,* red cross units, *Guardias de Asalto,* and labor groups took part in subduing the rebels. Some streets were cut off and outside telephone and telegraph connections were unavailable. Local telephone connections were also cut off intermittently from ten o'clock in the morning. There was heavy firing particularly around Plaza Cataluña and the government buildings in the heart of the city. The Barcelona radio service kept listeners informed of the progress against the rebellious soldiers, and the loyalty of those who had come to the aid of the Government with local orders for volunteers to go to civil hospital and give blood transfusions; also for opening of all pharmacies. It is understood that the rebellious troops endeavored to take the city at three-thirty this morning. A number of them were forced to find refuge in three large buildings around the Plaza Cataluña, upon which the office of the Consulate General fronts, namely Hotel Colon, department stores of Vicente Ferrer and the modern telephone building.

Loyal planes flew over the city and it is reported although not confirmed that they dropped bombs on the cuartel Atarazanas at the foot of the Ramblas where some eighteen or twenty soldiers were killed.

At eleven-thirty A.M. I took the two mile walk from my home to the Consulate General accompanied by an Englishman, Mr. Harskin whom I met en route. The streets of Diputación and Cortés were blocked to the east of Paseo de Gracia, barricaded with artillery pointed eastwards. Although no one was seen manning the guns it was reliably reported that they were manned by civilians nearby.

Heavy firing at that time was going on in the Calle Cortés near Hotel Ritz, and sporadic rifle firing from buildings in the neighborhood. We passed two dead horses. Some dozen mules were stationed near the front entrance of the Hotel Colon facing the Plaza Cataluña, and there were several empty automobiles and busses on and in the Plaza itself as well as two live mules. An abandoned street car was on the Plaza Cataluña and back of it the trolley wire was broken and hanging down. On the left side of the Plaza I noticed an abandoned machine gun with a dead man near it on the sidewalk. There was blood in several places of the street and while there was firing from buildings around the Plaza, I did not see anybody as I crossed the open square to the Consulate General. Upon my return from the office twenty minutes later, one of the mules in the center of the Plaza dropped to the ground apparently dead, evidently as a result of firing from one of the buildings on the east side. No soldiers of any kind appeared around the Plaza. After leaving it I met three red cross ambulances and four cars containing armed civilians with syndicalist (C.N.T.) markings on the cars. Very few people appeared onto the streets of the city during the day.

Every effort was made all day to report by telephone or telegraph conditions to the Embassy or the Department without success. The local correspondent of the London *Times* had been unable to transmit any information to his paper. There was a period during the afternoon when it was felt that the rebels were winning, with resultant tendencies towards destruction of private property. Anxiety was felt for the safety of the city. It was reported at half past six P.M. that the rebellious troops were surrendering and that it could be safely said that the attack on the local government had been unsuccessful.

During the day with the exception of activity concerned with the actual fighting, transportation of all kinds was paralyzed.

At eight P.M. the life of the city appeared to be assuming a more normal aspect but it remains to be seen whether or not the radical labor elements now in possession of guns and ammunition will confine their use to legitimate purposes or return them to the constituted authorities, or vest vengeance on their enemies such as church elements and adherents to the subdued Fascists.

At eight-fifteen P.M. President Companys announced over the radio complete rendition of the rebellious forces and just before he spoke, General Goded, reported to be the leader of the rebels stated over the radio that he was now a prisoner and that to avoid further bloodshed he absolved any of his followers from obligation to him.

It will be recalled that the officers of the present government headed by President Luis Companys were those who headed the revolution of October 6, 1934 in Barcelona, and were the ones to lead the suppression of the present revolt against their government today.

There were no instances of importance in connection with the protection of Americans.

At six o'clock five fires in the city could be counted, three of them reliably reported as churches. A woman at one of the convents whose husband is reported to have been an American citizen known to the Consulate, telephoned that she was being left behind by the nuns and asked for assistance. She was promised fifty pesetas and stated that she believed she could find shelter as she was penniless.

Lynn W. Franklin
American Consul General

Barcelona, July 20, 1936

Subject: Fascist Uprising in Barcelona

Sir:

Since writing the report entitled "Fascist Uprising in Barcelona, Spain," July 19, 1936, the inhabitants of Barcelona have spent another night and greater part of a day in the midst of armed revolutionary activity. Upon my arrival at the Consulate General this morning I found that the entrance of the building as well as the offices had suffered from stray bullets since my departure yesterday. More people were on the streets than the day previously. Evidences of the sharp fighting during the preceding afternoon were seen in the damaged condition of the Colon Hotel and the Telephone Building on the Plaza Cataluña and the additional bodies of dead mules in that neighborhood. The manager of the Colon Hotel informed me that American and other guests had been sent to the other hotels outside of the danger zone. I stopped at the Hotel Majestic which was more or less normal. The body of the machine gun attendant and the machine gun spoken of in my previous report had been removed. Some activity was noticed on the part of those patrolling the city and at one time there was a strong fusillade in the telephone building believed to be a final attempt to dislodge the rebels.

Upon my return from office an hour later in a round-about way I witnessed the opening of the Convent of Carmelites where rebel soldiers had been hiding since yesterday and who surrendered to the local army at 11:30 A.M. today. This convent was reported burned later during the day. One wounded person was brought out on a stretcher as I passed. Many of the Syndicalists' automobiles have rough looking women in them accompanied by armed men and the sign given by those who pass, on foot or in automobiles is the raised fist.

At three o'clock in the afternoon, when there was no particular personal danger in my opinion I sent Consul Horn to the authorities with a request for a cablegram to be sent.[17] The authorities accepted the cable to Washington but would not take any to the American Embassy in Spain. Mr. Horn met the British and French Consuls at the cable office. At the Consulate General the following letter was found, which translated, reads as follows:

> In a meeting held in the Generalidad with all the Consuls who it was possible to convocate it had been agreed to give maximum facilities to those foreigners who wish to abandon the country, in spite of the evident fact that the situation is becoming progressively normal. I am communicating this to you in this manner in view of the exceptional situation. [Signed] Secretary of Sr. Companys.

[17]Thomas S. Horn, assigned to Barcelona 13 March 1934 as consul, left September 1938, Department of State, *Biographical Register, 1944*, pp. 104–05.

I understand this may be depended upon to mean that the authorities will not put means of transportation or facilities at the disposition of foreigners but will give permission to go to those who desire to leave.

Since noon today there has been a marked change toward order and normalcy in the city and at the present writing (10:00) it is believed that the night will be a relatively quiet one.

The telephone at the Consulate General has not functioned but numerous calls have been received at my residence from members of the American and foreign colony generally.

The residences of all members of the Consular staff have been in the firing zone from time to time.

The Consulate General is giving assistance to American citizens who wish to send telegrams to their families regarding their safety.

Lynn W. Franklin
American Consul General

852.00/2177

Telegram   Barcelona, July 20, 1936

Since Sunday morning to date, the city of Barcelona has been the center of Fascist uprising and while greater part of rebels have surrendered, there continues a pursuit of rebels throughout the city making it dangerous for persons to appear on street. Larger portion of army cooperating with the guardia civil, labor groups and charge troops to capture rebels and maintain order. Many churches set on fire and feeling of anxiety growing. Believe that all Americans safe and desire this fact to be made known. No outside communication possible. Embassy in Spain not informed.

Franklin

Telegram   Paris, July 22, 1936, 1 P.M.

Consul Franklin reports that the troops in the barracks there revolted against the Government on Sunday or Monday. The revolt was suppressed with considerable casualties. In the city great numbers of armed Socialists and Communists are pursuing the Fascists throughout the city and in the process searching the buildings and houses. Considerable firing in the streets which makes it dangerous to go out. Consul Franklin reports he has been requested by the General Motors Company branch in Barcelona to order a small American freighter which is at Tarragona to come to Barcelona and take them on it. The Consul declined to do this because he considered it not a useful measure, also he feels he has no authority to do so; and furthermore, there are several hundred Americans in the city and the freighter could not take off more than 20 or 30. Consul has attempted to communicate with the Department twice by cable telling the Department that in a conversation with the President of the Catalan Government yesterday afternoon he was told by him that the circumstances made it impossible for him to guarantee the safety of American and other foreigners in Barcelona and that he would view favorably the Consul's action in requesting American ships to come to Barcelona to receive American citizens on board and would give them every facility in the port.

Straus

852.00/2193

Telegram   Paris, July 22, 1936, 1 P.M.

Consul reports that the French Consulate is attempting to evacuate the French colony which amounts to some 12 or 15 thousand people. Consul Franklin states that he does not feel personally able to recommend that ships be now sent to Barcelona for this purpose but that he would greatly like to have one or two American ships in the port in case of emergency. He has advised all Americans in Barcelona to remain indoors. Thus far no Americans in Barcelona have been injured. He was trying to communicate with the Embassy in Paris last night. He will try today to communicate with the Embassy in Paris. (We are trying to reach him but without success so far).

Mr. Wendelin has no further news except what he received from the Consulate in Gibraltar by way of Lisbon.[18] They say that the situation in southern part of Spain near Gibraltar is chaotic, at Málaga there has been much rioting and burning of churches and the extremist element seems to be in control. They have no definite information of the progress of the military revolt in that area and can only say definitely that the rebels hold the cities of Algeciras and Melilla in Africa.

Wendelin says communication with Lisbon so far today has been poor and he could not understand them.

Straus

---

[18]Eric C. Wendelin, Third Secretary of Embassy, Madrid, served in Spain from 25 October 1934 to July 1937, Department of State, *Biographical Register, 1944*, p. 230.

852.00/2209

Telegram   Paris, July 23, 1936, 10 A.M.

Franklin stated that there is relative calm in the city and no firing, although a good deal of pillage by irresponsible armed groups. The labor groups which had been armed had been sent outside the city to fight the insurgents. Although the local authorities had given orders through the news-papers and by radio that no foreigners were to be molested several automobiles owned by foreigners have been confiscated and many homes owned by for-eigners riddled by bullets. No injury or deaths reported of Americans or other foreigners. Franklin said that there was one element in the labor organization composed of downright anarchists who were armed and were a potential danger. He believes that unsettled conditions will last for some time.

He stated that Consul Jackson and family were safe in Madrid and that he was able to talk yesterday with Consul Davis and Vice Consul Wells at Valencia. Davis stated that Valencia was in the hands of the Communists but all Americans safe.

Straus

852.00/2278

Telegram   Barcelona, July 26, 1936

Sec. of State

Street cars and buses beginning to operate. Local authorities, evidently taking advantage of absence radical elements sent out of city towards Zara-goza, getting better control of situation in Barcelona. Foreigners and Amer-icans continue to evacuate, no violence to Americans reported. Embassy at Paris informed. Please inform Embassy at Madrid.

Franklin

852.00/2293

Telegram   Barcelona, July 27, 1936

Sec. of State

About the same as reported in my telegram of July 26, 6 P.M. Reported to the Embassy by telephone last night. No shortage of (#) or living necess-ities. Further churches being burned and certain amount of uncontrolled rob-bery and murder going on. Embassies at Madrid and Paris informed.

Franklin

(#) Apparent Omission

852.00/2337

Telegram   Madrid, July 31, 1936

Sec. of State

Consul at Barcelona requests transmission following information believes reliable: Barcelona forces near Saragossa. Severe fighting. 700 in hospitals at Lérida and 26 wounded brought to Barcelona yesterday.

Wendelin

852.00/2344

Telegram   Barcelona, August 1, 1936

Sec. of State

In my opinion reorganization of local government which occurred last night gives promise of better control over local conditions and at least as much security to lives and property of Americans and foreigners as the former administration was able to give. No Americans reported killed or injured to date.

Franklin

852.00/2475

Telegram   Barcelona, August 7, 1936

Sir:

Information received indicates Government forces not making advances of importance to date on Zaragoza front. No favorable reports regarding Zaragoza front allowed printed or spoken. Preparations going forward to send Government forces to Balearic Islands. Intensive manufacture going on of hand grenades. Local government modified by withdrawal of two Extreme Left representatives whose parties still cooperate with Government.[19]

Franklin

---

[19]The Catalan cabinet was changed on 5 August 1936. The following officials were dropped from the previous government: Juan Comorera (Economy), Estanislao Ruiz Ponsetti (Supplies), Rafael Vidiella (Communications)—all members of the PSUC (*Partido Socialista Unificado de Cataluña*).

852.00/2567

Telegram   Barcelona, August 12, 1936

Sec. of State

Danger of local conflict among governing groups much in evidence but forestalled to date. Assassinations continue in an alarming manner. Generals Goded and Burrill, who headed military revolt in Barcelona July 19 reported on reliable authority executed today after court martial.[20] Americans continue to evacuate and I hope most of those remaining will leave by the end of present week. No Americans injured or killed to date.

Franklin

852.00/2654

Telegram   Barcelona, August 17, 1936

Sec. of State

For the last ten days volunteers averaging 2,000 daily going to Zaragoza front from this district including women. There appears to exist today noticeable nervous tension among local authorities. Assassinations continue. Of three cases sick men mentioned one has typhoid. Recruiting going forward for troops to go to Mallorca. Americans continue to evacuate; I have discovered that we have 100 left of whom one half preparing to leave this week. French Consul discovered 500, British Consul 200 of whom they had no records or knowledge. Local conditions appear on the surface almost normal.

Franklin

852.00/2697

Telegram   Barcelona, August 19, 1936

Sec. of State

Situation unchanged. Last night group of fourteen desperate doomed men had occasion to escape from center of Barcelona, all killed. Day before yesterday 250 and 600 Government troops respectively reported killed in two

[20]General Manuel Goded Llopis (1882–1936) was in charge of the Nationalist uprising in Barcelona and was in fact executed as Franklin states on charges of treason and rebellion. For details see Thomas, *The Spanish Civil War*, pp. 235, 254–55, 403.

attacks on Mallorca. Ordinary mail being censored by military committee of anti-Fascists.

Franklin

Tarragona, August 22, 1936

TO: Lynn W. Franklin, Esquire, American Consul

Sir:

I have the honor to give you the following information.

The C.N.T. and F.A.I. organizations have requisitioned a number of industries in this province reportedly to a certain disappointment as it has been found in most of the cases that liabilities were in excess of recoverable assets.[21] They now seem to be modifying their tactics and instead of requisitioning they establish a supervision in such industries as they wish to keep under their control with the evident purpose of paving the way towards the total socialization (collectivism) of the economic resources of this province. Their aim is however being now greatly encroached upon by the U.G.T. (socialist) which is also establishing a control of its own in many other industries, in many instances by request, as reported, of the manufacturers or merchants themselves who thus try to avoid all sort of contact with the C.N.T. and F.A.I.

In Tarragona as from August 24 next, the C.N.T., F.A.I. and U.G.T. will take on for themselves the handling of all traffic through this port, in and out, ashore and on board. Prices are not established yet but all accounts have to be paid them by the ships' agents, the labor organizations disclaiming all sort of responsibility for marks or number of persons handled by them.

The summary executions have greatly increased in number during the last two nights all over this province. The doomed men are now usually taken in groups of two or three to neighboring villages and there executed, generally against the outside walls of the cemetery.

News from the Aragon war front are to the effect that the resistance of the rebels is proving to be sterner than anticipated, that the labor militias will not obey their officers and that a good many of the militiamen have been evacuated on account of venereal disease infected by prostitutes the men had taken along with them. It is also asserted that the militiamen never show

----

[21]FAI was the *Federación Anarquista Ibérica*, the largest anarchist political organization in Spain with its largest membership in Barcelona, where, in effect, it competed with the local government for control of affairs. This was the organization that would be destroyed in May 1937; see Chapter Two for details. See also Robert Kern, *Red Years/Black Years* (Philadelphia, 1978) for a recent history of Spanish anarchism.

willingness to go to the front alleging that their task is in the rear and that soldiers and armed police alone are to be employed in the battle line.

Caesar F. Agostini
American Consular Agent

To the Spanish Proletariat

The P.O.U.M. (Partido Obrero de Unificación Marxista—Labor Party of Marxist Unification) and the Actual Situation.

Events establish a new status of facts. A Worker's Government—Economic recovery of the country along Socialist principles.—A constituent meeting.—Workers', Farmers' and Combatants' Committees; expression of the New Democracy arisen out of the fight against Fascism.

The Spanish proletariat has lived through an epic; it is witnessing not only the greatest event in Spanish history, but one of the outstanding happenings of our present times. Spain's working classes are writing with their blood the red page of the gigantic struggle against the infuriated reaction. The Spanish gesture will act as a brake on international fascism rooted in every country, and has roused the solidary feeling of the proletariat of all nations. On the Spanish fronts there is at stake not only the destiny of the Spanish proletariat, but that of their brothers all over the world.

The light of the events has shown up in sharp contrast the firmness and determination and the weakness and errors of programs and tactics. It has been a severe but efficient test for the future of our generation. The circumstances that permitted the fascist movement to break out have not produced themselves spontaneously and independent of political conduct; it has been the corollary not only of a reactionary organization but also of omission and lack of political foresight on the part of those of whom such foresight was expected to safeguard the highest interests of the proletariat.

The generic and utopic meaning of democracy leads the lower middle classes and workers to believe that the opinion of the majority, expressed at the polls, would be respected by the middle classes at large. This is the myth of universal suffrage. The practice of parliamentary democracy in its most abstract interpretation facilitates and fosters the subversive organization of reactionary forces. In this way, in reality, democracy in the middle class sense of the word, becomes the assurance of easy success of movements like that actually fought by us. It means liberty to conspire for the middle classes.

The mission of the labor parties representing the people's foremost interests would have been to oppose such tactics. However, the strict policy of the *Frente Popular* (People's Front) which we have denounced at every occasion, robbed the workers' parties practically of all political independence, in as much as these latter submitted, and thereby subjected the proletariat to the control of the lower middle classes, thus abandoning their historical mission. In daily life the conduct of the workers' parties supposed formal acceptance of parliamentary democracy, that is to say, authorization of tactics of conspiracy among army and fascists. To entertain labor's attention which must always be vigilantly active, with revolutionary perspectives that were never to realize, was in no way conducive to face and resolve a situation. The history of these days will have great significance in the light of tomorrow's facts: It will tell how the gigantic movement surprised the great labor parties.

Fascism has been defeated more by the spontaneous action of the workers who have once more given proof of inexhaustible strength and vitality than by foresight of the lower middle classes and the traditional forces of the great laborist parties. The victory over the fascist reaction is the work of a class of people that could never be brought under one single party.

A day of revolution means years of events in the history of humanity. The rhythm of a revolution can change in a few hours the political situation. The changes worked since July 16 have not only exceeded the position and attitudes of the then prevailing parties, but brought the situation on a new plain [sic] which calls for political and social reconstruction work.

Socialism is the Sole Guarantee for Economic Recovery

The "gentlemen Patriots" who brought that horrible commotion over our country with the cry "Viva España," have converted it in ruins. The bankruptcy of liberal economy on which was based Spain's social structure, creates a very difficult situation for the morrow in the fields of production, exchange, and distribution. Once the fascist insurrection quenches, this will be the main difficulty of the country.

Is it conceivable to defend the possibility of economic recovery of a country in ruins by means of middle class liberalism? By no means. In the same way as at the present moment a series of vital problems have to be resolved, the republican lower middle classes, in order to mitigate, have to resort to measures that could be termed wartime communism. In plain language this is neither more nor less than a recognition of the impossibility of creating a new status with the help of the liberal doctrine.

However, the actual spontaneous and intuitive solution of the problems constitutes no premise for the reconstruction work immediately required. The situation demands that the problems be approached not in a provisional way, but be constructive and establish from now on a new order of things. Well-balanced socialism appears as the only way out.

A Workers' Government

The task imposed by the present moment cannot be fulfilled—we refer fundamentally to the reconstruction work—by a mixture of heterogeneous conjunctions. Its importance calls for a uniform judgment, a clearly defined program and practical solutions. The fundamental and decided contribution of the proletariat as a class towards defeating fascism makes them the legitimate beneficiaries of the new situation. The proletariat has manifested itself and claims the leadership of the nation, not only as a reward for the sacrifices, but because this alone guarantees the future. Despite desires to continue entrusting certain governmental functions to lower middle class factions, it is realized that to hope for stabilization and continuance of the actual political situation is pure utopia.

If economic recovery can be brought about only by applying socialistic measures, it is logical that such a policy can only be carried out by the adepts of socialism. Therefore, today more than ever the formation of a laborist government has become an absolute necessity, i.e., of a government composed of members of syndicalist parties and syndicates.

If the victory over the fascists cannot be credited to one laborist party or organization alone, but is the work of the whole proletariat as a class, it goes without saying that one party cannot at any moment assume the responsibility of all the working classes, not even if such a party represents the largest nucleus of workers.

Evidently such a government could be of a provisional character only, in preparation of a new state of things. A government must represent the large masses, workers, farmer combatants who fought for the victory, and it must lay the foundation for the new proletarian democracy.

A Constituent Meeting

The Parliament constituted by the popular movement of February 16 has been surpassed in the recent stirring events. Does anyone still believe in the possibility of reviving it? The very fact that nobody thought of calling it to meet is a recognition of its usefulness. Herewith appears the necessity to substitute it by new organisms expressive of the actual situation and forces.

The task of a laborist government, besides strengthening all the means of defense, struggle against and repression of fascism and laying the foundation for a new economy along the lines indicated, is to call a constituent meeting expressive of the fundamental change which occurred since the military-fascist rebellion.

The representation system of middle class parliamentarism gives the idle and the exploited, the fascist and the worker who fought for freedom, the military conspirator and the revolutionary soldier the same right to decide over the fate of the country. A revolution like the present established by itself a new conception of the right of representation.

Committees of Workers, Farmers, and Combatants

The peremptory and severe needs of the struggle have brought about the union of the worker's endeavours, in the battlefields and in the rear guard. Out of this union grows the strife for a fundamental change of conjuncture, calling for flawless organization, propaganda, and constitution of bodies representative of the workers, farmers and combatants, under which latter heading come militias, soldiers, and guards.

Systematic and speedy constitution of these committees is imperative, so that they may take up their functions at once and attend to the political and economic problems born out of the status created by the breaking out of the rebellion. These Committees will act as representative organizations in the constituent meeting that will decide on the course to be followed for the normalization of life in Spain and the new order of things.

The Partido Obrero de Unificación Marxista faces reality by offering a constructive way out of the present situation created by the military-fascist rebellion. The fighting spirit of the Spanish proletariat must be coupled with comprehension of the moment's requirements. The proletariat must offer the vast masses anxiously enquiring into the future a sure orientation and starting point. The P.O.U.M. offers this, thus harmonizing today's struggle with a constructive future.

The whole world looks on and awaits our decisions. And we hope to direct and carry out the social aspirations of the proletariat.

The Executive Committee of the
Partido Obrero de Unificación Marxista

852.00/2929

Telegram   Barcelona, September 1, 1936

Sec. of State

Following translation of decree of Generalidad of Catalonia issued August 28, indicative of growing feeling of unwillingness in Catalonia to recognize all of the acts of the central government at Madrid:

"In the present circumstances the work of government must answer to a unity of thought which collects in itself the might and social feelings of the proletariat of Catalonia. Therefore, on the proposal of the President of the Government and in accord with the Council, I hereby decree, only legal dispositions which are published in the official bulletin of the Generalidad of Catalonia shall have obligatory force in the territory of Catalonia." Signed by President of the Generalidad and the President of the Council.

Franklin

No. 874   Barcelona, September 2, 1936

Subject: Propaganda by Labor Groups

Sir:

I have the honor to enclose a translation of a leaflet distributed freely throughout this city by the propaganda office of the labor organization Confederación Nacional del Trabajo (C.N.T.) and the Federación Anarquista Ibérica (F.A.I.). These two organizations have a great deal of power in the present government of Cataluña. I am indebted to Mr. Francisco Font, Secretary of the American Chamber of Commerce in Spain for this translation.

Lynn W. Franklin
American Consul General

To the Lower Middle Classes

There is absolutely no explanation for the fear the lower middle classes have of us.

It is logical that the rich, the millionaires, the nabobs, the landowners, fear us. Because they personify injustice and represent the privileged classes. But the lower middle class citizen, the owner of a small business or industry, should come to realize that we are only the enemy of those who by exploiting others have heaped up riches which rightfully belong to those who produced them, i.e., the workers.

In Catalonia the lower middle class is extraordinarily numerous. We wish to preserve it and its function in society. We are convinced that within the new society that is now taking shape, this lower middle class will constitute a very important part in the mechanism under construction now by the working class, since capitalism passed on the 19th of July.

The owners of small businesses and industries are for the most part people who rose from the working class. They succeeded in emancipating themselves from factories and working places governed by capitalism, at the price of their sweat and through thrift and economy.

If they know where they belong; if the lower middle classes realize that their place is on the workers' side, they must not fear for the future. The future belongs to those who with their feet firmly set on justice, are about to build up a new life.

The *Confederación Nacional de Trabajo* and the *Federación Anarquista Iberica* tell them to fear nothing. They invite the lower middle classes to have confidence and to place themselves where they belong: side by side with the proletariat. This is their duty.

Memorandum

of Conversation with Mr. Scott Nearing: His Views on the Present
Political Situation in Spain.

September 6, 1936

Mr. Scott Nearing called, stating that he was a representative of the
"Federated Press" and that he desired to meet Americans representing American business interests in order that he might ascertain their views on the
present situation as affecting their property interests. Mr. Nearing was given
certain names but was informed that these persons might not be willing to
comment on the situation.

Mr. Nearing said that a great deal of sympathy was felt by the French
people for the Communist movement in Spain. When news reached Paris of
the 24 Italian planes which had been landed for the Spanish rebels in Vigo,
he said that a great demonstration meeting was held in Paris, attended by
about 100,000 people, and that the will of the meeting was that the French
Government should permit the sending of arms to the Spanish Government.
He said that the famous Spanish woman Communist, La Pasionaria, was
being acclaimed in Paris.[22] In Hendaye, the communist refugees from Irun
were welcomed by the French townspeople, and were assisted on their way
through France back to the Spanish border at Port Bou. The militiamen
refugees were disarmed on their arrival in France, but were also assisted to
return to Spain. Mr. Nearing thought that intervention by France was very
likely if the Spanish rebels appeared to be getting the upper hand. In the
possibility of intervention by Germany and Italy Mr. Nearing saw a serious
danger of another general European war. He had just come from Germany,
where the Nazi press of course supported the Spanish fascist movement but
where he saw few signs of any deep personal interest on the part of the
German people in the Spanish struggle.

At Port Bou Mr. Nearing said a very efficient control was being maintained over persons coming into the country, and that he had had to be
approved by three distinct committees before being allowed to enter. He was
impressed by the extreme youth of the communistic authorities at the border,
as well as by the genuineness of their revolutionary feeling, and expressed
the opinion that communism had already gone very deep in Spain.

With regard to the general situation, Mr. Nearing felt that the coming
of the new government of Largo Caballero was but a step toward a more
radical form of government which in time would develop if permitted into a

---

[22]Her real name is Dolores Ibarruri (b. 1895). She was a popular Communist leader whose
oratory won her the nickname La Pasionaría. After the Civil War she lived in exile in the USSR
and returned to Spain after Franco's death in 1975, where she remains as of this writing, a major
figure in the Spanish Communist Party.

soviet system. He expressed the belief that the fall of Madrid would not crush the communist movement, but would rather have the effect of turning the Catalan government farther to the left and perhaps stiffening their opposition to the fascists. He seemed to feel that the strength of communism in Spain centered in Cataluña for the time being, and he attributed the lack of a better communist showing in Asturias to the thoroughness with which the Spanish conservative government had put down the October, 1934, uprising.

It was obvious from Mr. Nearing's statements and general attitude that he was heartily in sympathy with the present government in its struggle against its fascist opponents.

Mahlon F. Perkins

Memorandum

of conversation with German Consul General, Dr. Otto Koecher, Barcelona.

September 17, 1936

I made my official call this morning upon the German Consul General, Dr. Otto Koecher. He said that he had been here about three years and that the German colony was formerly quite large, about 6,000 persons. However, on account of the recent troubles, this number was now reduced to about 1,500.

Mr. Koecher was very pessimistic in every respect with regard to the present situation in Barcelona. He said that soldiers returning from Irun were frequently hungry and robbing the houses and apartments of his nationals. Protests might be filed, but they were of no avail. He looked forward in the near future to a situation in which the foreign Consuls would no longer be able to extend any effective protection to the property of their respective nationals. He therefore felt quite in sympathy with the recent proposal of the British Consul General that the Consuls General having banking interests here should definitely warn the local authorities that they would close their consular offices and withdraw from Barcelona if any decree were issued taking over the foreign banks.

Mr. Koecher said that of course he took account of the fact that his own position, as well as that of German nationals, was perhaps on a less favorable basis than that of some of the other representatives.

Mahlon F. Perkins

No. 21   Barcelona, September 22, 1936

Subject: Withdrawal of American Naval Vessels from Spanish Waters

Sir:

There is, at the present time, communication by rail and by air between Barcelona and Marseille; but there is no reliable method by which the mail of this office may be transmitted to Marseille and thence to various destinations other than by a naval vessel. In view of this circumstance, the Embassy at Paris and consular officers in Spain have been requested to avoid the ordinary mails except for very routine correspondence and to transmit their official communications under sealed cover by naval vessels or by personal messenger over land routes. It is possible to communicate with American naval vessels when present at Marseille or at Villefranche by land wire through the American Consulates at those ports (in the latter case to Nice); but this method is not so certain or speedy as by naval radio.

Shortly after the outbreak of the present revolt, a British cruiser was moored at the Customs wharf in Barcelona and since that date there has been a communications service twice or thrice a week by means of British destroyers between this port and Marseille. All official mail from this office is transmitted by this service to the American Consul General at Marseille for despatch; and a considerable amount of mail is received by the same means. The radio service of the cruiser is also used at times in communicating with the U.S.S. *Quincy* and occasionally for other contacts with Mallorca, Valencia, etc. There is, furthermore, a British communications service by means of destroyers along the Mediterranean coast of Spain, of which this office may avail itself. By this means, mail is exchanged with the Consulate at Valencia and with the Embassy at Madrid via Alicante.

I should like to make it very clear that, in the extraordinary circumstances now existing, the functions which consular officers are performing in Spain depend for their effectiveness to a very great extent upon the mail and radio communications of naval vessels. These two services form, in fact, a unit for the purpose of the effective protection of our interests. At the present moment, that effectiveness is not seriously impaired here only by reason of the fact that our communications are being maintained through the courtesy of the British Navy.

With reference to the possibility of the evacuation of the Consular staff in the event of a direct and active menace to their safety, resort may be had to the British naval vessels in Barcelona and possibly to the ships of other navies that might be here; but the British Admiral has made it very plain to us that, in such an emergency, there would be a very heavy demand upon his facilities by British nationals themselves.

I should add that, on the three occasions when the U.S.S. *Quincy* has visited Barcelona it has been of the greatest assistance in the despatch of radio messages, in the conveyance of consular officers and for intelligence and consultative purposes as well as for evacuation purposes. On these occasions reciprocal services have been freely extended to meet British needs.

This despatch is not intended to deal with the subject of the withdrawal of American nationals from Spain during the present crisis or with questions arising from the use of our naval vessels for that purpose. It is intended simply to invite attention to the fact that, so long as Consular offices are kept open in Spain for the general protection of our interests the presence of our naval vessels must remain an indispensable adjunct to the effective attainment of that purpose unless we choose to rely indefinitely upon the British navy.

It also seems to me not inappropriate to make reference to the somewhat intangible matter of the maintenance of our national prestige through the presence of naval vessels. Despite its intangible character, there is a reality in this form of prestige which heavily reinforces the general protective purpose for which we are here. As illustrative of this policy in action, I may cite the daily practice of H.M.S. *London* which each day at sunset lowers its flag to the accompaniment of the national anthems of Britain, Spain, Catalonia, and of those other nations having naval vessels in the port of Barcelona. The residents of this city gather daily in increasing numbers to listen to this ceremony. Thus the British flagship under the command of Vice Admiral Max Horton, Senior Naval Officer, by the unostentatious, but very definite character of its undisturbed daily routine, exerts, we believe, a quieting effect that is not without its value.

Mahlon F. Perkins
American Consul General

No. 28   Barcelona, September 26, 1936

Subject: Article Published in *La Humanitat* of Barcelona

Sir:

I enclose herewith an English translation of an article published in *La Humanitat*, a radical daily newspaper in Barcelona, and reprinted yesterday in *La Vanguardia*, the leading daily published in the Spanish language. The article demands that an immediate halt be called to the reign of violence which has existed in Barcelona since the outbreak of the present revolution. The exigency of the situation is evidenced from the fact that this demand appears in a paper of the type mentioned.

Yesterday afternoon I talked with an American who had just visited the local morgue, where he viewed the bodies of six persons assassinated the day previous. He thought that an equal number might have been killed during the preceding 24 hours in other parts of the city. He furthermore estimated that in this district there has been some 10,000 persons executed since the beginning of the present troubles. It is against this sort of lawlessness that the article in question is directed.

Mahlon F. Perkins
American Consul General

Translation

of article from *La Humanitat*, radical newspaper in Barcelona

Enough!! Enough!!

It is absolutely necessary that the Catalonian Government, the Central Committee of the Anti-fascist Militia and the remaining responsible organizations mobilize all their effectives to put an end to the wave of terrorism which exists, even yet, in some zones of Catalonia.

There are functioning still flying squads, automobile pirates, moving gangs that spread terror in their path. Behind them, after each night's incursion, there remains a wake of abhorrence, of crime and panic. And a counter revolutionary atmosphere as well exists, which is the worst evil that could be inflicted upon the struggle against fascism.

All the personal vengeances, all the private hatred, all the insane fury of the sick and the degenerate, all the venting of the basest passions are being tragically settled in nightly incursions that dishonor the revolution and perturb the life and work of the rearguard.

The hour has arrived for saying: Enough! The hour has arrived for opening the fester and exterminating the evil, cost what it may. It is a case of conscience, it is a debt to humanity, it is a revolutionary necessity.

The worst enemies of the revolution are those who dishonor it. It must be added that not a single one of them is capable of taking a gun and going to the firing line. They prefer to fight with their man alone, unarmed, in the open and at night.

The hour has arrived for saying: Enough! The Government of the Generalidad, the Central Committee of the Anti-fascists and the rest of the responsible organizations must act.

852.00/3305

Telegram   Barcelona, September 29, 1936, noon.

New cabinet of the Generalidad of Catalonia composed of twelve members was appointed September 26th. All local labor factions fighting against the Fascists are represented in an attempt by the Government to centralize and strengthen its position. Announced program asserts a determination to attain early victory in the war and to obtain for the masses the benefits of a new social and economic order: civil and military heads of Government remain unchanged.

CONFIDENTIAL. Lack of unified leadership in the field and in civil authority in Barcelona afford little promise of success for the above named program. Embassy and Ambassador informed.

Perkins

CONFIDENTIAL

Barcelona, October 2, 1936

Subject: Civil and Military Disorganization in Catalonia

Sir:

I have the honor to state that all obtainable information points toward the existence of such a general state of disorganization as to effectively preclude substantial success in any direction.

On the civil side, the Government of Catalonia has been a little more than a name by reason of the activity of various extra-legal radical groups which have, to a large extent, usurped actual authority in this and neighboring cities. These consist primarily of labor organizations whose activities, prior to the present outbreak, were especially directed towards demands for higher wages, shorter hours, and better living conditions. In July they were given arms, assisted in crushing the revolt in Barcelona, recruited thousands of volunteers for the field, and took over to a large extent the "policing" of city. They have adopted, and are known by, alphabetical titles such as the C.N.T., F.A.I., U.G.T., P.O.U.M., etc. While usurping powers properly belonging to the Government, these factions are now striving for individual supremacy. They are torn by mutual dissensions and by personal enmities, but they may all be said to be of a communistic or anarchistic character.

The recent defeats of the Central Government troops in the field, coupled with the adverse results of such a state of affairs in Barcelona and throughout Catalonia, have apparently caused all factions to realize the truth of Benjamin Franklin's remark concerning what happens to those who do not hang together; for, as stated in my telegram above mentioned, a new cabinet has been formed which contains members of all important groups. This cabinet announces a definite purpose to do away with the hydra-headed authority which has been functioning here during the last two months. In so doing, it is a matter of conjecture to what extent those concerned appreciate the fact that they are abandoning the principles of "comradeship" for which they are fighting and are adopting, at least for the time being, the very principles of their "fascist" adversaries.

On the military side, it would appear that there is a similar disorganization, although the Consulate General is not in a position to ascertain the facts in the same way as in Barcelona where so much is apparent to the eye. However, all reports tend in the same direction. The militias are enrolled for no definite term of service. They are organized into groups of ten; these groups are then formed into *centuries*; and the *centuries* into *columns*, which do not consist of any definite number of *centuries*. Each of the various component groups has its delegate, with the result that a definite centralized authority is lacking and disasters occur through conflict or disobedience of orders. Many volunteers are becoming tired of campaigning and seek excuses to leave the front and return to Barcelona. The flags of the various organizations above named are used in the field and are seen more frequently than the flag of the Republic. There is no adequate hospital corps. Many young women volunteers have been allowed to go to the front presumably for auxiliary purposes of aiding the sick and wounded rather than for actually bearing arms. This course, as might have been anticipated, has had unfortunate results; for it has resulted in a large number of venereal cases, effectively incapacitating numerous combatants for the time being.

This Consulate General is not able to draw a comparison with conditions among the "rebel" or "nationalist armies"; but, from all that can be gathered, it is believed that there exists among them a more severe discipline, which of itself might account for the recent successes obtained irrespective of other factors.

It remains to be seen whether the lately awakened appreciation here of the necessity for organization and centralization of authority will bring about a definite improvement. The outlook, however, is not promising. The Government is endeavoring to bring about a social revolution while currently engaged in a war against a determined military opponent who has, for the moment, but one objective: to crush his enemies in the field. It is a case of diversified efforts against singleness of purpose.

Mahlon F. Perkins
American Consul General

———————

852.00/3351

Telegram   Barcelona, October 4, 1936, 2 P.M.

British cruiser *London* left port this morning and their destroyer service between Barcelona and Marseille is discontinued for the time being. Understand that all foreign vessels have left the harbor.

Yesterday on receipt of information from the Embassy American citizens coming in touch with the Consulate General were informed of the general tenor of the threatened bombardment but in the absence of a specific notice it was not deemed advisable to circulate any general warning. Representative of the American Export Line who arrived here this morning by plane has just been informed. Embassy informed.

Perkins

852.00/3353

Telegram   Barcelona, October 4, 1936, 6 P.M.

October 4, 4 P.M. For Admiral Fairfield. Department of State circular telegram October 2, 2 P.M. directs consular officers in Spain as follows:

"You will continue to evacuate American nationals and foreigners other than Spaniards under the same conditions as heretofore." This Consulate General has standing instructions to extend appropriate assistance to the nationals of ten other countries.

In the event of an American naval vessel coming to Barcelona to evacuate American nationals in connection with threatened bombardment of this coast, it is likely that numerous requests for evacuation would be received from consuls general of these other nations. It would therefore be advantageous for me to know at this time approximate passenger capacity of naval vessels whether destroyer or cruiser for purposes of transportation to Marseille or Villefranche. It is impossible at this time to form any estimate of prospective number requesting evacuation in such contingency.

Perkins

No. 53   Barcelona, October 13, 1936

Subject: Measures to be Taken by Inhabitants of Barcelona in the Event of Air Raids

Sir:

I enclose herewith an original copy, with English translation, of the instructions issued by the Department of Defense in Barcelona on September 21, 1936, outlining the measures to be taken by the inhabitants of Barcelona in the event of air raids.

Mahlon F. Perkins
American Consul General

Generalidad of Catalonia
Department of Defense
Instructions For the Case of Air-Raids

The Councillor of Defense of the Generalidad of Catalonia, in agreement with the Municipality of Barcelona, and in view of eventual air-raids has dictated the following instructions which must strictly be complied with by all citizens.

First, REMAIN CALM. Avoid at all cost mass panic. Let it be known to all that an air-raid is of no great importance, seeing that for an area of 1 square kilometer not less than ten thousand bombs would be needed to cause serious damage. Barcelona has an area of about 100 square kilometers.

With calm and presence of mind nothing will happen; the warning will be given sufficiently in advance to enable all to comply with the instructions given hereafter without precipitation; these measures are sufficient to make sure that nothing will happen, and undue hurry will cause only accidents and delays.

Second, WARNING SIGNAL. Will be given chiefly by potent sirens. The local broadcasting stations will give warning during three minutes. At night, all motor cars will sound the klaxon during the same time and the night watchmen will blow the whistles. Control will use portable sirens.

Third, RESPONSIBILITY FOR THE COMPLIANCE WITH THESE INSTRUCTIONS. In each building this responsibility, independent of that of each tenant, rests with an appointed representative of the anti-aerial defense, who may be anyone answering the following requisites in the order of their enumeration:

   a) elected by all the tenants
   b) Government, Generalidad or Municipal Official. If there be various, the oldest in years, being in active service.
   c) Janitors
   d) Any person in the nearest vicinity keeping premise open.

Fourth, ADVISING TENANTS. The representative of the anti-aerial defense is responsible for advising all the tenants, starting from the ground floor upwards.

Fifth, SHELTERS. In each building there shall be designated as one or more places in the basement, if any, or else in the first floor. They must have the necessary capacity and be separated from house fronts and patios. If basements are used, they must not contain any inflammable or otherwise dangerous matter. It must be borne in mind that a bomb of 100 kg. which is the model the fascists possess, cannot pass through more than two stories, causing damage in the third.

Sixth, EXTINGUISHING LIGHTS. In case of air raids during the night factories shall immediately extinguish all lights, and in all buildings doors and windows must be hermetically closed, so no light whatever can be detected from outside. Each family must provide itself with portable lamps or other forms of illumination, for the transit on stairs and shelters. The pressure of gas will be diminished and in each building the main pipes must be closed.

Seventh, COMMERCE. On sounding the alarm, all business places must be locked immediately, and the public inside must be given shelter behind the premises.

Eighth, JANITORS. Janitors must likewise close the house doors, with two minutes to take in passers-by who are in front of the building sounding the alarm.

Ninth, END OF AIR RAID. This will be announced in similar manner of alarm, and until this signal is given, nobody can leave the shelter.

Tenth, TELEPHONE DIRECTORY. In each building or shelter there shall be a list containing the telephone numbers of fire-brigades, nearest hospital and Commissioner of Public Order, so that all of these services can be called immediately, if necessary.

Eleventh, PERSON IN TRANSIT THROUGH BARCELONA. All motor cars connected with the anti-aerial defense on hearing the alarm must stop at once and remain isolated at parking places, or the sidewalks, leaving free the center of public thoroughfares for the transit of cars connected with the anti-aerial defense service. Conductors and passengers of tramcars, buses, cars, trucks, and other vehicles shall enter the nearest porter's lodge. The same applies to pedestrians who moreover may avail themselves of those underground stations designated as shelters, in view of the thinness of certain underground tunnels.

Twelfth, ANTI-AERIAL DEFENSE. The public is herewith informed that independent of defense by artillery and planes any air raid will be repelled by concerted machine-gun fire covering the whole city and thus avoiding low flying of enemy planes. It is, however, strictly prohibited to fire guns and pistols, and anyone disobeying this order will be seriously punished.

Thirteenth, FACTORIES, INDUSTRIES, THEATERS, HOSPITALS. Each of these constituting a special case, the corresponding committees will designate shelters and dictate the measures to be taken in case of air-raid along the lines of these general instructions, their committees being responsible for the observation of these precautions. In many cases, due to the particular situation of the premises, the public may remain in them, there being no necessity to seek refuge in special shelters.

Fourteenth, EMERGENCY LIGHTING. In the shelters in private houses, factories, industries, commerce, theaters, hospitals, etc., emergency lighting must be installed, to function before the general extinguishing of lights.

Fifteenth, RAILWAY AND UNDERGROUND TRAINS. As soon as alarm is sounded, underground trains will stop and the electric current will be shut off. Circulation of trains in Barcelona stations and nearby places will be suspended.

Sixteenth, PUBLICITY OF THESE INSTRUCTIONS. These instructions must be exhibited in janitors' lodges, workshops, commercial and any other place of amusement, factories, etc. that may shelter public. Moreover, cafes, theaters, etc., must also exhibit the special instructions dictated by their committees, with large conspicuous signs indicating shelters.

Barcelona, 21st September, 1936.

The Councillor of Defense
Felipe Diaz Sandino

2

A LIFE OF WAR AND
ECONOMIC REVOLUTION
(OCTOBER 1936–FEBRUARY 1937)

THE PERIOD FROM October 1936 to February 1937 was one that witnessed the birth of an economic revolution heavily dependent on anarchist and libertarian economic thought and the exigencies of war unique in modern European experience. In Cataluña and the nearby region of Aragon, but also in other Republican zones, collectivization of industries and farms, with a heavily communalistic emphasis, provided a unique experiment in radical economics and business. This development, while mostly affecting agriculture, was also clearly seen in the industrial sector. Central to any understanding of Barcelona, these developments impacted the great Catalan city.

Collectivization usually began with a group of workers in a particular factory spontaneously taking control of the plant, running it, dividing among themselves the profits of the enterprise, and making sure the owners never returned to power. During the fall and winter of 1936–37, reluctant and surprised governments in Madrid and Barcelona created appropriate legislation to legitimize and expand upon these individual actions. In the course of several months, most unions in Barcelona became involved, as did such larger organizations as the UGT and CNT, leading ultimately to the collectivization of whole industries and not simply individual businesses. Thus, the CNT took charge of many food production facilities, creating a network of supply committees in Barcelona. Various Catalan communities also experimented with certificates and coupons as replacements for money, since many anarchist leaders vowed to create a money-less society. While this effort failed, bartering became serious business, particularly as the war dragged on, when the supply of currency (especially coins) declined sharply. In fact, by the end of the war peseta and mill coins were not to be found in any Republican zone. Owners of business enterprises, particularly factories, were killed, brushed aside, or sometimes absorbed into the egalitarian management of their businesses. In effect, a collective capitalism replaced a more traditional form of economic activity. By this process of collectivism a group of workers continued to operate a facility for profit, much like a privately owned business, yet shared any earnings amongst themselves rather than with the investors in the enterprise. This process of collectivization within the Republican zone was most extensive and clearly most militant within Cataluña. There a drive for a complete restructuring of the economy—i.e., sharing of the wealth of all enterprises with their workers and the deposit of all assets in worker banks—exceeded the economic theories of the day and the practices of the more conservative Republican government and, initially, of the Generalidad. To a large extent support for new economic methods emerged in Cataluña more than anywhere else because of the significant proletarian population and the existence of industrial enterprises, conditions that when combined in a highly politicized environment made new experiments easy to carry out.[1]

The Generalidad sought to regularize the situation by issuing a decree on 24 October 1936 that authorized operational control of businesses by workers. They would work with and audit units of production (such as companies, shops, and plants), which could still remain in the hands of their original owners. An Industrial and Commercial Credit Bank was created for the purpose of providing funding and credit facilities to these workers. While these labor committees could not and did not provide the kind of professional management that they usually replaced, their enthusiasm was unlimited in the early days of the Civil War.

A new society was being born out of a revolution. To capture the mood typical in a collectivized company, one has only to turn to the U.S. consular files for examples. In December 1936, for instance, the Consulate was informed by the workers of the United Shoe Machinery Company that they had collectivized the plant. The letter began by referring to the consul as "Comrade" and after citing clauses in the decree of 24 October as justification concluded with the following paragraph:

> We do not wish to end this circular letter without calling your attention to the importance in the economic-social order represented by the new structure of the economy of our country, and there is no doubt that the system of collectivization of our firm, likewise as is being done in many others, is the fruit of the economic-social revolution we are carrying through and the essential base for saving our economy, since it will permit, counting with the sympathy and cooperation of all the Spanish proletariat, the reconstruction of the collective, and this will be the best compensation to our efforts toward the salvation of our country. Health!
>
> The Council of Enterprise.[2]

This kind of correspondence highlighted yet another concern of American diplomats, namely the protection of foreign investments in Barcelona.

---

[1] The literature on anarchism, libertarianism and collectivization is voluminous. Some of the more important recent works include César M. Lorenzo, *Los anarquistas españoles y el poder* (Paris, 1972); José Peirats, *La CNT en la revolución española*, 3 vols. (Paris, 1971); Vernon Richards, *Lessons of the Spanish Revolution, 1936–1939* (London, 1972); Antonio Rlorza, *La utopía anarquista bajo la segunda república española* (Madrid, 1973); John Brademas, *Anarco-sindicalismo y revolución en España (1930–1937)* (Barcelona, 1974).

[2] Department of State Records, National Archives, 852.00 file.

Like other diplomats, those of the United States complained about the seizure of assets belonging to foreign nationals. The Americans protested the expropriation by workers of typewriter firms, automobile factories, and eventually of the telephone company, an American operated enterprise.[3]

Collectivist economics dominated Republican economic activities throughout most of 1937. Opinion regarding the success of collectivization remains mixed; if a consensus had to be identified, it would be that the program of workers running factories did not prove as successful as anarchist and libertarian theory suggested. Furthermore, the results of the program in the agricultural sector were mixed, although no final conclusion can be drawn because the program continued through only one planting. However, even with this new form of economic activity, products were made, crops grown, people employed, and the economy survived. For the historian, one of the most interesting by-products of this unique economic experiment was a vast quantity of literature dealing with the economics of collectivization in Spain. A few facts suggest the effect of the war on Republican economics in general. The loss of markets, interruptions in the flow of raw materials, the depleted labor force resulting from workers joining the armies and militias—all led to economic disorders. In turn, these disruptions caused a reduction in overall output of between 60 and 75 percent from September 1936 to October 1937 when compared to the output of January 1936. Production subsequently rose in some industries and declined in others. Luxury items, for example, experienced a decline while war-related production (bullets and weapons, for instance) increased. In general, by about November 1937, depletion of inventories contributed enormously to a disrupted economy. By February 1937, the conversion of the Catalan economy from a peacetime one making consumer goods and industrial products into a wartime one dedicated to supplying armies had been effected.[4]

For each Catalan the most important issue for the remainder of the war was simply basic survival in uncertain financial times during which assassinations, aerial bombardments, changing currencies, lack of sufficient quantities of food and jobs made life difficult at best. The economy of Barcelona, as it slowed dramatically in the fall of 1936, forced many organizations to do makeshift machining and supplying of raw materials. Lipstick cases were converted into cartridges; bread was made from anything but wheat. Collectivization throughout Cataluña disrupted centuries-old commercial patterns and inevitably caused a sharp decline in hard currency. Invariably, the economic curse of inflation drove upward the cost of living. Between July 1936

[3]For treatments on collectivization in Catalonia and in Barcelona the most useful works are Frank Minz, *La collectivisation en Espagne, 1936–39* (Paris, 1967); Albert Pérez Baró, *30 mesos de col-lectivisme a Catalunya (1936–39)* (Barcelona, 1970); Pedro Voltes Bou, *Historia de la economía española,* vol. 2. See also Michael Seidman, "Work and Revolution: Worker's Control in Barcelona in the Spanish Civil War," *Journal of Contemporary History,* 17 (July 1982): 409–33.

[4]A convenient source of statistical data is Tamames, *La República: La Era de Franco,* pp. 301–30.

and March 1937 the cost of living doubled, while wages rose a mere 15 percent. Lines formed at bakers' and butchers' shops while a black market flourished. Women demonstrated in the Barcelona streets demanding additional supplies of bread and other food staples during April 1937. These demonstrations did not change either the lack of food or increase the availability of additional ration tickets. Meanwhile, trade union organizations called on their members to make more sacrifices for the war effort. Stanley Payne cited statistics indicating that industrial production declined almost steadily month by month from July 1936 through September 1938, down to a third of its prewar level. Catalan unemployment increased from approximately sixty thousand in July 1936 to about eighty thousand by the end of the year. The decline in the economy had outpaced the ability of recruiting efforts to absorb all the extra men into military units, and many women had no alternative careers to pursue when out of work. With only slight fluctuations in the unemployment figures, conditions remained the same throughout 1938. Out of a prewar work force of about 600 thousand, unemployment hovered at around 15 to 18 percent of available labor (both male and female). Such statistics illustrate the fact that life for the average citizen in Barcelona was becoming more complex and difficult.

In summary, four reasons account for this general situation. First, there was unemployment despite the demands for manpower to fill armies. Second, inflation took its toll due to the loss of productive capability and the insufficient supply of necessities. Third, there was an influx of 700 thousand refugees into Cataluña. Fourth, inefficient administration of the economy became a common problem for many companies and government agencies.[5]

The Nationalists made significant military progress during this period. They pushed northward toward Madrid, taking Toledo in September, the same month that Franco was appointed head of government of the Spanish state and declared generalissimo of all the Nationalist armies. The battle for Madrid was fought in November; the Republicans were able miraculously to hold on to the capital despite actual fighting in some of the city's outskirts. In February 1937, Málaga in southeastern Spain fell to the Nationalists, a major victory for Franco. By June, the Basque country was well under the control of the Nationalists. Thus by mid-year, residents of Barcelona, while not threatened directly by invasion, could see clearly that the war would be a long one in which the Nationalists had already made significant progress. Within the diplomatic community concern for the viability of the Republic was expressed, although more was to be felt by the end of 1937.[6]

---

[5]Carr, *Spain*, pp. 658–59; Broué and Témime, *La révolution et la guerre d'Espagne*, p. 275; Payne, *The Spanish Revolution*, 257–58.

[6]For discussions of the war during this period, especially useful are Thomas, *The Spanish Civil War*, and Broué and Témime, *La révolution et la guerre d'Espagne*.

852.00/3660

No. 53   Barcelona, October 13, 1936

Subject: Interview with Mr. Martin L. Glidewell, Agent in Barcelona for
     American Steamship Companies

Sir:

I have the honor to enclose herewith a memorandum of an interview
on October 12, 1936, with Mr. Martin L. Glidewell, Agent in Barcelona for
American steamship lines which contains certain comments by him in regard
to the present political situation in Spain.

Mahlon P. Perkins
American Consul General

Memorandum

October 12, 1936

Mr. Glidewell said that he had just returned from Gibraltar and certain
ports in southern Spain where he had been shipping on one of his steamers
a large amount of freight for the United States which had accumulated on
account of the absence of steamers for the past several weeks.

In his opinion, the war will be over by the end of the year and it would
then again be possible for business to take a new start in Barcelona. There
was no doubt but that the insurgent forces would win and that they would
put an end once and for all to communism and other isms so prevalent in
Catalonia. He said that the program for social and economic changes here
was an impracticable and impossible one, even if there were no war and there
existed a free field in which business men now refugees in Italy and other
places who would return to Barcelona the moment that it was safe for them
to do so.

Mr. Glidewell believed that the insurgents would not compromise with
the Catalonians and that they would immediately proceed in this direction
after the fall of Madrid. For the time being he would conduct his shipping
business from Genoa, which was a central point for the shipping of his line
visiting Portugal, Spain and Italy. He thought that in the process of taking
over Barcelona there might well be local disturbances and that the best plan
was to watch developments from day to day. After the crisis was over he
would return to Barcelona but in the meantime his office would be left in the
hands of his Spanish representatives.

In the territory which is now under the occupation of the insurgent
forces, Mr. Glidewell said that efforts were being made to restore normal
business conditions as soon as possible.

No. 64

Barcelona, October 17, 1936

Subject: Political Conditions in Barcelona

Sir:

With reference to my despatch No. 37 of October 2, 1936, entitled, "Civil and Military Disorganization in Cataluña," I have the honor to state that the continued progress of the armed forces attacking the Government has served to make still more keenly felt here the necessity for the laying aside of factional differences and a concentration upon unity of effort and the avoidance of non-essentials. However, it is doubtful whether any very effective measures have been taken and also whether any measures taken at this late date will prove of any avail.

Within the last few weeks, Barcelona presents, superficially at least, a more normal appearance. There are fewer groups of armed irresponsibles wandering about the streets and there is less of a tendency on the part of the militia police to interfere with the free movements of the population. There are many more motor cars in evidence than a month ago and the Confederación Nacional del Trabajo (C.N.T.) has put into operation a fleet of some 75 taxicabs for the use of the public.

Running counter, however, to this superficial tide of apparent "normalcy," there is a deep undercurrent of discouragement. Not only the few people "in the know," but groups increasingly larger are beginning to realize, in spite of the suppression of unfavorable news, that the game is up. This morning a long line of small children, carrying large bags, marched by the Consulate General: these proved to be some of the children that have been sent here from Madrid and neighboring cities on account of the shortage of provisions in the capital and fear of injury to them in case of bombing and street fighting. It is obvious that, with such scenes before their eyes, the population generally cannot long be kept in ignorance of the fact that their cause is lost. Even here in Barcelona, many kinds of food supplies are running short; long queues may be seen waiting to buy provisions; only small amounts of sugar, potatoes, etc., may be purchased at a time; and cards are necessary in order to make even these purchases. Meat and eggs are practically not to be had, although small quantities may be had at prices beyond the reach of the average purse.

Banking, finance, and commercial relations are handled by make-shift devices. The wages of labor are, in many instances, being paid, as reported in connection with the affairs of American concerns, by illegal levies upon banking accounts. The limitation upon the amount of commercial paper to be discounted is substantially set aside by a decree which transfers such loans to a new account and allows the further extension of discounts up to the amount originally permitted. Goods continue to be manufactured for which there is practically no market. It may be said that the community keeps going from what momentum still remains from the much impaired structure of the capitalistic system of a few months ago. Since that system is anathema to the elements now in control here, there is apparently little consideration given to the economic future of this great manufacturing center of Spain; for it is presumed that it is the intention to build a new social and economic structure to replace the former one.

Perhaps the most serious single item in the economic situation is the question of the textile industry which employs between 200,000 and 300,000 people. All cotton in Catalonia has been commandeered; for the mills must be kept going. There is little disposition to pay for cotton even were there the disposition to do so. Large amounts of manufactured goods are accumulating; probably not more than 5% can be sold outside of Spain, and the Spanish market is in ruins at the moment. It is reported that no cotton is *en route* from the United States and other countries toward Barcelona; insurance is almost prohibitive; and the importers have neither cash or credit sufficient to make importations. Since the mills must be kept going, there would seem to be no alternative, in the opinion of bankers, but the issuance of fiat money to maintain the workers, such currency being based on the value of the accumulated manufactured goods. Even with the possession of the commandeered cotton now here, supplies may be exhausted early in November. The economic future is therefore a dark one.

With military defeat staring them in the face at present and the prospect that the military forces opposing the present government will forthwith proceed to the reduction of Catalonia, and with the economic situation as above outlined, it would seem that the acute crisis for this part of Spain is yet to come and that this crisis will not be far off. The picture thus painted is possibly blacker than the facts may warrant; but it represents, as nearly as I can do so, the condition in which Barcelona finds herself after 90 days of "Revolution."

Mahlon F. Perkins
American Consul General

852.00/3518

Telegram   Barcelona, October 20, 1936

Sec. of State

President Azaña arrived Barcelona from Madrid last night by motor car; three members of his Cabinet also in Barcelona. Local situation superficially unchanged. Reliably informed that white forces from Zaragoza have advanced half way towards Lérida. For some time one foreign consul general has had codes and confidential files on board naval vessel just outside of harbor, and another has been communicating, and continues to do so, by radio from his office with flagship in similar position. We desire constantly maintain close contact with American naval vessel at Villefranche or other nearby station. Please repeat above to the Secretary of State and American Embassy at Madrid. Could you kindly mail copies radio news service.

Perkins

852.00/3555

Telegram   Barcelona, October 24, 1936, 4 P.M.

Following telegram has been received from Ambassador Bowers.

October 23, 11 A.M. Reported by the French press that Azaña in speech to militia in Barcelona said fall of Madrid not important and foreseen. Also that he has established himself and government in Barcelona. Please inform me of the facts and keep Embassy promptly informed of any significant words or activities of Azaña hereafter. Bowers.

To which I replied as follows:

October 23, 5 P.M. Your cipher telegram of October 23, 11 A.M. Azaña has made no (repeat no) public statements since his arrival to our knowledge. Perkins.

Embassy at Madrid informed of the above telegrams by telephone yesterday. Also to the Ambassador as follows:

October 24, 3 P.M. My October 23, 5 P.M. On the 22 I paid informal courtesy call upon President Azaña who has established himself in the local Parliament Building as if prepared for an indefinite stay. His arrival here has injected a new and uncertain factor into the field of local politics. The treatment accorded him by the local press seems hardly consonant with the essential importance of his presence here. President Azaña desired me to send you his very kindest wishes.

Perkins

852.00/3573

Telegram   Barcelona, October 26, 1936

Sec. of State

No further developments in connection with the presence here of President Azaña.

I have gained distinct impression that only a small percentage of the Barcelona population have other than a most limited local outlook or even yet adequately appreciate the present precarious status of their cause. Sunday, however, there was held in the bull ring a mass meeting of all radical organizations with the exception of the Marxists which was dedicated to "the triumph of the proletarian revolution"; even such bitterly opposed groups as the UGT and CNT met in the interest of the "unity of the proletariat."

Perkins

852.00/3586

Telegram   Barcelona, October 28, 1936

Sec. of State

Minister of Marine Prieto arrived Barcelona yesterday by plane from Madrid and returned the same day.

Air transit from here to France has lately been freely available but I now understand that although service has been augmented reservations must be made days in advance and may be suddenly requisitioned by the government.

Decrees appearing today call for military service drafts years 1932 to 1935, inclusive, and order general turning in of firearms in the hands of people within eight days.

Local situation though superficially calm and presenting a more normal appearance physically than a few weeks ago contains definitely explosive elements and must be watched constantly. Reported commencement of the formation of local governments in Aragon, Valencia, et cetera, seem to indicate intention to concentrate on the defense of localities in the face of existing and impending military reverses.

Perkins

852.00/3671

Telegram   Barcelona, November 3, 1936

Admiral Hatfield & Sec. of State

It is reported that Prieto's visit was to seek military assistance from Catalonia but that he found disorganization here rendered visit futile. For some days there have been rumors of American Bellanca planes being equipped by Government forces for military purposes but no verification yet obtainable.

Decree of Catalan Government of 24th ultimo calls for "collectivization" of all industries controlled since July 19 last provided employing one hundred or more persons and industries employing less than one hundred if abandoned or owners fascists, also enterprises employing less than one hundred if majority of workmen and owners agree to collectivization or if three-fourths of the workers vote in favor. Reference my despatch No. 88 dated October 31 subject socialization of industry. I have requested that American interests be protected.

Perkins

No. 97   Barcelona, November 6, 1936

Subject: President Manuel Azaña in Barcelona

Sir:

With reference to my telegram of October 24, 4 P.M., I have the honor to state that I called informally upon President Manuel Azaña on October 22nd at the Parliament Building after arrangements had been made through President Companys of Catalonia. I was accompanied by Consul Franklin. There was no discussion of political topics; but, in reply to his inquiry, my appreciation was expressed of the degree of protection that it had been found possible to give to American interests in the present emergency. The President inquired whether there was an American naval vessel in port and was informed that they had been withdrawn from Spanish waters, only to be recalled in the event of some specific emergency requiring their presence in specific cases of need in connection with the safety of American citizens.

President Azaña appeared wholly calm and unperturbed in outward manner in spite of the grievous state of his country and of the very considerable personal peril in which he must unquestionably find himself. His attitude was of the utmost cordiality consistent with the dignity of his position; and I was deeply impressed with the apparent sincerity and elevation of his character.

During the two weeks that the President has been in Barcelona, the local press has hardly paid him the attention which his position would seem to warrant. He has given out no public statements or made any public appearances. On the contrary, he has either kept, or been kept, in the background. This may be due to the fact that, as there is one President of Catalonia, President Azaña does not desire to embarrass in any way the head of the local government. For some days, he is reported as having actually withdrawn from the city and taken up his residence in the vicinity of the Castle of Montjuich, whence he may make motor trips to the Monastery of Montserrat, some 25 miles in the country. It is also said that the decrees which must have the Presidential signature have been brought from Madrid by airplane for him to sign. Although various ministers have been going back and forth between Madrid and Barcelona, it cannot be said that the government has in any sense established itself in this city.

Numerous rumors have been afloat with regard to the President; that he has been deprived of most of the presidential guards coming with him from Madrid; that he is virtually a prisoner; that a certain radical organization served notice that his place was in Madrid and that he must return within 8 days, etc.

Whatever truth there may be in these rumors, it is certain that President Azaña must feel himself in a most unenviable position and must hardly know which way to turn. Caught between two extreme elements, he seems practically shorn of all power and with hardly more influence than can be exerted by his own personality. My impression is that notwithstanding the excellence of his character, the President lacks the daring and the force to make himself felt in the midst of times that are too tempestuous for any but the most venturesome and hardy political leaders.

Mahlon F. Perkins

852.00/3718

Telegram Barcelona, November 7, 1936

Admiral Fairfield & Second Assistant Sec.

Contact was made with the Embassy by telephone at 11:30 this morning and I was informed that insurgents are in the outskirts of the city, members of the government are leaving for Valencia.

Barcelona remains apparently calm inasmuch as local press conceals gravity of Madrid situation. Some ten thousand volunteers have been sent out in the last few days presumably for defense of the capital but in all probability they are destined for the defense of the Valencia, Catalonia, Llano and adjacent hinterland. Although some of the population have lost their early enthusiasm as a result of depression and doubt as to any eventual betterment of living conditions under a "red" regime, there is not, as yet, any evidence here of a disposition on part of labor groups and Government to compromise the struggle.

Perkins

852.00/3732

Telegram   Barcelona, November 9, 1936

Sec. of State

Yesterday parade of radical organizations consisting of Anarchists, Socialists and Communists occupied between four and five hours of passing the Consulate General. Demonstration was in honor of the Soviet anniversary November 7, was orderly and non-military and did not arouse much display of enthusiasm on the part of the bystanders who were far less numerous than might have been expected. In the afternoon the President of Catalonia in a broadcast hailed "Glorious Russia and the Glorious Republic of Catalonia." Evening of the 7th Soviet Consul General held reception attended by officials of the local government.

CONFIDENTIAL. Soviet steamer of about 3000 tons has arrived at Barcelona and according to reports is unloading munitions of war. Unverified reports of two other Soviet steamers at southern ports. Also that munitions arriving here in small lots by sailing ships and motor trucks from France.

Perkins

852.00/3866

Barcelona, November 10, 1936

Subject: Recent Contacts Between Soviet Russia and Catalonia

Sir:

With reference to my telegram of November 9, 5 P.M. concerning the local celebration of the Soviet holiday of November 7th, I have the honor to enclose herewith copies of the pictorial section of the Barcelona *La Vanguardia* of today together with an article describing this celebration. Lack of time prevents a translation of this news item being enclosed.

The parade through the principal streets of the city was noteworthy for its complete orderliness and for the degree of unity that was manifested in the full cooperation of the various radical labor organizations which composed it. The anarchist-syndicalist group (F.A.I. and C.N.T.) which had refused to take part in the parade of October 6th, took perhaps the most conspicious part in the day's celebrations.

There has latterly been considerable evidence of a drawing together of Catalonia and Soviet Russia, especially on the part of officials here. This seems to have been due largely to the force of recent circumstances. The success of the insurgents has been steadily paring down the territory under the control of the Government until it has reached a point where, with the fall of Madrid, the principal bulwark remaining to the Government will be the Mediterranean littoral, containing the two large industrial cities of Barcelona and Valencia. It is in this part of Spain that the radical movements have been extreme and active. With the realization of the fact that the victory so confidently expected a few months ago is vanishing from sight, it has been but natural to look more and more to foreign support; and the most likely direction in which that may be found appears to be Soviet Russia. Transportation from Russia to Catalonia may easily be had by an all water route from Odessa to Barcelona; and supplies by this means have already arrived as reported in my despatch No. 59 of October 16, 1936. The spirit of cooperation, as well as actual means to that end, have no doubt been promoted by the arrival some two months ago of the new Soviet Consul General Antonov Ovscenko as reported in my No. 41 of October 4, 1936.

However, in this relation, the adage of "any port in a storm" may well be borne in mind. There are rumors already that the anarchist-syndicalists are not very enthusiastic over this new trend in affairs and that they view the participation of Soviet influence and the equipment of Catalonian militia with Soviet arms as something that must be carefully watched lest the Communist organizations be built up to a strength which may prove a menace to the present predominant position of the F.A.I. and the C.N.T.

Another factor which may militate eventually against Soviet Russia acquiring anything of long term value here is the Catalonian character which is individualistic and materialistic. It is the business acumen and acquisitiveness of the Catalonian which is responsible for the growth and recent prosperity of Barcelona in contrast with some other portions of Spain. It is said that the employees of some of the large enterprises that have been "taken over" for the benefit of the workers are already beginning to question where they are going to come out in the long run and are now highly skeptical about matters that but a few months ago aroused great enthusiasm. The view is held by competent observers that the Catalonian cannot, from his very temperament, be long persuaded to embark upon social and economic courses of an idealistic nature if such programs do not produce pesetas.

Mahlon F. Perkins
American Consul General

Barcelona, November 18, 1936

Subject: Article by Mr. Lawrence A. Fernsworth Concerning Conditions
in Spain

Escape of Catholic Primate of Catalonia

There is as yet the untold story of how the Catholic Primate of Catalonia,
the aged Cardinal Vidal i Barraquer, Archbishop of Tarragona, and his eccle-
siastical entourage, were rescued from a red mob with machine guns and put
safely on an Italian ship for Rome in the early days of the civil war. The
story has heretofore been kept secret for fear that terrorists might wreak
vengeance on those responsible for the cardinal's escape. It was told to your
correspondent by the man who made the safety of the cardinal his personal
affair and as to whose identity it may be said that he is one of the leaders of
the Catalan left party with an important position in the present Catalan government. Indeed in those early days when passion was running riot the Catalan
government made it its special business to try to save the entire Catalan
episcopacy and as many of the clergy as possible. It saved all but one of the
eight Catalan bishops, and placed more than 500 priests, including most of
the monks of Montserrat, aboard Italian ships for Italy.

The saving of Cardinal Vidal was related as follows by the man in
question.

"A few days after the rising, when it was apparent that mobs were
getting out of hand, I drove to Tarragona to see the cardinal and try to induce
him to depart with me at once. He did not realize his peril and refused to go.
The next day, July 21, I sent heavily armed cars to the episcopal palace under
orders to take the cardinal and his household away whether they desired to
leave or not. They were vacated to Poblet, the historic old monastery known
as 'Catalonia's Escorial,' and suitably housed in a mansion nearby where they
were provided with every comfort.

"For reasons which it would be indiscreet to relate in detail, the cardinal
and his followers felt obliged to leave their retreat some fifteen days later and
were on the highway in a motorcar bound for nearby Montblanch in the hope
of finding refuge there. They were met and captured by a band of terrorists
bent upon taking their lives. Word of what had occurred reached Montblanch
and a delegation of citizens under my orders and armed with carbines and
machine guns, was immediately organized to go to the rescue. We finally
got them away from the mob and they were rushed to Barcelona and placed
aboard an Italian ship in the harbor."

The Bishop of Barcelona, Manuel Irurita, owes his life in part to the
Anarcho-Syndicalist leader, Buenaventura Durruti, who got him safely out
of the episcopal palace here, and to Major Pérez Farrás, who was condemned
to death as the leader of the Catalan forces in the military rising of 1934.

Major Farrás personally saw the Bishop safely aboard an Italian ship. This is likewise an untold story and of interest in view of a message from Rome some time ago expressing doubt as to the fate of the Bishop.

Of the six other Bishops, the Bishops of Gerona and Vich were safely ushered out of the country, the Bishop of La Seo de Urgel, who is also the co-Prince of Andorra, and the Bishop of Solsona, found safety in Andorra for a short time and later went to France, while the Bishop of Tortosa was put aboard a vessel at Castellón. The Bishop of Lérida was the unfortunate victim of a mob. In the early revolutionary days a state of complete anarchy prevailed at Lérida, but the Catalan government has now imposed its authority there. Aside from these eight bishops, there appears to be some doubt as to the fate of the auxiliary bishop to the Archbishop of Tarragona.

A large number of priests still remain here, more or less in hiding, and some under the protection of the Catalan government. A number of them are in a home for the aged in this city. Your correspondent knows of two cases of priests who have abandoned their frocks, taken wives and become members of the Catalan militias.

Lawrence A. Fernsworth

852.00/3960

Telegram   Barcelona, December 2, 1936, 7 P.M.

I am reliably informed that during the past few weeks there have been increasing quantities of munitions arriving from France largely by motor truck. Some thousands of foreign volunteers have also arrived: these are mostly French but consist also of Russians, Germans, Italians, Poles, Belgians, and other aliens of radical sympathies. Some of these groups have been observed by ourselves. I have little doubt that these volunteers have been a factor in prolonging the resistance to Madrid, and from this vantage point the struggle appears to be presenting a more international aspect than at any time hitherto.

The port of Barcelona is almost bare of shipping. Although evidence of an effective blockade is lacking, small Spanish craft are being seized along the coast and traffic is reduced through apprehension. Street lights of the city are being colored blue and places of refuge arranged against air raids.

Perkins

852.00/4212

No. 128   Barcelona, December 2, 1936

Subject: Article by Mr. Lawrence A. Fernsworth, Concerning the Secret Reign
    of Terror in Barcelona and Catalonia

Sir:

    With reference to my despatch No. 47 of October 8, 1936, I have the
honor to transmit herewith a copy of a further article by Mr. Lawrence A.
Fernsworth, Barcelona correspondent of the *London Times*, concerning the
secret reign of terror resulting in numerous "executions" in Barcelona and the
rest of Catalonia since the beginning of the military uprising on July 19th.

    Mr. Fernsworth states that this "reign" may have cost some four thou-
sand lives in Barcelona and twice that number in all Catalonia. There is no
question but that this estimate is far too small. I have heard the number placed
as high as seventy-five thousand and I believe that the correct number would
be between these two extremes.

    Mr. Fernsworth also states that this reign of terror "seems to have well
nigh ended." I consider that this statement is quite erroneous. My telegram
to the Department of November 25, 5 P.M. reports the execution of three
Spanish employees of the Armstrong Cork Company at Palamós as recently
as November 17th. I am constantly hearing of the disappearance of persons
of whom no trace can be found and I am also meeting from time to time
persons who are daily living in fear of their lives. In this connection, reference
is made to my confidential despatch No. 118 of November 20, 1936, entitled
"Case of Don Piu Valls Feliu." I am furthermore in almost daily receipt of
reports that the number of bodies at the morgue which are obviously the result
of assassinations continues high and that there are many victims whose bodies
never reach the morgue, but are disposed of clandestinely. I am therefore
wholly unable to accept Mr. Fernsworth's statement in this particular. As I
have previously stated, I have the highest regard for this writer's veracity;
but I believe him to be so blinded by his political sympathies that he is at
times unable to assess the facts from a realistic point of view.

    The leaders of the Government in Catalonia are without a doubt opposed
to, and revolted by, the secret reign of terror existing here. There have been
notable instances in which they have taken measures, even at personal risk,
to save life; but nevertheless they have been unable to suppress a savage
proscription which has cost the lives of many thousands of persons wholly
innocent of any crime whatsoever.

    I am not in a position to comment upon the executions and cruelties
which have been perpetrated by the opposing faction in this civil war, and I
have no information upon which to question Mr. Fernsworth's position that
the misdeeds of the insurgents have been even more heinous than those

committed within the ranks of the "Government." The atrocities committed by both sides turn back the clock of civilization by centuries.

Mahlon F. Perkins
American Consul General

Reign of Terror

A secret reign of terror which since the beginning of the military uprising on July 19 has cost some four thousand lives in Barcelona and may well have cost twice that number or more in all Catalonia seems to have well nigh ended as a result of the firm stand taken by the Catalan government in collaboration with the various proletariat parties such as the Socialists, the Communists and the Anarcho-Syndicalists.

It is an ugly chapter which has horrified many well meaning revolutionists. There was a time when every morning saw bodies scattered in the outlying parts of the city. The victims were of many kinds—persons considered as dangerous fascists, the victims of private vengeance and persons executed for plain motives of robbery. The sponsors were also a varied assortment. There were the secret revolutionary committees which questioned persons brought before them as dangerous to the revolution and decided whether they should be released or executed. There were uncontrollable private gangs of gunmen who evened old scores with employers, with secret policemen considered to have persecuted workers, and workers who had records as "scabs" or as squirrels, as they are called in Spain. Many priests also fell victims.

There is evidence that much of the terrorism was conducted by plain gangsters, criminals who crawled out of their holes or flocked here from various parts of the world for motives of robbery and plunder under the cover of revolutionary terror. Such gangs frequently invaded the homes of wealthy persons under cover of night, robbing them of all that was valuable; in other cases [they] resorted to blackmail and they dealt death as suited their purpose. The dregs of Marseilles, of Paris and of Berlin seemed to have poured into Barcelona to prey on the terror-stricken wealthy.

The Catalan government did its utmost to prevent the slaughter. It deprived nightwatchmen of their keys to houses so that they could not be overpowered. It imposed summary justice where culprits were found. It brought pressure to bear on the extreme revolutionary parties to put an end to the business. Finally it succeeded in organizing a government in which the Anarcho-Syndicalists and other extremists were represented and pledged to obey no other orders but those of the government, respecting its authority in every particular. As an additional remedy a number of popular tribunals were instituted to try publicly and with celerity persons accused of fascist and other revolutionary activities.

The impetus given to this class of terrorism, however, was too great to permit its being ended over night. The irresponsible gangs bent on vengeance and robbery are still leaving their trail in the city and throughout the region although in diminished degree. No better picture of what is occurring could be given than that portrayed in a manifesto just broadcast by the Regional Federation of Anarchist Groups, and which is all the more interesting inasmuch as it shows the very organization at whose door such crimes are laid as a matter of course, as being one of the organizations most concerned in the rapid ending of them.

The manifesto declares that "we cannot understand how, in the name of the social revolution, it is possible to commit all manner of social excesses and we are obliged to put an end to such things. Groups of individuals are going from town to town perpetrating all manner of misdeeds, doing whatever they please; with equal facility they rob and murder or by inconfessible methods obtain quantities of money. That cannot be tolerated, and much less can it be tolerated that such acts be branded as Anarchistic. The only purpose is to discredit the F.A.I. (Anarchist Federation), one of the organizations leading the revolutionary movements in Catalonia. We are partisans of strict and implacable revolutionary justice. If it be necessary to kill, we kill, always provided it be for justifiable cause. But the business of seizing a man and killing him for no other reason than that he is a Catholic does not harmonize with our ideas."

The manifesto ends with a warning to those elements "who have chosen Catalonia as a field of action, and in the name of the F.A.I." that their activities will be ended "at whatever cost."

A tragic incident at Martotell a few days ago is an example of the kind of acts denounced. A gunman visited the house of a wealthy and respected resident named Manuel Borras, demanding a sum of money and giving warning that he would come on a certain day to collect it. On the appointed day the town's acting mayor and a militiaman notified of his arrival went to the house to question him. He showed a Socialist union identity card, but at an opportune moment he whipped out his gun, shooting down both men, the maid servant and the wife of Borras, killing the latter. He then escaped. The two men died of their wounds.

Accusations made in connection with the dismissal and imprisonment last week of the Catalan General Commissioner of Public Order, Andreu Rebertes, the supreme police power in the region affords another example of terrorism perpetrated under revolutionary cover. In a sensational article the Anarcho-Syndicalist newspaper openly charged that he had ordered the assassination of persons who in one way or another stood in his way, such as his mother-in-law, on the pretext that they constituted "antifascist repression." Says one paragraph of this accusation:

"It is proved that he ordered the assassination of Juan Solans, secretary of the chief of services, of Comrade Eroles (a high police functionary), as well as the elimination of our companion Aurelio Fernandez, general secretary of the interior junta of security, and of Comrade Portela, chief of the passport section. These constituted a great obstacle to the ambitions of Rebertes. Rebertes' ambition apparently consisted in making himself one of the leaders of the just frustrated separatist plot to overpower the government and proclaim a Catalan Republic with "fascist tendencies."

As suggested in the Anarchist manifesto, some of this terrorism was undoubtedly the work of provocative agents bent upon discrediting the revolutionary movement. It is the sort of thing well understood in Spain. Moreover, neither Barcelona nor Catalonia must be taken as isolated instances but the whole situation must be viewed in perspective in relation to the situation throughout Spain. There has been bloodshed and assassination everywhere, both in government and in rebel territory. The killings on the rebel side have been attended by unheard of cruelty which have had no counterparts on the government side. There have been no wholesale slaughters in a bullring, as in the case of Badajoz, no such case as that of the left deputy Manso who was put in a bullring and made to undergo the tortures of the chief actor in a bullfight until finally slaughtered; no invasion of hospitals and the wiping out of sick and wounded with bombs as occurred at Toledo.

To the credit of the Catalan left Government it must be said that in the early days of the terrorism it managed to save the lives of hundreds [of] priests and other churchmen and also of nuns, notwithstanding its anticlerical tendencies. It gave safe conducts to many, protected some 500 priests who were put aboard Italian ships for Rome. It managed to get seven of the eight Catalan bishops safely out of the country, going so far as to rescue the Catalan Primate, Cardinal Vidal, from a mob at the point of a machine gun, and sending him to Italy.

                                                                    Fernsworth

---

852.00/3978

Telegram   Barcelona, December 3, 1936, 3 P.M.

Ambassador Dodd has telegraphically requested through Embassy at Paris that I telegraph him confidential information already sent to the Department concerning Soviet Russian participation in Catalonia. Following is submitted to the Department for transmission, should the Department feel so disposed:

"To the best of my knowledge, two Soviet steamers have arrived at Barcelona, the first in October brought food supplies, the second in November brought some 70,000 rifles and several million rounds of ammunition. Some volunteers of Russian nationality have arrived, but not in such large numbers as those of other nationalities, such as French, Germans, and Italians.

Other radical labor organizations here are jealous of the growth of outside communist influence and are suspicious that communists may have been involved in the recent death near [omission] of the anarchist General Durruti who headed a column from Catalonia. There has been a sporadical number among people here upholding Soviet assistance but I believe there is a growing feeling that this is an illusory hope and that in consequence the position of the Soviet Consul General is not as strong as it was in October."

Perkins

852.00/3987

Telegram   Barcelona, December 4, 1936

Sec. of State

This morning's press announces that President Companys is leaving today for a brief visit to Paris accompanied by several other officials. He desires to be there in connection with the activities planned for the 6th by the French proletarians "in favor of the lawful Spanish Government and against the rebellious instruments of Fascism." His secretary has informed me that the President expects to return to Barcelona on the 8th.

Perkins

852.00/4000

Telegram   Barcelona, December 5, 1936

Sec. of State

President of Catalonia has returned to Barcelona as a result of his motor caravan consisting of about 40 cars meeting with difficulties in obtaining entry at the frontier. He did give out that his journey will be shortly resumed as distinguished persons in the French Government desire to receive him in a friendly manner.

Perkins

852.00/4194

No. 138   Barcelona, December 8, 1936

STRICTLY CONFIDENTIAL

Subject: Abortive Trip of the President of Catalonia, Señor Luis Companys,
      to Paris.

Sir:

Señor Luis Companys, President of Catalonia, left Barcelona for Paris
on December 4th with a very large retinue occupying some forty motor cars.
The public had been prepared for his departure by means of a brief item in
the press of December 3 in which the correspondents were reported as making
inquiry of Premier Tarradellas concerning a prospective visit of the Catalonian
President to the French capital.

On the following morning, Barcelona was startled by the news that
President Companys had returned. A public statement was given out that,
although there had been difficulties at the French frontier, President Companys
expected to resume his journey in a few days inasmuch as distinguished
persons in the French government desired the visit and were prepared to
receive him in a friendly manner. The report was also circulated that the
difficulty was due to the number of motor cars and the size of the retinue;
that President Companys had not been refused personal entry into France,
but that he naturally could not with any dignity proceed himself and submit
to the size of his entourage being limited.

It seems highly improbable that President Companys should have undertaken this journey without definite prior arrangements having been made in
Paris and I do not think that the reports circulated give by any means the
whole story. It has been suggested to me that the prospective visit was arranged
for the purpose of bringing about a closer understanding between Catalonia
and the left Government in France with a view to facilitating and increasing
the flow of various forms of assistance to the Spanish Government in its
present struggle; and that, had it not had such a purpose, President Companys
would never have been allowed to depart from Barcelona. In explanation of
the failure to cross the border, it is said that the French Government learned
of threats made by Fascist elements in France (the Croix de Feu) to assassinate
President Companys either en route to Paris or upon his arrival there. Not
wishing to run the risk of any such catastrophe and fearing the political
repercussions that might ensue, it is said that the French Government were
unwilling to assume responsibilities of the visit at this time.

The foregoing must, of course, be taken as pure rumor. In view, however, of the obvious dangers to France of the creation of a "Fascist" Government south of the Pyrenees, I must say that the report contains certain
elements of plausibility in which the public statements are lacking.

Mahlon F. Perkins
American Consul General

852.60/22

No. 139   Barcelona, December 8, 1936

Subject: An Instance of the Administration of the Decree of Collectivization

Sir:

The Department may be interested in the attached report from the acting manager of the Singer Sewing Machine Company concerning a meeting on November 27, 1936, between members of the Worker's Control Committee from his office and a Board set up within the Catalan Council of Economy to consider applications for collectivization. This meeting took place prior to the announcement of the Council of Economy reported in my telegram under reference, but if correctly described it is extremely interesting as indicating an attitude moderate but lacking in self-assurance of these local authorities toward foreign property interests. The desire to extend to such interests a proper respect is undoubtedly strengthened where there is a material interest to consider such as the maintenance of a continued supply of raw materials. Fortunately most of the local businesses in which American capital is represented in large amounts are in this kind of position. The meeting described by the local manager of the Singer Company is also suggestive in that it shows that primary [to] every other consideration at the present time is the necessity to keep Labor conciliated.

Mahlon F. Perkins
American Consul General

Compania Singer de Maquinas para Coser

November 27, 1936

Hon. Consul General of the United States,

Hon. Sir:

As we informed you yesterday afternoon, a committee of the personnel of this Branch Office has been today at the office of the Councilor of Economy in order to expose before the Board composed by Messrs. Capdevila, Martin Barrera and Ruiz Ponseti, the form in which this Company carries out its business in Spain, and see if according to these data its collectivization could be realized.

After hearing the Committee the members of the Board stated among other things that extreme care should be exercised since a foreign firm was concerned, and that the committee should bear in mind that one of the principal points would be the indemnification of the foreign firm to the last peseta and that they should see from where they were going to get the money for payment.

The Board asked them what idea they had for the development and increase of the business at the time when stocks should be exhausted, and they mentioned the idea of undertaking the manufacture of similar machines in Cataluña, in a form similar to that of another firm in Barcelona. The Board replied that they should take into account that they could never make use of the trade mark on account of the risk that would be incurred, unless they should reach an agreement with the Company and the latter should recognize them as its concessionaires and should furnish them with anything needed, against a means of payment.

In order that the Board might better judge, it was informed that this Enterprise could not be controlled, because the Head Office in Spain is at Madrid, where the general administration of the business is taken care of, and for the reason that the legislation there is different from that of the Catalan territory; also that here in Barcelona it was not possible to know the cost price of a machine, nor the expenses it carries with it; that if this Company had not a portfolio of outstanding payments for the machines that have been sold on installments amounting to a considerable sum, by closing and selling its shops and stores and withdrawing from the banks the sums in its account current, the Company could have left more than 300 employees without work, which measure would have had a bearing on the national economy. In view of these statements, it seems that the Board was more inclined in favor of the collectivization, but as it noted a difference in opinions it suggested that a general meeting be called of all the personnel of the Company in Cataluña, to decide by means of a vote for or against collectivization.

As a consequence of the above statements, next Tuesday it is proposed to hold a meeting of the Regional Committee of Barcelona with the Sub-Committees of Badalona and Tarragona, and after discussion convoke an Assembly for Sunday, December 6th, and to act in conformity with the Decree as determined by the vote.

As regards the argument which they submitted to the Board that if this Company had not a credit of such importance for machines sold on the installment plan, which represents a considerable sum, it would have closed its doors, I beg to ask that it be permitted to us to say to you that if the Company had not developed its business on the basis of installment and cash sales, and had it engaged only in cash sales, it would not have needed to keep open so many establishments, nor to have as large an organization as it has, and then, the number of employees being less, it would not have found itself in the situation that it is now facing. As regards prejudging the case that the Company by closing its doors would have left more than 300 families on the street, it is a gratuitous statement, because it has thought of it, and this is what is called anticipating developments and forming in hypothesis an opinion based only on a supposition and not on reality.

This report we submit to you is just as it was reported to us, and for this reason we consider somewhat outside of the limits of the Decree the reply of the Board to the effect that in order to compensate the Company the Committee should see where they would get the money for payment in case of it being collectivized. Since articles 36 and 37 of the above mentioned Decree clearly specify that for the purposes of compensation there shall be separated what represents foreign investment or participation and entirely recognized as such by the Generalidad, and, even though the Decree states that its value shall be estimated in national currency, we recall that according to your statement under the general policy of protection to property followed by the Department of State at Washington all American property subject to seizure for the needs of war or for other reasons must be promptly and completely paid for.

Without prejudice to furnishing you with all information possible, we would appreciate a reply from you, in order that in writing to our Head Offices at Paris and Madrid, we may give them the authorized opinion from you in this matter of such transcendental importance to the Company.

Luis T. Gavilanes

852.00/4086

Telegram   Barcelona, December 12, 1936

Sec. of State

Prime Minister made public announcement today that Cabinet meeting on the 9th would be the last since political problem has come to a head. Reason given is that the situation has daily become more insupportable on account of lack of discipline and of a sense of responsibility. Minister stated: "I am not disposed to continue with this state of affairs, since I cannot or will I ever be able to decline to have fall on me responsibility for acts of government which often are carried out by irresponsibles and by those who now call themselves uncontrolleds. For this and other reasons which for the time being it is unnecessary to make public you may consider the present Catalan Government in a state of 'crisis'."

Perkins

852.00/4255

Barcelona, December 12, 1936

Subject: Reign of Terror in Catalonia

Sir:

I have the honor to refer to my telegram of December 12, 6 P.M., and to my despatch No. 128 of December 2, 1936, entitled "Secret Reign of

Terror in Barcelona and Catalonia," and to state that all available information supports the belief that the cruelties described in this despatch are continuing with unabated ferocity. Some weeks ago there was reason to believe that executions and assassinations were diminishing; but, since the insurgent attack in the Bay of Palamós (November 17, 1936) they have been again increasing because the spirit of retaliation has been aroused. In the country districts the rabble is in control; and I have been informed that even here in Barcelona the Chief of Police has admitted that he is almost powerless to prevent these crimes of violence. It has been suggested by a competent observer that, if one were to go over a list of the members of the fifty leading business firms of Barcelona, it would be found that there are not five per cent of such members who had not either been killed or forced to flee the country. The principal cause appears to be either class or religious hatred, although it may also be said that the personal grudges of a generation are in [the] course of being wiped out. People are reported to have been killed for simply belonging to a religious charitable society; recently the houses of members of the Rotary Club were searched, presumably for the reason that this organization is considered to be composed of the "bourgeoisie." Almost no one who has held in the past any position of responsibility does not know at what hour he may be arrested and possibly executed either with no trial or with merely the pretense of one.

I have been told from reliable sources such stories as the following: one member of a radical organization boasted that he was personally responsible for "bumping off" some 200 persons. One of his comrades protested that he did not believe that the number could be so great as claimed, but that, even if the number were only 100, he was willing to admit the person responsible was "a pretty big man."

Another recent boast was made that a lucky find had been made that day of two priests and several "seminarists." The priests were shot and the others forced over the railing of a bridge. When they attempted to hold to the edge, guns were brought down breaking their fingers and compelling them to drop to their death below.

As having a very definite bearing upon acts of this kind, I enclose a translation of an article appearing in *La Vanguardia* of December 9, 1936. In this President Luis Companys of Catalonia makes specific charges of crimes in which those assassinated were actually his own friends. When a point has been reached when such atrocities are openly denounced by the highest official of Catalonian Government, it needs but little exercise of the imagination or of the power of inference to picture the true facts.

Mahlon F. Perkins
American Consul General

Translation

From front page article of *La Vanguardia*, December 9, 1936. Selection entitled: "Generalidad of Catalonia Declarations of President."

Among other things, Luis Companys said to the newspaper men:

"I was just now reading some letters sent me from Tarragona, Tortosa and other towns of the coast reporting to me some lamentable happenings which have taken place down there.

"In the town of Garcia, for example, two or three men were assassinated, tried men of the left, old friends of mine, and the instigators are old town leaders who now have entered certain organizations. In other towns the seizures continue, illegal taxes are imposed and they want me to maintain terror. Valor and the rifle, exclaimed the President in terms of lamentation, should be at the front, where fascism must be overcome.

"It is supposed that the instigators of the assassinations of Garcia must already be in prison, for in regard to crime law must be quick and thundering. It is too important to all to save the honor and the glory of the Revolution, to win the war and to outlaw assassinations.

"Naturally the general aspect of Catalonia has increased in tranquility and confidence, but the last vestiges must be brought to an end and in a lightning-like manner. And in this sense I have urged the zeal of the authorities."

852.00/4150

Telegram   Barcelona, December 17, 1936

Sec. of State

Formation of new Catalan cabinet announced today, Prime Minister continuing in office and labor organizations obtaining eight out of eleven members. It is hoped that this reorganization will enable the government to function with less internal dissension and with more authority.

Perkins

852.00/4322

No. 152   Barcelona, December 17, 1936

Subject: Fall of the Catalan Cabinet

Sir:

I have the honor to enclose herewith a copy, in English translation, of an article in *La Vanguardia* of December 13, 1936, dealing with this subject.

Although the language of this article is, perhaps from the necessities of the case, not very specific, it appears fairly obvious that the Cabinet has not been able to function as effectively as is considered necessary by reason of a lack of support by certain powerful radical labor groups. The reorganization announced today, as reported in my December 17, 6 P.M., which gives a larger measure of representation to these groups, may constitute a cabinet commanding sufficient authority to enable President Companys and Prime Minister Tarradellas to be content to carry on with their responsibilities.

Mahlon F. Perkins
American Consul General

No. 43   Barcelona, December 19, 1936

Subject: Comment of a Spanish Attorney of Barcelona upon the Recent
             Catalonian Regulations Governing Trade and Industry

Sir:

I . . . enclose . . . a strictly confidential memorandum entrusted to me by a prominent Spanish attorney of Barcelona, in which he gives his considered views of the legal and other aspects of certain of the recent decrees of the Government of Catalonia governing the trade and industry of this province. I do not feel at liberty to give any indication of the identity of the author of this memorandum inasmuch as he states that it would without question cost him his life if this fact were known. I must also request that the memorandum itself be also kept strictly confidential since it is possible that the identity of the author might be traced if the contents were to become public.

Although the views expressed by the writer are perhaps nothing more than might be expected to come from a conservative temperament of any nationality, I nevertheless consider them extremely valuable comments by an intelligent man who has lived many years in this province and knows both his people and his country. I may also say that these views, taken generally, seem amply to confirm the observation made in the final paragraph of my despatch No. 124 (November 25, 1936) in which it was suggested that all the recent governmental measures of this character boil down to an attempt by the "have not's" to distribute among themselves the property of the "have's."

Mahlon F. Perkins
American Consul General

Translation

Dear Sirs:

In accordance with your verbal request I have the honor to explain to you herewith my personal opinion under the legal and doctrinal viewpoint, in connection with the regulations dictated by the Government of the Generalidad of Catalonia regarding the industry and trade of this country, especially as far as the interests of your Company in Spain are concerned.

This regional government published in its official bulletin, after July 19 last, a series of decrees and orders which have altered fundamentally the individual guarantees covered by the existing laws throughout Spanish territory protecting private ownership and stimulating the development of the economic life of the country. I am therefore going to study such regulations in synthesis, their obligatory force, and the legal status derived therefrom.

Antecedents

The municipal elections which took place in April, 1931 resulted in a change of the political regime of the country to an unexpected extent, by substituting for the secular and traditional Monarchy, the Republic. This change was worked out by mere political evolution, without any fight or bloodshed.

Although this was a matter of pride for the new regime in fact it was the basis of the present developments as the intention of establishing a Republic of a bourgeois type as in France, without experiencing the violence of a true revolution, deceived a large part of the left wing and the extremists started working on the establishment by violent means of a new social order which was looked upon with favor by the governments, whose components were much too busy with their speeches in Parliament and their theories to pay due attention to the progress of the sovietization of a large part of the country.

Under the circumstances Spain witnessed what in similar cases has nearly always occurred everywhere, i.e., that the men who have not been free for a long time do not know how to make a discreet use of their freedom and have abused it with corresponding consequences. It is what used to happen in those countries where wine was not produced: the men were often inclined to drink excessively, whereas the people in countries where wine is the current drink are rather sober. The youngsters who had not had the opportunity to experience the thrills of a true revolution abused this liberty and the revolt became unavoidable with the cruelty which characterizes the beginning of all revolutions and with all kinds of violences due to the ignorance and the ferociousness of the people excited by the rebellion.

Paying no attention to the existing foreign influences which are not to be considered here, it must be recognized that the present Spanish revolution is not a political one but a true social revolution with the spirit of revenge and destruction of the masses full of the desire to destroy all that represents control, authority, hierarchy, tradition.

As a consequence of the foregoing the leaders of socialism took the public power with communists and anarchists, all anxious to destroy a social order based on capitalism and began to dictate regulations of an executive character intended to apply with a feverish haste some theories not well digested in the periods of persecution as well as some methods from other countries whose people, civilization and living conditions were quite different or even opposed to those existing in Spain, with the chaotic result that exists now here.

Regulations of the Government

The foregoing antecedents have been brought here in order to explain satisfactorily the reasons of the regulations dictated by the Government of the Generalidad of Catalonia since July 19 last, as otherwise it would be difficult to understand same.

Under the point of view of theory and doctrine all these regulations would have no legal force not only [on] account of the fact that the same were issued against the fundamental laws of the Spanish State (Constitution, Civil and Commercial Codes, international treaties, etc.) which are still in force in spite of the so called "state of alarm" declared and maintained by the Parliament of Madrid, but also on account of the violation of the Statute of Autonomy of Catalonia as the regulations dictated by the regional government exceed the boundaries of said Statute and are often against the rules issued by the corporations depending directly from the Administration itself.

Without having derogated the *status quo* existing before July 19, 1936, without having formally declared in Catalonia a state of siege and therefore without having followed the regulations prescribed for this case, the government of the autonomous region had no hesitation in considering as nil the national and regional laws passed by the respective parliaments, under which the legal order of the region was organized, and had besides no hesitancy in dictating new regulations the spirit of which was against the fundamental principles of any society organized within the frame of the European civilization, with the deliberate purpose of favoring a certain social class to the prejudice of the others.

Such is the new legal regime and it must not be forgotten that often what is legal cannot be reputed to be fair.

Spanish citizens residing in Catalonia, whether or not Catalans, as well as concerns having a national character and residing within this territory, are unable to escape from the fulfillment of such regulations which have been dictated with legal force, as a strong pressure is exerted on them and any resistance in this connection is always suppressed by violence.

The foreigners residing in Catalonia and the foreign concerns established in this territory are in a position to oppose the fulfillment of said regulations by means of the intermediary of their respective Consulates. Generally speaking this is the best protection especially taking into account that up to the present the Government of the Generalidad has avoided putting itself openly against foreign governments whose consular representatives have been protecting their nationals against any excess of the hot headed people.

It is to be recognized that since things have gone too far many consular protests have been presented—some quite energetic—and then the Government has been forced to take some action. However, nobody can tell what is likely to happen in a situation far more violent produced by dispute or by hypertension of the anarchists succeeding in getting an absolute control of the situation during more or less time, without the counter-weight of a force susceptible to oppose against them.

Such is the situation *de facto*.

Analysis of These Regulations

The list of these regulations is already very large and their transcription would be annoying and perhaps worthless. However, it is very interesting to set up a summary of the most important regulations not only taking into account the consequences thereof but also the threats which they represent for the immediate future. Their description marks the revolutionary period which began on July 19 and which has not yet finished.

The official bulletin of the Generalidad of Catalonia of July 25, 1936, contains the regulations which were issued with a view to normalize the industrial activities of the region and accordingly the Permanent Committee of Industry was authorized to intervene and dispose of the cash on hand and industrial means for making the payments ordered. It is undoubtedly a confiscatory measure against private ownership with the only purpose of insuring the payment of wages irrespectively of whether the workers have worked or not during the week.

On the following day, i.e., July 26, salaries under 6,000 pesetas per year were increased by 15%. On the 28th the General Commissariat of Insurance was established and all the companies were included without paying any attention to their nationality, as it had already been ordered on the 23rd to private banks operating in Catalan territory. On the 31st salaries were once again regulated and all remunerations over 1,500 pesetas per month were forbidden. A decree of August 11 referred to the owners and managers of industries abandoned, inviting them to resume their duties before the 15th as otherwise the business and other means of the owners or associates would be confiscated. On the 25th all companies supplying electricity, gas and water were intervened, a delegate of the Government being appointed whose powers, as well as in the case of other industries, were fixed in another decree of the 28th.

It is to be remarked that when dictating measures of such importance the Councilor (i.e., the regional Minister) who signed said important decrees, tried to justify them by stating that they were intended to meet the needs of the moment.

It is needless to point out the confiscatory character of such arbitrary regulations. When the Government of the Generalidad has issued or authorized orders of taking over a business (*incautación*)—remark that they do not use the word confiscation—official interventors have been appointed and at least have authorized the establishment of workers committees which jointly with the official interventors have assumed the duties of the management disposing of the financial resources without paying any attention to the rules and precautions formerly established by the owners with the banks where the funds were deposited. In this connection the Commissariat of private banks was created in order to impose on the banks under its control the policy dictated by the Councilor of Economy (Regional Ministry).

Covering the possibility that the foregoing may prove of not sufficient value, the decree of August 21 is intended to give legal force to the new appointments made of representatives as a consequence of the appropriations, interventions and/or confiscations made in accordance with the other decrees mentioned herein and their execution.

All the foregoing took place *manu militari*, without paying any attention to the private interests injured, to the nationality of the affairs or to the loans guaranteed by these concerns whose securities are largely in the hands of the public and often owned by people of rather poor financial standing. What has happened to these people? Even the movement of funds to meet the payment of the coupons due has been stopped.

Notwithstanding the importance of the decrees herein considered, none is so remarkable as that issued on October 24 regarding the collectivization of industries employing over 100 workers and establishing the workers control on all enterprises without exception. Said decree which is the materialization of an ideal—rather theoretical than practical—of a certain social party, accepts openly the socialization of the heavy industries and represents only the expression of the personal ideas of its author faced with the preoccupation of the masses, full of bluff and with an absolute lack of sense of reality. Although I doubt whether this decree may some day be normally applied, it is interesting to quote the most remarkable articles which will afford quite a clear picture of the present situation here:

Article 1: In accordance with the rules contained in the present decree, the commercial and industrial enterprises of Catalonia are hereby classified in: (a) *Collectivized enterprises* in which the responsibility of the direction falls upon the workers who compose same, represented by a Council of Enterprise and (b) *Private enterprises* in which the direction is in charge of the owner or manager with the collaboration and censure of the workers committee of control.

Article 2: All the commercial and industrial enterprises which on June 30, 1936 employed more than 100 workers with fixed salary and also those enterprises employing an inferior number of workers the owners of which have been declared rebels or have abandoned the enterprise shall be obligatorily socialized. Notwithstanding this, the enterprises of less than 100 workers can be socialized if the majority of workers and the owner or owners agree to such determination. The enterprises of more than 50 workers and less than 100 can also be socialized whenever three quarters of the workmen agree to do so.

The Council of Economy may also resolve the socialization of other industries which by reason of their importance within the national economy or for other characteristics make it convenient to free same from the action of private enterprises.

Article 9: In the enterprises in which there are foreign subject interests, the Councils of Enterprise or the workers control committees, in each case, shall communicate it to the Council of Economy and the latter shall call together all the interested parties or their representatives to treat the matter and determine what is most convenient for the due safeguard of those interests.

Article 32: In every socialization of an enterprise whether it treats of national or of foreign interests, whatever its importance may be, a balance sheet and inventory of the situation will have to be drawn up, based on duly audited account books of the enterprise accompanied by the detailed and appraised audit of the goods and stocks and landed property of every kind belonging to the enterprise in question.

Article 35: Once the firm's assets have been set up as per inventory and after deducting the liabilities should the result be positive, the balance shall be registered at the Board of Economy of the Generalidad for the purpose of concretion of the usufructuaries and the corresponding social compensation.

Article 36: For the purpose of this compensation, all that is represented by foreign contributions or participations shall be separated and also that which belongs to popular savings and lending institutions, credit establishments and that which corresponds to private individuals and other national concerns, and to this end the Board of Economy shall publish the corresponding advertisements on the understanding that any participation whatever it may be must refer to a date after July 19 ultimo.

Article 37: The social compensation corresponding to the first case mentioned in the preceding article shall be entirely recognized by the Generalidad. Its value shall be calculated in national currency.

Legal Value of These Regulations

All of these decisions of the Government of the Generalidad to which we have made reference in the preceding paragraphs as well as all the others not mentioned here, represent a frank acceptation of the socialization of Catalonia, that is to say, they aim to drive towards the collectivity of the individual rights taking it for granted that the public power is sufficiently strong as to modify the conditions of civil life. By this I refer to the incompetency of the Government of the autonomous region to pass laws dictated in quite a dictatorial way and therefore arbitrary. On August 9 a decree-law was approved whereby the Government of the Generalidad granted itself the authority to legislate by decree on all matters formerly reserved to Parliament—regional or national.

The legal situation created as a consequence of such decisions of the regional government is the one resulting from the establishment and maintenance of an extraordinary case of *force majeure cui resistere non potest*, considering this not only in the light of the old Roman conception adopted in Article 1105 of our Civil Code from which the character of force majeure is attributed to any event that could not be foreseen or even foreseen proves to be unavoidable, but also to the more extended modern conception especially in matters of contracts in accordance with which force majeure is defined as any fact independent of the will of the debtor which he could not foresee and which makes him unable to meet his obligations.

All this class legislation mentioned has brought up in government terminology in Catalonia words like "appropriation," "collectivization," "control," "attachment," etc. most of which were unknown in our private right and even abolished as the penalty of confiscation formerly suppressed and now reestablished. Our modern right only accepts the case of expropriation on the ground of public utility and against the corresponding indemnification excepting the text of the Agrarian Reform Law where the expropriation of certain large rural properties is established without indemnification with a view to distribute them among the farmers and start their cultivation.

The legal value of all this legislation essentially revolutionary and disturbing is nil on account of its origin as the legislative power lies with the national or regional Parliament without any possibility of accepting as good the confirmation of the legal status created, made by the regional Government itself abusing its authority. *Quod ab initio vitiosum est, tractu tempore convalescere non potest*. This does not mean that such a legislation is not obligiatory for same is being imposed by violence.

This legislation, abruptly promulgated, does not aim to impose a true communistic regime nor to suppress the existing capitalism; it is only intended to sovietize the country, suppressing the present capitalists, without paying attention to the utopia consisting in the intention to enforce by violent means the economic laws in which the organization of the civilized world lies, which laws are as inexorable as the sidereal laws.

The legal value of this series of laws promulgated by the revolutionary Spanish Governments and their rather chaotic regulations may be considered merely as temporary if the force which has created them vanishes and the situation becomes again normal.

This assumed, several of the facts which have taken place during this period would undoubtedly prove irreparable. For instance, the appropriations of money and other effects, funds deposited with banks and disposed of to pay wages unearned, losses derived from the enormous decrease in the efficiency of the workers, losses derived from the unsuccessful management of industries in the hands of control committees whose members had not a good training in the line, the modifications made in the buildings which are being devoted to other purposes different from the ones for which they were erected, etc.

In fact, however, neither the collectivizations of industries already made nor the socialization of other concerns, especially enterprises of small importance, nor the appropriation of properties, can prevail if a reaction against the present revolutionary situation arises. Whatever may happen it would be unwise not to weigh duly the importance and seriousness of some of these measures especially those contained in the decree of October 24 last regarding the collectivization of certain industries and the establishment of workers control committees, and not to pay attention to Articles 9 and 36 outlined above.

We do not know whether there is a real intention to have the provisions of said decree executed; probably not. We also do not know whether they will impose it on certain industries. Probably not, since they do not dare insist in the case of certain industries, especially war industries and enterprises where foreign interests are involved. At any rate and in order to secure some protection against any possible irreparable measure it is advisable to adopt these precautions *ad cautelam* that in case of need could prove efficient against any action of the public power.

My personal opinion is to the effect that the decree in question may be self propaganda of the Councilor who dictated it, with a view to have an instrument of opposition or a flag to be used in future political campaigns.

852.70/6

No. 166   Barcelona, December 29, 1936

Subject: Communications Between Palma de Mallorca and the Mainland

Sir:

There is now a weekly mail service by French commercial steamer between Marseille and Palma; and mail for the latter port may be sent to the Consulate General at Marseille for transmission instead of to this office.

There is also a regular air line functioning between Genoa and Palma. It is suggested that telegrams concerning the welfare of American citizens might be sent to the Consulate General at Genoa for relay by air. However, if such telegrams are of great urgency, they may be sent to this office for possible relay by British naval radio; but I am averse from making such requests except in cases of extreme urgency and importance.

It should be borne in mind that welfare inquiries for the Island of Ibiza should be sent to Palma de Mallorca in care of Mr. Noble Clay, who is the temporary representative of this Consulate General in that city.

The Island of Menorca is still under the control of the Government forces. This Consulate General is able to communicate with Menorca by cable; but I am not informed as to its steamship connections with the mainland.

Mahlon F. Perkins
American Consul General

852.00/4460

No. 167   Barcelona, December 29, 1936

Subject: Visit of Consul L.J. Callanan to Palma de Mallorca.

Sir:

With reference to my telegram of December 16, 11 A.M. mentioning the visit of Consul Leo J. Callanan to Palma de Mallorca, and with reference to my confidential despatch No. 135 of December 5, 1936, entitled "Possibility of an Attack upon Barcelona by Air and/or Sea," I have the honor to enclose herewith a memorandum by Mr. Callanan containing notes made by him regarding his visit to Palma.

Particular attention is invited to Paragraph 1 reporting Mr. Noble Clay's estimate that there may be 8 or 10 bombers capable of undertaking raids from Mallorca to the mainland; also to paragraph 7 reporting Mr. Clay's opinion that attacks may be expected on the Catalan coast as soon as Madrid falls.

As stated in my December 16, 7 P.M., there was an air attack made on that date in the vicinity of Port Bou on the French frontier, evidently with the purpose of interrupting traffic communications into Spain. There have been one or two subsequent raids in the same area but apparently without any serious damage.

Mahlon F. Perkins
American Consul General

Memorandum

Notes on Palma de Mallorca, as of December 16, 1936

The city was quiet and orderly. Clay said that there were from 30,000 to 35,000 men under arms, but there was little evidence of them except in the case of groups of recruits in civilian clothes drilling in the streets and a few soldiers in uniform. Clay estimated that there are about 20 airplanes in Mallorca, a few of which are seaplane or flying boats, and that of the 20 about 8 or 10 are bombers capable of undertaking bombing raids from Mallorca to the mainland.

It was said that there are about 200 Italians in the Mallorca forces principally connected with aviation. About 60 of the number are commissioned officers and pilots while the balance are mechanics and aircraft men. All of these are in Mallorca under assumed names being officially in Ethiopia on leave of absence. It was stated that even the mail of these men to and from Italy is routed via Ethiopia.

The cotton mills have experienced a shortage of raw cotton; there is no white wheat flour to be obtained on the island and there have been periodical shortages of coffee and sugar. A small single sheet daily paper is published printed on locally made paper.

Whereas some 10,000 motor cars circulated in normal times in the island the number is now said to be less than 1,000. This is understood to be the result of the strictness of the authorities in issuing permission for cars to circulate and is intended to conserve the gasoline supply which, consequently, is understood to be still considerable.

The outstanding difficulty faced by the Mallorca authorities is that of obtaining foreign exchange for the purchase of necessary supplies abroad. There appeared to be no special arrangement concerning the exchange of goods between Mallorca and countries sympathetic to the Franco regime, but a certain interchange of products with Italy was currently practised. For example, it was said that early in December something over a million pairs of shoes had been shipped from Mallorca to Italy and that the resulting credit in Italy would be applied to the purchase of commodities required in the island.

The electric company, which is unable to arrange payment for coal from abroad, is operating on fuel composed of local lignite mixed with almond shells.

Concerning the future it was Mr. Clay's opinion that attacks on the Catalan coast were to be expected from Mallorca as soon as Madrid falls. In addition to the planes mentioned above, available for such use, there are three ships available for carrying troops, the capacity of each being roughly 1,000 men.

Mr. Clay also said that a large aerodrome is under construction and that a concentration camp for prisoners is being prepared.

December 29, 1936

L.J.C.

852.00/4248

Telegram   Barcelona, December 31, 1936

Sec. of State

Within the past week, some 4000 foreign volunteers of various nationalities have passed through Barcelona for the front. Estimate over twenty
thousand such have passed since October 31. These arrive by rail from France
and are grouped according to nationality. There appear to be no (repeat no)
Russian contingents.

Security for person and property throughout Barcelona is definitely
worsening and, with increasing refugees from Madrid, it will be difficult, if
not impossible, to preserve from occupation, furnished apartments vacated
by evacuated American citizens.

Perkins

852.00/25

No. 170   Barcelona, December 31, 1936

Subject: Collectivization of Industry

Sir:

I have the honor to refer to . . . the collectivization of businesses in
Cataluña in which there are foreign interests, and to enclose herewith for the
Department's information a copy of an order dated December 12, 1936, by
the Councilor of Economy concerning General Motors and a resolution dated
December 9, 1936, by the President Delegate of the Council of Economy
concerning the United Shoe Machinery Company.

There is also enclosed a copy of my letter of December 31, 1936, to
the President of the Generalidad de Cataluña regarding these developments.
It may be noted that the Consulate General has not received a reply from the
Government to its letter of November 21, 1936, a copy of which was enclosed
with my despatch under reference.

Mahlon F. Perkins
American Consul General

Order

Considering that the workers of the collectivized enterprise General
Motors, located at Barcelona, Mallorca No. 453, in conformity with the
provisions of article 15 of the Decree of Collectivization of October 24, 1936,

have proposed to this Consejeria the appointment as Interventor of the Generalitat de Catalunya in said enterprise, of the comrade Joan Jimeno i Inglada, domiciled at San Adriá del Besós, Calle República, 29, making use of the authority granted me by said Decree, I have decided:

To appoint as Interventor delegate of the Generalitat de Catalunya in the collectivized enterprise General Motors, the comrade Joan Jimeno i Inglada, in accord with the workers of the said enterprise.

Barcelona, December 12, 1936.

The Councilor of Economy
Joan P. Fabregas

852.00/4453

Barcelona, January 5, 1937

Subject: Foreign "Volunteers" in the Spanish Civil War

Sir:

I have the honor to . . . state that the almost daily procession of these groups of foreign nationals has been for some weeks perhaps the most conspicuous feature of the life of this city.

In a news bulletin issued by the U.S.S. "Raleigh" on December 19, 1936, an item emanating from Paris contained the following statement:

> French Parliamentary Commission estimated that nearly sixty thousand foreigners are serving in the rival armies. The estimated were: Thirty thousand Germans and more than a thousand Frenchmen and Irishmen on the rebel side; and twelve thousand Frenchmen, two thousand Germans, two thousand Belgians, two thousand Poles, and ten thousand Russians on the Loyalist side. In addition, the rebel General Franco has transported nearly twenty-five thousand Moors from Africa.

I am not in a position to make any comment in regard to the number of foreign troops on the rebel side. Neither can I comment in regard to the number of Russians on the loyalist side; for such Russians would naturally not enter Spain through such a northern port as Barcelona. The total 18,000 of the remaining Frenchmen, Germans, Belgians, and Poles, is not far from the estimate of over 20,000 of various European nationalities reported in my telegram under reference.

The appearance of these volunteers varies greatly. Some are sturdy young men of obvious military value, but others present a pathetic spectacle and have evidently come to fight in Spain because they are destitute. I am told that many of the Poles have been at work in coal mines in France but have latterly been thrown out of employment, perhaps for seasonal cause. A few days ago there arrived in Barcelona the first contingent of English volunteers, a group of 23 young men, some not more than 18 or 19 years of age. These had been picked up in France, whither they had presumably drifted from home. I am told that the foreign volunteers, after but a few days training, are sent into the front lines in advance of the Spanish troops and that they are sometimes referred to as "carne de cañon" or cannon meat.

A recent article in the London *Times* mentinoed the fact that, in some areas occupied by the insurgent forces, more German was heard among the soldiers than Spanish. It might be said, without much exaggeration, that at present among the soldiers in the streets of Barcelona, more French is heard than Spanish. In almost all press items relating to the subject of foreign troops in Spain, emphasis is placed upon the large numbers of German and Italians engaged with the insurgent forces, and upon the Russians engaged with the loyalist side. Comparatively little attention seems to be given to foreign volunteers of other European nationalities who enter Spain across the French frontier to fight with the loyalists. This may be due to the fact that such volunteers do not arrive by sea and enter in small detachments of a few hundred men at a time.

Although I do not feel qualified to comment with any assurance upon the political aspects of this question, I may suggest that the French Government's ability to continue with the non-intervention policy in the face of considerable opposition from the more radical groups in that country may have been possible only because of the passage of this somewhat equivalent number of loyalist volunteers over the French border.

Both sides in the present struggle naturally welcome the arrival of foreign reinforcements. It is perhaps premature for them to begin to speculate how it will be possible to "liquidate" such numbers of foreigners after the war has come to an end. Unquestionably a considerable fraction of them are not the kind of immigrants that would be permanently valued in any stable society.

The shipment of munitions and supplies by rail from France is, of course, not a matter so easy of observation as the arrival of volunteers. However, I am constantly hearing of such shipments; but thus far I have had no means of forming any estimate whatsoever of their volume or the frequency of such a flow through this area.

Mahlon F. Perkins
American Consul General

No. 177   Barcelona, January 6, 1937

Confidential

Subject: Issue of Catalan Currency of 20,000,000 Pesetas

Sir:

    I . . . enclose . . . copies of the following documents: (1) Decree of September 21, 1936, by the President of Catalonia authorizing the issuance of 20,000,000 pesetas in paper currency; (2) Decree of December 4, 1936 by the Premier of Catalonia authorizing the Counsellor of Finance to place this issue in circulation; and (3) Order of December 7, 1936 by the Premier directing the issue to be placed in circulation through the Bank of Spain. The dual office of Premier and Counsellor of Finance is held by Señor Josep Tarradellas. There is also enclosed a single specimen (5 peseta note) of the new issue.

    From Article 1 of the Decree of September 21, 1936, it will be noted that this issue is secured largely upon confiscated stocks of gold and securities, possibly a somewhat shaky foundation. I understand that these notes do not circulate outside of Catalonia and that they are spoken of derisively by the man in the street. However, in view of the penalties attached to non-acceptance, I have not heard of their tender ever being refused. Today I have been privately informed that another 100,000,000 pesetas of these notes have already been printed, though not yet issued.

    The economy of Catalonia is in such a state of disorganization as the result of the new social and financial experiments now in effect that it may be expected that new and larger issues of notes will have to be forthcoming to maintain the situation. I understand that the payrolls and other expenses of "collectivized" enterprises are being financed by the Generalitat in numerous instances. Till now many concerns have been kept going from the bank accounts "taken over" at the time of the revolution. Some of these reserves are now running low and yet the enterprises must be kept in operation. Hence arises a necessity for official support and for issues of currency.

    The economy of industrial Catalonia depends upon the export of its manufactured products to other parts of Spain to a greater degree than upon its exports abroad. Both of these markets are enormously affected by the present civil strife; and I apprehend the development of a very critical economic situation in this province which may prove a greater threat to its general well-being than the menace of military attack.

Mahlon F. Perkins
American Consul General

No. 179   Barcelona, January 6, 1937

Subject: "Menos Comités y Más Pan."

Sir:

Some two weeks ago there appeared a definite shortage in the bread supply of Catalonia. Long queues, mostly composed of women and children could be seen at the approaches to the various bakeries, as it is not the local custom to bake bread in the home. I am informed that, in many cases, purchasers began to form in line as early as 3 A.M. although actual distribution did not commence until several hours later.

It appears to be a question whether the shortage is real or only a factitious [sic] one created by radical elements to bring about dissatisfaction with the officials responsible for provisioning the city. Whatever may have been the source of the shortage, the women of the city, after a few days of privation, formed a procession, which marched to the Generalidad, shouting "Menos Comités y Más Pan. Que gobierne un Gobierno: el de la Generalidad." (Less Committees and more bread. Let there be one Government, that of the Generalidad).

The next day there was an abundance of bread and the queues disappeared. However, after several days, there has again appeared a shortage. It is impossible to trace the ramifications of local dissensions leading to situations such as the one under discussion; but it is certain that the problem is a difficult one for the Generalidad, a "Government" which is in the unenviable position of being held to responsibility while lacking any real authority.

I may remark that the slogan "Menos Comités y Más Pan" adopted by the women of Barcelona reveals, quite naturally, a somewhat different grasp of the realities than the suggestion attributed to Marie Antoinette to "Give the people cake if they have no bread."

Mahlon F. Perkins
American Consul General

852.00/4741   Barcelona, January 30, 1937

CONFIDENTIAL

Rear Admiral A.P. Fairfield, U.S.N.,
U.S.S. *Raleigh*

Sir:

I wish to thank you for your letter of January 24 and I am taking advantage of the opportunity offered by the passage through Barcelona today of Commander Chandler to send you a few further notes.

The reports which you have heard of the bombardment of Barcelona are almost wholly propaganda. It is true that on two or three occasions there has been a little cannonading at night, but not enough to cause one to get out of bed. It is said that a few people were injured on the water front, but of this I have no authentic confirmation.

Local dissensions among the radical groups have, however, resulted in some actual bloodshed. A local fight took place here near the Rambla in which some seven persons were killed or wounded. At Fatarella, near Tarragona, there has been considerable disorder. Two of the C.N.T. from Barcelona were killed and their coffins were paraded past the Plaza Catalunya in an imposing funeral in which several hundred of the C.N.T. took part, all fully armed and prepared for trouble. I am told that negotiations looking toward reconciliation and consolidation of these organizations are taking place, as the vital need of unity is, of course, recognized by the more intelligent. The outcome, however, is problematical.

To a shortage of bread, gasoline, and other essentials there may now be added a serious shortage of coal, which is handicapping train service. With the progressive general disorganization here, such conditions should grow worse instead of better, unless acute necessity spurs the "authorities" to action.

I have carefully noted the arrangements of your schedule of ships between February 1 and February 18. We have no present intention of evacuating Barcelona between those dates and, of course, hope that we shall not be forced to do so at any time.

Colonel Fuqua is very much improved and hopes to be able to leave the hospital within a few days. I shall be most pleased to convey to him your kindest regards and best wishes for a speedy recovery.

Mahlon F. Perkins
American Consul General

No. 220   Barcelona, February 4, 1937

Subject: Incipient Anti-Foreign Sentiment in Barcelona

Sir:

I . . . enclose herewith the text of an editorial in English translation, entitled "Our Enemies," appearing in the *Diario del Comercio* of January 27, 1937, a paper which formerly confined itself to commercial matters, but which now has ventured into the realm of politics. The writer obviously seeks to stir up a feeling of general hostility towards foreign nations on the ground that Spain has been little more than a colonial field for exploitation at their hands.

There is also enclosed a poster entitled "The Stranglers of the Poor Spanish People—The True Reasons For The False Neutrality." This poster has been recently issued by the Propaganda Office of the Generalidad of Catalonia and has been widely disseminated throughout the business sections of Barcelona. Until recently there has been practically no evidence of a desire to create any general anti-foreign sentiment among the people. The development of any such tendency will be carefully observed.

Mahlon F. Perkins
American Consul General

No. 219   Barcelona, February 4, 1937

Subject: Operation of the Collectivization Decree in Catalonia

Sir:

I . . . enclose a copy of my letter . . . to the President of the Generalidad, whose reply will be mentioned elsewhere herein, concerning the collectivization of General Motors and United Shoe Machinery plants in Barcelona, and to submit below some observations and comments on the operation of the Collectivization Decree.

In the absence of specific assurances from the Catalan Government that prompt and full compensation can be expected by American interests for damage suffered through collectivization—considerable damage [having] already been sustained in several instances—it becomes pertinent to consider the provisions of the Decree itself which refer to foreign interests. It will have been noted (a copy of the decree accompanied my despatch No. 88 of October 31, 1936) that foreign interests are mentioned as indicated below:

Art. 9: It is here provided that the Council of Economy, having been notified of the foreign interest in a given enterprise, will call a meeting of the interested parties in order to determine the best method of safeguarding their interests.

Arts. 32 to 35: These indicate the method by which the assets and liabilities of all collectivized enterprises, including those in which there are foreign interests, are to be determined.

Art. 36: This article provides for the segregation of all that is represented by the foreign interest in each enterprise, as of July 19, 1936.

Art. 37: Provides for the recognition of foreign interest by the Generalidad, and stipulates that its value shall be calculated in national currency.

A first important point would seem to be that wherever the "recognition" or "protection" of foreign interests is mentioned it does not mean that foreign interests are recognized as exempt from collectivization or are to be protected from the results of collectivization. This is apparent from the fact that at least the two American organizations mentioned in the first paragraph of this despatch have already been collectivized. Thus, the safeguarding of foreign interests through meetings of the interested parties, as provided in Art. 9, cannot be regarded as involving the exercise of choice or discretion by representatives of foreign interests in agreeing to or opposing collectivization, and cannot be taken to mean the protection, in the sense of preservation, of private property.

Articles 32 to 37 refer to the "segregation" of foreign assets, the "recognition" of foreign interest and the "calculation" in pesetas of the value of foreign participation in collectivized enterprises, but nowhere does it appear categorically that the foreign owners may expect to realize the value, for their free disposal and use outside of Spain, of the capital and assets they possessed in Catalonia before July 19, 1936.

The operation of the Collectivization Decree has been thus far so lacking in uniformity and so subject to abuses that it is impossible to analyze its workings or to estimate its ultimate effect on foreign businesses. It will be noted that Articles 1 and 2 of the decree specify that enterprises employing more than 100 workers at fixed salaries are automatically subject to collectivization, and that those employing between 50 and 100 workers may be collectivized if three-fourths of the employees so desire. However, any enterprise may be so collectivized if a majority of the employees, with the agreement of the owner or owners, so desire.

Although it is not clear what real or imagined advantages would accrue to the workers if a small business was collectivized rather than operated by its owner or manager under the control of a Committee of Workers, as provided for in Article 1 (b) of the decree, it is apparent that under existing conditions, a majority of the employees could obtain the agreement of the owner or owners by intimidation and threats. On the other hand, instances have come to the notice of the Consulate General indicating that small businesses which have not been collectivized are completely at the mercy of their employees, the authority of the owner or manager being practically nil. The effect seems to be that, instead of the workers approving the acts of the owner or manager in the pursuit of a policy determined upon by him, the workers frequently take the initiative and require compliance in their decisions by the nominal head of the business. This is particularly true in matters concerning wages and hours, and in regard to claims for indemnification made by former employees who take advantage of the present economic and commercial confusion to present such claims.

A specific instance of the collectivization of an entirely American concern is found in the United Shoe Machinery Company. The director, a Spanish citizen, left the country in the early weeks of the revolution because his life was in danger, and the organization fell under the control of a workers' committee. Notices were published demanding the presence of the Director, and later, of the President and the Managing Director, both of the latter being American citizens and in the United States at the time. Official records of the company were seized by the workers' committee, and two Spanish officers holding powers of attorney from the company for the exercise of certain functions found that they had no voice in the affairs of the business and that their actions were closely watched by the workers. For their own safety they ceased any attempts to oppose the actions of the committee.

In December a circular was issued in the name of the United Shoe Machinery Company, S.A., announcing the collectivization of the business and the names of the three managing "comrades" designated in conformity with the Collectivization Decree. A translation of the circular is enclosed herewith (Enclosure No. 1). It will be noted that the circular promises to "recognize" and "respect" the foreign interests that may exist in the enterprise.

Consequent upon the collectivization of this enterprise, the Consulate General has been notified by the local representative of the accounting firm appointed by the shareholders to audit the books for 1936 that they had been informed by the "new" company that their services would not be required, and that they would not be allowed to complete the audit of the 1936 accounts. The termination of the services of this auditing firm, a British concern, would appear to remove one of the remaining safeguards of the foreign interest in the business, or in any event cannot be regarded as increasing whatever protection may still be effective.

The Barcelona company of the Boston Blacking Company, a subsidiary of the United Shoe Machinery Company, and the General Motors plant have also been collectivized.

Other American firms which have been affected by the Collectivization Decree, although they have not been collectivized as yet, are the Singer Sewing Machine Company, the Royal Trust Mecanográfico (Royal Typewriter Company), the Hoffman Pressing Machine Company and the Western Electric Company. The Hoffman Pressing Machine Company is under the control of a workers' committee and the manager has found unavailing his efforts to guide the affairs of the business toward what, in his opinion, is the benefit of the owners. The manager of the Western Electric Company office, the employees of which have thus far been content with the treatment they have received from their employers and have not initiated action under the Decree of Collectivization, has received a letter from the bank handling the company's account which forces him to consider the operation of the business in accordance with the terms of the decree. A translation of the bank's letter is enclosed herewith (Enclosure No. 2). In view of the circumstances in his particular case, the Western Electric Company manager obtained an interview with the Counsellor of Economy in which he pointed out that his concern was entirely American and asked for a categorical statement concerning the application of the decree to foreign enterprises in general and to his own company in particular. The Counsellor failed to meet the issue squarely and practically admitted that the pressure from the various syndicates in the matter of collectivizations was so great that the Government was not in a position to clarify the status of foreign enterprises.

In the case of the Royal Trust Mecanográfico application has recently been made by the employees to the Counsellor of Economy for the collectivization of the enterprise, and the resulting situation provides an example of the lack of uniformity characteristic of the operation of the Collectivization Decree. The local manager of this company has explained his position to the Consulate General as being that of one entirely in charge of the operations of the company in Catalonia and answerable to the General Manager, normally stationed in Madrid, who is at present out of Spain. It therefore developed that the Counsellor of Economy refused the application of the employees on the ground that the powers of the Barcelona manager were not sufficient to permit him to act for the company and that only the General Manager could appear in the collectivization procedure as representative of the owners. In view of the manager's statement that he is in complete charge of the company's affairs in Catalonia, and that the decree does not, of course, extend beyond the boundaries of Catalonia, it would seem that the local manager is being eliminated from the matter, and, in view of the practical impossibility of an appearance by the General Manager, that the outcome is likely to be collectivization without any voice or participation by any representative of the owners.

Closing down the Barcelona branch, as an alternative to standing helplessly by while the business is collectivized, has been considered by the Royal Typewriter Company and the possibility of so doing has been discussed by the Barcelona manager in a memorandum, a copy of which is enclosed (Enclosure No. 3). The memorandum points out that, while the employees might be agreeable to the withdrawal of the company upon payment of the required indemnities to the employees, there would be no assurance against future claims and probably the syndicates would object, in any case, to the closing of the business by the owners.

The only expressions from the Generalidad of Catalonia in reply to this Consulate General's requests for information are found in the letters of the First Counsellor dated November 5, 1936, a translation of which accompanied my despatch No. 121 of November 21, 1936, and January 27, 1937, a translation of which is annexed hereto (Enclosure No. 4). Repeating that foreign interests are protected by those provisions of the Collectivization Decree which are discussed elsewhere in this despatch, the First Counsellor, however, in his letter of January 27 states that there can be no distinction in the operation of the decree between "enterprises partially or entirely foreign." This presumably is intended to mean that no distinction is made between Spanish enterprises and enterprises partially or entirely foreign.

The question of the time and manner of the compensation of foreign interests has been referred to the Department of Economy for consideration.

In spite of the statement of the First Counsellor in his letter of November 5, 1936, that the decree does not project anything new within the Republican Constitution, there remains a doubt concerning the legality of the method of its enactment and of its legal force under the constitution of the Spanish Republic.

Respectfully yours,
Mahlon F. Perkins
American Consul General

3

DESCENT INTO CRISIS
AND THE MAY DAYS
(FEBRUARY–MAY 1937)

ALTHOUGH THE CIVIL WAR remained far from Barcelona throughout the spring of 1937, political conflict was intense within the city. Communists still competed with the Anarchists for control in the city, and this competition resulted in more deaths by assassination and execution. Law and order were continuing to crumble. Over one hundred fifty murders in Barcelona that spring went unpunished by the authorities. Thus terrorism continued to generate tension for all residents, a fear expressed in some of the papers below. Various factions increasingly found a need to clash in the streets in order to make their power or desires known, a development that resulted in a major crisis in May 1937 that can best be described as a mini-civil war limited primarily to the city of Barcelona, although minor outbursts were reported in surrounding communities. Because this fighting changed the nature of life in the city, it is worth reviewing briefly. Moreover, the events of that May were significant for the course of the Civil War as a whole.

Labor organizations played a major role in Catalan politics, a role more extensive than in any other part of the Republican zone. It was in Cataluña that labor competed most directly with the legally established authorities. Simply put, the PSUC (Communist-dominated Socialist Party in Cataluña) and parts of the remaining lower middle class were allied with President Companys' government against the Anarchist elements of the FAI. Their rivalry for political power accounted for most of the violence behind the battle lines of the Civil War in Cataluña that spring. By April, the government of the Republic sought to expand its influence in Cataluña, particularly in those areas dominated by the Anarchists, in order to strengthen and coordinate the war effort against Franco's Nationalists. The Republic felt this objective had to be achieved in Cataluña for the government to survive. Moreover, the Communist party, then on the ascendancy within the Republican government, sought to crush its own political enemies, most of whom were anarchist and in Cataluña, primarily in Barcelona. Consequently, the Communists, acting in the name of the Republic in most instances, sent in or cooperated with the *carabineros* of the Republic and occupied the Catalan cities of Puigcerdá and

Figueras in mid-April. On 25 April, Roldán Cortada, an important leader of the UGT and a leading member of the PSUC, was killed. His murder increased tensions among the radical elements while generating hostility toward Republican and Francoist groups, both of which were blamed for his death. The PSUC sought to improve its position with a show of strength at his funeral, organizing a mighty parade which the POUM—Marxist yet noncommunist party—and the CNT saw as a threat. The police attempted to reduce the state of tension in various parts of Cataluña by arresting Anarchists. This led to sporadic street fighting. Rumors spread that the Republic had issued orders to disarm all workers, who in turn disarmed some police. Friction continued with a considerable number of outbreaks in Barcelona, leading many people to expect open fighting in the streets. Residents bought extra food if they had sufficient ration cards and many stayed home as the anticipated conflict approached.[1]

The Commissariat for Public Order, under the command of Rodríguez Sala, a member of the Communist-dominated PSUC, seized the CNT-UGT-dominated Telefónica building in the Plaza de Cataluña on 3 May. The tall building dominated the area of central Barcelona and was a communications center. When word went out of the building's occupation, workers went on strike throughout Barcelona. They constructed barricades, armed themselves, and protested what they clearly thought was a direct assault on their authority over the city and its proletariat revolution. By evening, they easily had control of the city. To reduce tensions and ensure control, President Companys announced over the radio that he was repudiating the seizure of the telephone building by the police. The CNT agreed to call for calm among all workers at the same time. Members of the Republican government also appealed to reason and proposed a cease-fire. However, on the morning of 5 May, the workers still occupied their barricades, and all normal activity in the city had come to a halt. As the despatches and telegrams below illustrate, Barcelona was a city at war, with fighting taking place from house to house, in the side streets, and across the major plazas. Both the Catalan and Republican governments realized that they now faced a major crisis that threatened to hamper the war effort and, even worse, give the Nationalists the opportunity to take advantage of a division in the Republican zone. Despite the danger, more radical elements disagreed with the combined CNT-Generalidad position than was assumed by any group trying to bring peace quickly to Barcelona.

The confusion and misinterpretation of various political views, which had become more polarized with each passing hour, caused the eventual disorganization of the workers' strike, a split in the ranks of those fighting against the forces representing government. This development made it possible

---

[1]Bolloten, *The Spanish Revolution*, pp. 368–402; Jackson, *The Spanish Republic and the Civil War 1931–1939* (Princeton, 1965), pp. 368–71; Thomas, *The Spanish Civil War*, pp. 646–65.

for order to be restored in Barcelona because no strong coordinated resistance to the government was either possible or actually mounted. During the crisis, leaders of the different groups gunned down each other while their own forces fought. Bodies of key leaders appeared in various parts of the city. Antonio Sesé, a leader of the UGT, died in this manner. Other bodies of local leaders turned up after 6 May, when the fighting ended.

The Republic pushed forward as quickly as possible to restore its authority. The restoration of power was made easier by the inability of the Catalan government to control the disorder within the province. Thus the Republican government sent five thousand men throughout Cataluña to take over public order and defense, assigning a large portion of this force to Barcelona. With such an influx of armed men, virtually all fighting came to a halt.[2]

There remains some debate about the number of casualties suffered during the May Days in Barcelona. Estimates run from two hundred fifty to eight hundred fifty dead; the real figure was probably closer to five hundred. At least twice that number were wounded. (It would not be surprising if the final count of the wounded doubled that figure.) Bodies of important individuals who died in the fighting kept turning up for days afterwards in empty buildings, deserted lots, and along roads. Domingo Acaso died in the violence. On 6 May, the body of Camillo Berneri, one of the outspoken members of the "counter revolution," was found, shot by the UGT. Later the remains of Alfredo Martínez, secretary of the Revolutionary Youth Front, were also identified. Both Berneri and Martínez had criticized Communist rule in Cataluña and probably died because of their beliefs.[3]

Eyewitnesses of the fighting called it serious and widespread, and said it completely disrupted normal patterns of life in Barcelona. George Orwell, a member of POUM's militia, said that first most workers "went out into the streets in a spontaneous gesture of defense" in order to regain control of the telephone building, thereby ensuring their influence over all local telecommunications. Second, they wanted to disarm the *Asalto* guards, a special force created by the Republic to combat urban violence and who now were pitted against the proletariat forces wishing to dominate the city. Robert Louzon, a French journalist who happened to be in Barcelona at the time, agreed with Orwell's interpretation, adding that without a doubt the workers had controlled 90 percent of the city. Yet he also argued that they lost the struggle in the end because they remained on the defensive, never attempting to destroy their enemies completely. Confused, unorganized, and unwilling to expand their

---

[2]See Broué and Témime, *La Révolution et la guerre d'Espagne*, pp. 281–86; Cattell, *Communism and the Spanish Civil War*, pp. 133–42; Constancia de la Mora, *In Place of Splendor: The Autobiography of a Spanish Woman* (New York, 1939), pp. 319–20; Salter, *Try-Out in Spain*, pp. 135–36; Carlos Semprún-Maura, *Revolució i contrarevolució a Catalunya, 1936–1937* (Barcelona, 1975), pp. 211–73.

[3]On casualties of the May Days, see Thomas, *The Spanish Civil War*, pp. 650–65; Bolloten, *The Spanish Revolution*, pp. 403–30.

power, the radical groups simply buckled under the threat of force from the
Republican government. The extent of the Republic's victory, and consequently of the Communists', proved significant.[4]

Daily life had been altered during and as a consequence of the fighting.
The change in power simply continued the frustrating experience of going
about daily routine. One eyewitness later wrote that on 4 May, the first day
of fighting

> the housewives went out in order to get their provisions, then returned
> rapidly to their homes while the merchants who had opened their doors
> hastily closed them again. The streets, one moment alive, again became
> empty and those people who had been bold enough to show themselves
> at the windows were begged, politely but in a tone which would not
> permit a refusal, to immediately close them again and to retire into the
> interior of the apartment. This was done without wasting time. And the
> battle began. . . .[5]

This pattern of behavior continued long past the May Days as the Republic
consolidated its control over Barcelona and surrounding towns. Arrests continued and sporadic fighting was not uncommon. In sum, for a citizen in
Barcelona, the tensions of the May Days continued for weeks into the summer.

As a consequence of the fighting, property damage was severe around
the Plaza de Cataluña during the two first days of warfare, not to mention
the tragedy for those families who lost members in the struggle. In the days
that followed, shortages became common; rubbish and bodies were cleared
from the streets; and the barricades were dismantled as best as possible. The
city kept its warlike appearance, however, because the main avenues still had
sandbag emplacements, and buildings damaged by earlier fighting remained
unrepaired.

In short, the events of May represented a major turning point in Republican affairs and an important period in the history of Barcelona. The power
of the Anarchists was broken, Communist dominance over the Republican
zone ensured, and the local economy damaged even further. The mini-civil
war had exposed all the rifts in the political life of the Republic while suggesting that the Nationalists were increasingly more united in their efforts to
win the war. Yet the events also signaled the determination of the Republican
government to control better the remaining resources of its zones. For citizens
of Barcelona, however, the street battles damaged their properties, caused
more shortages, changed the political environment of the city, and brought
the hazards of war closer to home.

---

[4]George Orwell, *Homage to Catalonia* (New York, 1952), passim; Robert Louzon, *La
Révolution prolétarienne*, 10 June 1937; Santillan, *Por Qué Perdimos la Guerra*, p. 164.
    [5]Marcel Ollivier, *Les journées sanglantes de Barcelone (3 au 9 mai 1937)* (Paris, 1937),
p. 16.

852.00/4792

No. 224   Barcelona, February 9, 1937

Subject: Local Dissensions as Evidenced in the Barcelona Press

Sir:

    I . . . enclose . . . [a] translation of a letter, dated January 30, 1937, received from an unknown person now held in detention in this city according to the allegations of the writer. The letter discusses the state of disorganization, dissension and confusion now existing in Barcelona and arising from the inability of the various groups to work together for a common end. His method of proving his point is simply to refer to the articles appearing daily in the local censored press. I do not find that he has exaggerated the facts.

    In relation to this general subject, reference is made to my despatches No. 200 of January 22, 1937, entitled "Speech by President Azaña at Valencia" and No. 208 of February 1, 1937, entitled "Enough Disunion."

Mahlon F. Perkins
American Consul General

Barcelona, January 30, 1937

Dear Mr. Consul:

    I have no doubt that in writing you as I am going to do now, in these times we are going through, it may result in something difficult and dangerous for me. I know, furthermore, education and common sense and in their name I beg your pardon for sending you this letter. This letter is the fruit of patriotism and desperation. An alleviation to my poor soul, frightened in the face of the monstrous acts which I have witnessed like many other Catalans. I know that since you do not know who am I, this letter loses a large part of its value. I do not forget, besides, the neutral mission of diplomats. I know everything, I understand everything. But my impulses are stronger than my will. Pardon me.

    My brother has been killed and my father is in jail at Monjuich. Reasons? To have another brother who is a priest, who was also killed on the road of Vich on August 22 last. As regards myself, they have done little to me: they expropriated all my belongings (my small shop among them), I have been two months arrested in a "Checa" of the Plaza Lesseps, with only bread and water, and lately they make my life impossible with threats. Reasons? The same, to have a brother priest. But, naturally, you who are living here know hundreds of dramas of this nature. Thousands of unfortunate persons are wandering throughout Catalonia, besieged with hunger, and we will die without knowing what crime we have committed.

    You, dear Mr. Consul, I am entirely aware that you fulfill wonderfully your mission in this unfortunate zone of Spain. Although not familiar with law, from my youth I have known what a diplomat is and I also know what International Law is. Furthermore I am following with interest, led by my desire of justice, many things occurring inside and outside the frontiers.

In addressing you, therefore, I do so quite conscientiously. With the conviction that I may modestly increase your loyal knowledge, that you in turn, complying with your high mission, may inform your state, which through other sources secures information from here.

Allow me to contribute once to this advisory function. I take one day at hazard as I could have done any other day. On my table local newspapers of this morning accumulate. In front of so much absurdity and sewage, it occurs only to me to tell you: "Have you see them?"

I will make no more comments. I have said what it is my duty to say as a civilized man to a representative of a foreign nation. Perhaps that nation receives these papers. On the chance that this may not be the case, I will point out the news of today.

Notice in the *Noticiero* of last night in which is reported the arrival of an additional 500 foreigners to fight on the side of the reds. (This occurs daily!)

Article on the 3rd page of *El Diluvio* of today in which it plainly talks about the chaos existing here (Title: "For the Rearguard").

Editorial of the *Diari de Barcelona* (Fantastic!)

Les Noticias, in its 2nd page, showing the fight between Syndicates (Transports and Leather). On page 4 a terrible article against the P.O.U.M.

Page 3 of *La Publicitat* with a note of the Rabassaires, showing clearly the uneasiness among peasants.

Editorial of *Solidaridad Obrera* attacking England, etc. On the 1st page see article entitled "Present Day Valencia" commenting on certain statements made by the Minister of Agriculture regarding robberies, crimes, etc. perpetrated in Valencia. On the 2nd page Azaña is attacked. On the 3rd page, under "Sea Compass," it is clearly set forth that the war in Spain is of an *anti-capitalist* nature and at the same time they make charges against *La Batalla*. On the same page, a letter is published from the Youths of Freedom addressed to the Consul of the U.S.S.R., which letter, according to *Treball*, has been returned to the senders by the Consul himself. On page 4 there is an anti-capitalist outburst in an article on the glass industry. ("In Spain," Alvarez del Vayo said, not long ago, "everything is anti-Bolshevist!!") On page 5, in an article entitled "Establishing Positions," an attack is launched against the Socialists. On page 7, "International Chronicle," it is promised that the Revolution will be unleashed in Portugal. And, finally, on the last page, see an article (a tremendous thing at that!) regarding the Aragon battle front, and another one entitled "We Are We" which is simply delightful.

I am not pointing out anything contained in today's editions of *La Batalla* and *Treball* as I would have to underline the entire newspaper—such is the fierceness with which they make charges.

Before all this, Hon. Consul; before this anarchy; before this worldwide scandal, it is not, not possible to remain silent. Yesterday at La Fatarella—a humble hamlet in the province of Tarragona—people were put to the sword; the enormous case of refusing to unload the last Russian ship which arrived in Barcelona, for the reason that each syndicate wanted to get hold of the goods (shots, people killed, etc.); the question of house rents (demonstrating the prevailing anarchy); the shooting which took place a few days ago on the Ramblas. Today in the open air. . . . What will it be tomorrow?

And at the same time "poor" Azaña has been undusted and taken to Valencia to deliver his speech! That speech in which they wanted to give the impression to the world that nothing was going on here.

Hon. Consul: Excuse me. Please . . . send the Catalan press to your country! It is the only thing humbly requested of you by your most obedient servant,

[There is an illegible signature]

852.5018/3

No. 227 Barcelona, February 10, 1937

Subject: Disorganization in Barcelona

Sir:

I . . . enclose herewith two lists of food stuffs some of which may not be purchased at all and some of which may be purchased only rarely or in small quantities in Barcelona. These lists were prepared independently by Mrs. Ashdown and Miss Haynes, clerks in this office.

It is obvious that many of the most important items of provisions are giving out. Were Barcelona under siege, this condition would not be surprising; but the facts are that there is ready access to the surrounding country and to France both by railway and highway, and that there has been no very effective blockade of this port by sea. It is a matter of common knowledge that the country towns are well stocked with most kinds of provisions. The causes are to be found in the ineptitude of the system, or lack of system, in the local "Government" and in the fact that certain groups are endeavoring to obtain complete control of the provisioning of the city to ensure their predominant political and financial position. In this relation, reference is respectfully made to my despatch No. 201 of January 22, 1937, entitled "Arrival of the Steamship 'Rion' from Soviet Russia."

Another phase of the present disorganization is the financial status of "collectivized" industry. I have been informed from a reliable source that, whereas some twelve million pesetas had been gathered in the general "collectivization" of industry that began in the autumn, it would not now be possible for the "collectivizers" to meet a payroll from their own resources of twelve thousand pesetas. The informant stated that Barcelona was reaching the stage of "decomposition." To my inquiry as to just how a city decomposed, the reply was made that this was the "black question mark."

Mahlon F. Perkins
American Consul General

List of Foods Impossible to Buy in Barcelona

Potatoes	Soup Bones	Bacon
Sugar	Dry Beans	Salt Pork
Flour	Tin Salmon	Tin Sardines
Beef	Tin Tuna Fish	Eggs
Veal	Cheese	Olives (loose)
Pork	Crackers of any kind	Bananas
Fresh Sausage	Lard	Carrots (you can buy one for soup)

List of Foods that Can Be Bought if Willing to Stand in a Queue *Anywhere from 45 Minutes to 2 or 3 Hours*

Bread (price has risen from 80 centimos to Ptas. 1.35 per kilo)
Fish (price has risen from Ptas. 5 per pound to Ptas. 15)
Codfish (only certain days a week and only ½ pound per person. It is sold wet.)
Frozen Meats (only certain days a week)
Fresh milk (one litre per family)
Fresh vegetables are plentiful, cabbage, lettuce, leeks, cauliflower, beet root, parsnips, spinach. (The prices of these have risen anywhere from 100 to 200 per cent)
Tomatoes and condensed milk can be bought occasionally but the tins are opened in the shop. That is done to prevent people buying more than one at a time.
Oranges and apples are considerably dearer than last year.
Foreign cigarettes and matches cannot be bought.
Unmarked items can no longer be bought in Barcelona. Items marked (x) can be found only very rarely. Items marked (#) are becoming scarce. Most Important Items preceded by -.

Food Stuffs
-Meats:
      Fresh Beef
      Fresh Veal
      Fresh Pork (x)
      Cold Storage Beef (x)
      Good quality Fish (x)

> Cod Fish (x)
> Ham (x)
> Chickens, rabbits, etc. (x)
> Bacon (x)
> Mutton

-Fresh eggs
-Cold Storage Eggs (x)
  Canned Soups
  Bouillon Cubes
-Sugar, neither brown nor white
  Dark Brown Molasses Sugar (x)
-Wheat Flour
  Corn Meal
-Bread (x)
  Brown Bread
  Crackers
  Cookies (x)
  Flour made of Rice (#)
  Italian made Spaghetti, Macaroni
  Rolled Oats
  American Breakfast Foods, such as
      Post Toasties, Puffed Wheat (x)
-Butter
  Nesco
  Good Quality Cheese (x)
-Potatoes
-Chick Peas (one of principal items
      Spanish diet)
-Beans
  Fresh Peas (#)
-Milk (#)
-Canned Unsweetened Milk
  Canned Sweetened Milk (x)
  Canned Sardines
  Canned Tuna Fish
  Canned Salmon
  Tomato Juice
  Coffee (#)
  Tea (#)
  English Mustard (x)
  Bananas
  Wines (#)
  Good Cognac
  Rum
  Gin

Miscellaneous
  Soap (#)
  Toothpastes (#)
  Foreign made Listerine
  Small Size Toothbrushes (x)
-Essential Chemical Substance for
      making gas masks
  Foreign Magazines
  Foreign newspapers, except
      occasionally *L'Humanité*
  Books in English (#)
  Hats for Women of This Year's
      Models
-Matches (#)
  Foreign Cigarettes
-Anthracite Coal
-Coke
-Carbon de Bois
-Gas for Cooking Only Some Hours
      and in Some Sections of City (#)
-Shoes (#)
  Pig-skin gloves (except pre-
      revolutionary stock)
-Gasoline (x)
  Alcohol for Burning (#)
  Camel's Hair Material

Medicines
Many German made Chemical Prod-
      ucts and Medicines Now
      Exhausted

852.00/4684

Telegram   Barcelona, February 15, 1937

Sec. of State

    Saturday 10 P.M. we witnessed from our residence overlooking city
brief naval bombardment residential business section Barcelona with harbor
fort returning fire. This morning inspected ten damaged buildings. There were
several deaths and casualties among noncombatants. Valencia informed.

                                                              Perkins

852.00/4920

CONFIDENTIAL

Barcelona, February 16, 1937

Rear Admiral A.P. Fairfield, U.S.N.
U.S.S. *Raleigh*, Villefranche

My Dear Admiral Fairfield:

Today's pouch brought your letter of February 3, 1937, confirming your prospective return to Villefranche on February 18th, as stated in your earlier letter of January 24th.

About 10 P.M. on February 13th, there was a brief naval bombardment of the central portion of Barcelona which lasted about 20 minutes. A copy of my report to the State Department is being sent to you. There is a general feeling of alarm among the local population, the more so as this attack came so soon after the loss of Málaga. On all sides there is a cry for unity, general mobilization and the abandonment of the mutual dissensions by the various radical factions. Whether the imminence of a common danger will bring about the desired end, time alone can tell. If things continue to go adversely for the "Government," it will not be long before the local leaders will be facing the question of how to save themselves. Just what form this process will take and what results are apt to ensue generally as regards the population of Barcelona are questions to which we are giving considerable thought.

The French Consular steamer still continues to make frequent trips to Barcelona and is entering the port.

Mahlon F. Perkins
American Consul General

852.00/4949

CONFIDENTIAL

Barcelona, February 27, 1937

Rear Admiral A.P. Fairfield, U.S.N.
U.S.S. *Raleigh*, Villefranche, France.

My Dear Admiral Fairfield:

Supplementing my letter of February 16, 1937, I may say that the loss of Málaga and the recent bombardment on the night of February 13th are still exerting a stimulating effect upon Barcelona. There is more animation and outward emotion evidenced in the streets than for some months. An attempt is being made to organize a "Popular" army and the new recruits are constantly drilling upon the side-walks during the rush hours. Although the cry is for unity, the dissensions of the various "parties" appear to be sharper than ever with various rumors as to the likelihood of open hostilities between them. All are agreed that the war must be won, but each has its own plan and insists that its way is the only right one.

I understand that lately seven ships have arrived in Barcelona. Three of these are from Soviet Russia and I am reliably informed that they have brought 1000 bales of cotton, considerable wheat, and large quantities of arms and munitions. It would therefore seem that the "blockade" is far from being effective.

Consul Davis at Valencia tells me that the presence of the Government there has had a steadying effect and that, as long as the Government holds, it would seem that there is a fair prospect of the maintenance of the elements of order. I regret that I cannot speak as optimistically with regard to Barcelona. This "Post Málaga" stage of Barcelona is difficult to analyze. The present swing seems to indicate a growing and very general desire to curtail the extreme activities of the "uncontrolled groups"; but the very realization of the drift of public opinion may serve to drive these groups to attempt the seizure of complete local control before the tide against them runs too strong. At present it is largely a battle of pamphlets and hand-bills: we hope that the release of emotion will be restricted to these methods.

I have just read the foregoing to the Belgian Consul General who has dropped in. He has been in Barcelona some three years and says that he fully concurs in this outline of the situation.

The *Raleigh* press news, which we are receiving regularly, is very much appreciated and frequently gives us the first news of events in other parts of Spain and of items in other countries relating to Spanish affairs.

Mahlon F. Perkins
American Consul General

No. 241   Barcelona, March 8, 1937

Subject: Popular Demonstration of February 28, 1937

Sir:

There occurred here on Sunday, February 28 a popular demonstration in the form of an enormous parade in which some 100,000 persons took part. The demonstration may be said to be the reaction of the people to the loss of Málaga and the bombardment of Barcelona. All military and labor organizations participated in the parade, as well as units of the new Popular Army which is being recruited.[6]

With the exception of the C.N.T. and the F.A.I., none of the organizations carried their own emblems and the national Republican flag was more in evidence than it has been for several months. There was considerable cheering from the bystanders for the National Guard and for the *Guardias de Asalto*, but such tokens of approval were not forthcoming for some of the more radical labor organizations. This has been interpreted as indicating that although the new Popular Army is being recruited "to win the war," it is nevertheless being regarded by the people primarily as an additional safeguard for the preservation of local peace and order.

Mahlon F. Perkins
American Consul General

852.00/4932

Telegram   Barcelona, March 13, 1937

Confidential

Catalan Government has been making marked efforts to effect reorganization of Department Internal Security with a view to obtaining control over lawless elements. These efforts meeting with popular approval which is perhaps as much interested in this phase of the situation as in the progress of the war.

Reliably informed that munitions as well as volunteers are still being brought across the French frontier, although latter in smaller numbers. Reports generally indicate that Government is meeting with constant military reverses. Local atmosphere is pessimistic and most foreign observers consider defeat as only a matter of time.

Reported four planes dropped eighty bombs this morning neighborhood of Barcelona, causing considerable damage.

Perkins

---

[6]An important publication in the city, *Noticiero Universal*, editorialized on 1 March 1937 on the need for "a regular army, a sole command, a sole service of public order, a sole flag— the Republican flag, interlaced with that of the four red stripes," p. 1. The stripes refer to the four provinces of Catalonia. Another paper noted that the enthusiasm for a unified military force was "one of the great miracles of the revolution. But it is simply due to the fact that the people today realize that it is not a force of oppression; that it is a force of defense," *La Rambla*, 1 March 1937, p. 1, reflecting the views of the Partit Socialista Unificat de Catalunya.

852.00/4954

Telegram   Barcelona, March 16, 1937

Sec. of State

We observed from our home this morning's air bombardment of southern section of the city resulting in 1 killed 18 wounded according to official reports and destruction of several unimportant houses. Some 20 bombs dropped.

Franklin

No. 258   Barcelona, March 29, 1937

Subject: Resignation of Government of Catalonia

Sir:

I have the honor to refer to . . . the present unsettled condition of the Catalan Government under the Presidency of Luis Companys, and to enclose a translation (1) of the note of Companys published in yesterday's newspapers outlining his position, as well as (2) a memorandum regarding local comments, together with (3) a translation of a leaflet being distributed this afternoon and attributed to the POUM.

With reference to these so-called Cabinet Crises, it is believed that the CNT and FAI now are insisting on having seven out of the eleven cabinet positions in the Catalan Government with the UGT the other four positions; leaving out the Left Republican Party and the local supporters of President Companys. It is thought that the public will insist on President Companys having at least a majority of the cabinet members of the groups not belonging to the anarcho-syndicalists (CNT and FAI). With the present and continued dissension in the local government it is impossible for the present for Catalonia to cooperate closely with General Miaja, Commander of the Madrid forces, against the insurgents and assure proper protection to those residing in Catalonia.

Lynn W. Franklin
American Consul

Free Translation of a Statement issued by Mr. Luis Companys, President of the Generalidad of Catalonia, appearing in *La Vanguardia*, of March 28, 1937.

Eight months have elapsed since the revolt of the military element at the service of international fascism and of the other privileged elements who had directed, corrupted and denaturalized the legitimate tradition of the Iberian peoples. The popular masses and the loyal forces stopped and defeated the revolt of those who today are being maintained only by the help rendered to them by the foreign countries that have invaded Spanish territory.

The revolt brought about, as the effect of a long political process, an intense commotion of public vengeance with the purpose of making sure that it would not be possible to revive an unfortunate past, and with the noble and ambitious purpose of securing, assuring and establishing the foundations guaranteeing the economic victories that would carry the Republic to the first line in progress and human liberties.

The protest of the people, which broke out in a painful moment of its history, has been very intense, and its development has not been free from the disturbances and experiences that accompany all profound and fruitful commotions. With the direct assistance of the syndical organizations and anti-fascist political parties in a compromise agreement of responsibilities and duties, we have been watching the revolutionary process and the necessities and requirements of the war, the basic objective, since all the other possibilities depend upon victory. And among errors and successes there has been carried out, with the cooperation of all, a work that in spite of the difficulties encountered during such complex times, has evidently improved and strengthened the social resources in all the aspects of the new order, of the new economy, and of the efficiency [of] the new instruments of combat.

But the rhythm of the efforts should be accelerated, since the war is being prolonged on account of foreign help and the new problems should be prevented from piling up on the previous ones. It is necessary to take resolutions, meditated and appropriate, but rapid, under the superior and only direction a responsible Government, whose authority arises from the popular and democratic base of the forces of the majority in Catalonia, can take.

This need for a Government that can govern and impose itself upon those making its work difficult has always been restrained by considerations or actual situations that may not be denied nor disregarded. And while this is understood and even logical, on account of the difficult historical days we are undergoing, it is also certain that it is not possible to lose a further minute, and just in order to avoid sacrifices and insure the victory of our desires it is necessary, urgently necessary, to put an end to all kinds of confusion.

Public opinion has, at least, the right to be respected, and when a program is launched, which furthermore is commented or strengthened with the assurance that it will be made effective, there is a duty of fulfilling it. And at this time of the present crisis, as an experiment and as recognition of changes and guarantees for the future, we should recall the course of the previous crisis, their programs and the engagements repeatedly agreed upon.

After the first Government, formed solely of republican parties of the left, there was formed on September 26 the first Council of the Generalidad in which participated all the syndical forces and anti-fascist political parties and there was published the program that, among other things, and as a basis, established the collectivization of the large rural estates, respect for small agrarian propèrty, the collectivization of the large industries, public services and transports, the partial devaluation of urban property by means of a reduction in rents or the establishment of equivalent valuations, the seizure and collectivization of abandoned establishments, workers' control of private industry and respect for the Catalan middle class. And in making public this program the following was stated:

> The Council will make the necessary dispositions for the greater success of the war and the forms of the new economy, and invested with the unanimous representation of all the anti-fascist people, it will impose itself on all those who for any reason pretend to act outside of the discipline imposed by the circumstances and without which we could not win the war (our supreme objective), nor solve the serious economic problems arising therefrom.

On October 27 there was published in the *Diari Oficial de la Generalitat de Catalunya* the Decree of Collectivization which had been prepared by agreement in the Council of Economy with representation and with the assistance of all the syndical forces and anti-fascist political parties, presented by the proper Councilor to the Government, which approved it after much discussion, and because it was considered, as was stated as the transactional basis of satisfaction and guarantee that would permit the facing of other problems of interior character and of war, since it would cause to disappear suspicions, that with the approval of said decree might be overcome, and which otherwise could have no possible solution.

On December 17, and in the face of the same situation of a lack of effectiveness in the management of Government and compliance with the decrees, another crisis took place, the present Government being constituted in which are represented the CNT, the UGT, Esquerra party and Rabassaires. The Council bound itself to make effective the program of the previous Government which it had not been possible to carry out nor had it been imposed on anyone; and in the public declaration made, the following was stated:

> The Council will put into effect the program agreed upon and made public upon the constitution of the previous Council and which this latter began to apply, but which is not yet fully effective. In this connection it will develop the immediate program of social realizations mentioned in said manifest, and of public safety, confidence and arrangement of the rearguard under the sole superior direction of the new Council, in which will participate the greatest majority of the syndical and anti-fascist political forces.
>
> In order to win the war and direct the program of economic changes asked for by the working people and the popular anti-fascist masses, the Council requests the assistance and cooperation of all Catalonia and declares that it will enforce its decisions.

The Council believes that in these times what the country wants is action and not words, and refrains from making any other statement. It hopes that the work it is going to start will speak for it.

The present Government, like the previous ones, has not failed to point out the rules for governing the political and social life of our people, and the decrees approved with the unanimous accord of the councilors are numerous, and I take pleasure in pointing out the effort, the extraordinary scope of the decrees published by the Councilor of Finance, which were not only approved by all the councilors, but were also discussed and finally agreed upon and accepted by the syndical representatives who had offered some resistance and made remarks, some of which were incorporated in the legislative work of the first councilor.

But the efforts of the Council to bring into effect its decisions were not successful, inasmuch as at the meeting of the Council of February 27 there was given to the press a declaration of Government which was approved by all the councilors after much discussion of each paragraph, and in which the following was stated:

The President of the Generalidad has submitted in denunciatory terms, the urgency for the Government to act with full authority and with the energy required by the problems it has to solve, and upon which depend the victory and the future of our people. The Council, in taking into account the words of the President, has examined in all its aspects the situation of defense, public order, and economy; after hearing the opinions of the responsible elements of the different groups, it has unanimously decided:

First, to ratify, in a public declaration, its firm decision to carry out the social changes that constitute the aspiration of our people and which were incorporated in its program. The Government expects that it will continue to merit the confidence of public opinion to carry out this program completely.

Second, taking into account that the syndical forces and political organizations which form the Council are the authentic representatives of the popular will, the Government will not permit any interference, nor will it allow to remain unpunished violations and acts contrary to its decision, or contrary to the new social order.

Third, the Council, though appreciating the value that private or collective suggestions may have, cannot tolerate the effectiveness of other decisions than those determined by the Government.

Fourth, the Government of the Generalidad hopes that all political and social organizations will understand the necessity of fulfilling its dispositions, subordinating their private and collective interests to the necessity of winning the war. The Government of the Generalidad also believes that it must make public its confidence in the work of coordination of all our efforts with the Government of the Republic with the purpose of organizing rapidly the regular Army under a single command.

And this declaration ended with the following words:

> Fifth, the Government declares that on making these decisions public it
> does not limit itself to making a further declaration, but announces imme-
> diate and energetic action which will correspond to its contents.

In meetings of the Government, after making these statements public,
it approved the decrees of Interior Security on the withdrawal of arms, and
of mobilization.

At present a new crisis in the face of a large number of legislative
dispositions approved with the unanimous vote of the Council, and which
were largely discussed in meetings and assemblies, but which it has not been
possible to carry out and which in certain aspects have not been complied
with and in other cases trespassed or deformed still exist.

We have all emphasized the great importance of the days we are going
through, not only for Catalonia but for Spain and for all the world. And this
conviction puts us under the obligation of leaving aside group interests and
even ideal aspirations to the benefit of the union of the anti-fascist elements
and for the prime purpose of winning the war, a matter which is constantly
emphasized in the press and in public meetings by the men of the different
political and syndical parties. And it also obliges us not to yield, but to
confront the manifestations or symptoms that may obstruct, disturb or delay
the work of the Government, whose Councilors must have full authority to
develop their initiatives if they are to be considered responsible men, since
there exists no responsibility when the necessary authority is not conferred
for the performance of the functions entrusted.

The new Government to be formed will be invested with the necessary
confidence of the respective organizations and parties to act from the first
moment with authority as such. This is an indispensable requirement for its
constitution under my presidency.

I have deemed necessary to limit myself, in this note, to calling to mind
the compromises and guarantees of previous political events, and I have
commented upon them in a smooth and simple manner, which is not contrary
to the firm resolution of adopting a line of conduct adequate to the needs and
to the situations that may present themselves.

Luis Companys

March 29, 1937

Memorandum

Synopsis of Local Press

On Saturday, March 27, President Companys gave publicity in the press
to the note he had announced. In this note he makes a detailed statement of
the steps taken in connection with the constitutions of the Government of the

Generalidad since the Revolution of July 19, 1936, and makes special reference to the program his government proposed to carry out and the difficulties encountered for its fulfillment. He states that the new government to be constituted should have the necessary confidence of all organizations and parties in order to have complete authority, which is an indispensable requirement if it is to be constituted under his presidency. This requirement would seem to imply that if further difficulties are caused by the syndical organizations he would be likely to resign his position.

Yesterday, March 28, a meeting was held in the Tivoli by the Sindicatos del Transporte CNT. At this meeting Companys was the object of violent attacks on the part of those who spoke. In this meeting Companys was referred to as a man who is not worthy of any confidence since "a man who when speaking to another is constantly looking at the floor and does not dare to look at the face may not be relied upon." They added that the Generalidad is asking for the return of arms, but that although they have many they will not give a single one. The *Hoja Oficial* of today, when giving a statement of this meeting does not mention a single word about this. This is further evidence of the existing dissentions among the parties constituting the government, and especially of the desire of the CNT to predominate in all aspects.

On account of several occurrences during the last month the armed forces here (police, civil guards, etc.) do not seem to be very friendly to the syndical groups. Again, on the 26th of this month a member of the police on duty at a garage was seriously wounded by some men who attempted to withdraw a car from that garage having no authority to do so and therefore with the opposition of the police. It is reported that this man has died and there seems to be ill-feeling against the CNT and FAI by the police forces. The statement is made by some of them, and probably it is the general feeling, that they are quiet only for the sake of discipline but that they are ready not to leave one of these "people" alive and that it should not be a surprise if later on they should be compelled to do it. In that case what happened on July 19 will be nothing as compared with what would occur—they state.

Lynn W. Franklin
American Consul

Free Translation of a Leaflet Distributed by the POUM

To the Comrades of the CNT
To the Comrades of the FAI

It would be nothing short of shutting the eyes in the presence of real facts if anybody denied that the counter-revolution is raising its head and that it has succeeded in stopping the impulsive course followed by the revolution after the 19th of July. The attack against the Committees, the temporary suspension of CNT and the definite suspension of *El Combatiente Rojo* in Madrid, the taking over of our broadcasting station in the capital of the

Republic, the governmental arrests of revolutionary leaders, the attempts to reconstitute on the former basis the old army of the bourgeoisie, the contemplated reorganization of the services of Public Order, the press censorship established by the Government of Valencia, the temporary suspension of *Nosotros* in Valencia and of our central mouthpiece *La Batalla*, the arrest of the Regional Committee of the CNT in Euzkadi and of the staff of their newspaper there: all these facts are actual signs of the advance made by the counter-revolution.

Under such conditions we arrive at the present crisis of the Government of the Generalidad, while a crisis of the Central Government is announced as imminent. The reformers will no doubt take advantage of the situation to launch a new attack against the revolutionary conquests of the proletariat and with a view to strengthening the position of the democratic bourgeoisie. Watch out, comrades! Previously we were eliminated from the Government. Now, as we had already foreseen, the attack is directed against you. Will you stand for it? Upon the energy we display in defending our positions depends the victory of the reformers of the progress of the revolution. The moment is grave and decisive. And, in our opinion, there is only one way out of this— the Workers' Revolutionary Front, made up by the CNT, the FAI and the POUM, and the constitution of a Government of Workers and Peasants, the only one that can give satisfaction to the workers as well as win the war and make the revolution.

The only obstacle to it might be your traditional non-political policy; but inasmuch as the circumstances have forced you to participate in governments, follow it to the end, throw overboard the ballast of bourgeoisie parties and work for the constitution of a Government of Workers and Peasants. This is the only revolutionary way out of the situation. By keeping up the present game we enhance the positions of the reformers and the triumph of the counter-revolution.

Long Live the Workers' Revolutionary Front!
Long Live the Government of Workers and Peasants!

Barcelona, March 27, 1937

852.00/5069

Telegram   Barcelona, April 4, 1937

Sec. of State

New government formed last night by President of Catalonia but without settling differences causing resignation of former cabinet. Present cabinet may be said to carry same proportional representation of labor groups as previous one. Relative calm exists among people of Barcelona.

Perkins

852/5010/4

No. 269   Barcelona, April 6, 1937

Subject: Economic Conditions in Catalonia

Sir:

I had yesterday a conversation with a foreigner who has lived in Catalonia many years and who, by reason of his business activities, is in a position to speak with authority in regard to the economic conditions of this region. He reports the existence throughout the country of a deplorable lack of the primary foodstuffs of the people: bread, meat, cod-fish, and even olive oil. It is not merely that the prices of these articles have risen: they are frequently not to be had at any price. Villages often go many days without any supply of bread whatsoever. This is a tragedy to the common people; for perhaps in no country more than in Spain is bread the staple food. The shortage of feed for animals and poultry is so acute that the farmers are killing the young pigs and selling the small chickens rather than attempt to raise them to the customary size for marketing.

My informant states that, even under ordinary conditions, Catalonia has had in the past to import large quantities of grain, amounting annually to some 700,000 tons of wheat and 300,000 tons of corn. A considerable portion of this has come from areas now under Nationalist control. It will be necessary to import heavily from other countries, primarily France. But Catalonia has little credit abroad by reason of the revolutionary economic changes that have occurred here; and, moreover, the province has very little to export in way of payment of purchases in foreign countries. The shortage of olive oil is due largely to its export abroad, principally Russia, in order to pay for war supplies and other imports. Within the past ten days over a million pesetas have been transferred from Barcelona to Valencia in order to pay for Russian exchange. Thus funds that should be used for the purchase of grain are being partly dissipated for war purposes.

This situation, bad enough in itself, is being aggravated by the assignment, among the various towns and villages of Catalonia, of large numbers of refugees from Southern Spain. In one instance, I am told, the number of refugees so assigned has exceeded the number of the resident inhabitants.

In all these circumstances, which are daily becoming worse, my informant sees a state of affairs full of danger. He states that the "authorities" are at a loss how to deal with these difficulties and he fears what may happen at any time when the people's hunger reaches the point of desperation.

Mahlon F. Perkins
American Consul General

852.5018/5

No. 270   Barcelona, April 6, 1937

Subject: Living Conditions in Barcelona

Sir:

I . . . enclose herewith for the Department's information a translation of a portion of a letter sent recently from Barcelona by a Spanish lady to a friend in France. The letter describes not only the bitter living conditions caused by the lack of foodstuffs and other necessaries, but also suggests the depressed state of mind of many of the residents of Barcelona as a result of the hardships of the Revolution.

This despatch relating to conditions within Barcelona itself may well be read in connection with my despatch No. 269 of even date, entitled "Economic Conditions in Catalonia."

Mahlon F. Perkins
American Consul General

Translation of Enclosed Portions of Letter:

The worst is that even those who have money will not be able to get food. Since fifteen days ago the lack of food has increased, and not only is there no bread, but we do not find rice, sugar, oil, and for the milk we make a very long queue and there is not enough for all. Chick-peas, beans, cod-fish . . . for six months they have not been seen. Potatoes was the first thing that was finished; there are no tomatoes, fish, and as regards meat . . . once per week, a small quantity, and very expensive. We have vegetables, which is something, and fruit (oranges), chocolate and marmalades. We are living; but when I see the children losing in their health . . . I suffer enormously.

Barcelona is a dirty city; it has in its streets a rabbling appearance. There are multicolor flags, without knowing which one among all we are serving; red, red-black, republican, catalan, those of the Consulates . . .; something awful! Of the joyful city, nothing remains.

When will all this have an end? Perhaps you know better than I; sometimes I am entirely at a loss. Have we lived good days at other times? How many years ago?

Who will be living at the street? I think that all Spaniards that were living there are dead; and all those who lived around here, in fine houses, also.

852.00/5172

Telegram   Barcelona, April 17, 1937

Sec. of State

New cabinet unexpectedly announced last night consists of a reshuffling of the cabinet under the same premier which resigned March 26. Friction during past three weeks has been continuous and it is hoped differences have now been sufficiently composed to eliminate danger of local hostilities and permit reasonable degree of cooperation. Problem of Government control over arms still retained by labor groups has not yet been solved.

Perkins

852.00/5387

No. 294   Barcelona, April 20, 1937

Subject: Air Bombardment of Sunday, April 18, 1937

Sir:

At about 3 P.M. on Sunday, April 18, 1937, an air raid occurred in the vicinity of the Customs House at Barcelona. From such inquiries as I have been able to make, it appears that about 50 bombs of small size were released from a single airplane. The press reports that the casualties were six killed and forty-nine wounded. The material damages are reported as slight, but I am privately informed that some damage was done to two or three merchant ships at the docks adjoining the Customs House. The continuous explosion of the numerous small bombs made a noise resembling rolling thunder.

Shortly after the raid, Vice Consul Flood visited the area attacked. A copy of his memorandum is enclosed herewith. There are also enclosed photographs of the effects produced by the bombs, as published in the pictorial supplement of *La Vanguardia* of April 20, 1937.

The alarm signals of a further air raid on Monday, April 19, 1937, were given at about 6 P.M., Barcelona's "rush hour." The people speedily sought the *refugios*; but the attack did not take place. Enemy planes had been detected at Tarragona heading for Barcelona and a warning had been communicated to this city.

Mahlon F. Perkins
American Consul General

Memorandum

Bombardment of April 18, 1937

About 4:30 yesterday afternoon I went down to the port district to see what damage had been caused by the aerial bombardment. At the corner of the Paralelo and Paseo Colon, next to the Aduana, there were between 30 and 40 marks where bombs, or pieces of bombs, had dropped.

These bombs must have been very light and small (such as a 25-kilo size) or else they exploded before contact, judging from the dimensions of the marks. They were mostly from 4 to 8 in. in diameter and 1 to 3 in. deep.

Entrance to the port was blocked at the railroad tracks, but from what could be seen, there apparently was little damage done, aside from shrapnel marks on the Aduana building and broken windows and street lights. One bystander told me a large bomb had fallen in a factory building between the Aduana and the power station, on the Paralelo, but entrance to the building was barred, and I could not confirm this.

A mass of broken glass between the street car tracks on the Paralelo, about a third of a mile up from the Aduana, at a considerable distance from any street light or building, indicated that a street car or automobile had been struck.

D. Flood

852.06/5388

No. 296   Barcelona, April 21, 1937

Subject: New Cabinet of Catalonia, April 17, 1937

This new government takes the place of the "stop-gap" government reported in my telegram of April 14, 11 A.M., a government which never actually functioned by reason of the "sit down" policy of the anarchist groups. The new government, although containing the same proportional representation of the C.N.T. as that which resigned on March 26, is obviously much more acceptable to that organization, which, during the past three weeks, had entirely withheld its cooperation.

A glance at the lists of the two cabinets will show that the new one is largely a reshuffling of names. Many of the members are the same; some have merely exchanged positions; and there has been added, however, a High Council of War and a new Department of War Industries, both under the direction of President Companys.

From the comments made by the daily press, it may be inferred that the new Government takes office under favorable auspices and with a better promise of cooperation than has existed for some time. There seems to be a greater realization than hitherto of the deplorable consequences of disunion and of the very real danger of eventual defeat in the war, unless local differences are put aside. During the past three weeks, the possibility of local clashes between the two main groups, the C.N.T. and the U.G.T., has been by no means absent; and the sudden announcement of the formation of a new government has been received generally with a feeling of relief.

Mahlon F. Perkins
American Consul General

852.00/5423

No. 310   Barcelona, April 30, 1937

Subject: Declaration of the Generalidad Concerning the Abnormal Situation
    of Public Order in Catalonia

Sir:

I have the honor to refer to my telegram of 11 A.M. today, copy attached, in which I have quoted the notice issued to the press by the Generalidad of Catalonia concerning the abnormal state of public order now prevalent in Barcelona and certain other parts of Catalonia. I did not attempt to give a precise interpretation of the text of this notice because I did not feel sufficiently informed to do so with any assurance of accuracy as to the purpose of its issuance. It is difficult to state whether it is an act of despair in the face of the insurmountable difficulties of government or a last appeal for a composure of differences. The rumor has come to me that President Companys has threatened that he will turn over his authority to a certain military leader, now in Barcelona and recently from Madrid, in the event that the "Government" definitely feels that its authority has gone. In any event, the notice indicates the existence of a state of affairs so alarming that the Government feels it necessary to make public acknowledgment thereof and substantially admit its inability to assure order.

Rumors of clashes in various parts of the city have been numerous. It has been reported that, on the night of the 29th, one man was shot near the Principal Palace theatre; that a garage held by the Generalidad was attacked by members of the FAI, two being left on the ground; that another clash occurred on the Plaza Universidad; etc., etc. Since my arrival in Barcelona on September 5th last, there has been no period in which so much evidence of actual disorder has been manifest.

As indicative of the sort of thing that is going on, there is enclosed herewith a copy of a memorandum by Consul Franklin detailing notes of various occurrences within the last 48 hours within the knowledge of the guards of the Consulate-General on duty this morning. The Department's attention is particularly invited to the reported radio notice issued last evening by the Government, warning all persons against being on the streets after 10 P.M.

As of possible interest in connection with the general situation existing here for many months in greater or less degree, the Department's attention is respectfully invited to my telegram of September 19, 6 P.M., 1936.

Mahlon F. Perkins
American Consul General

True Reading of Telegram Sent

April 30, 11 A.M. Following notice appears in the morning papers. "The Council of the Generalidad in view of the abnormal situation of public order, cannot continue its work under the present danger and disorder arising from the existence of groups that in some parts of Catalonia endeavor to impose themselves through coercion and compromise the revolution and the war.

Therefore the government is suspending its meetings and hopes that immediately all those who are not directly under the authority of the Council of the Generalidad will retire from the streets in order to make possible a rapid disappearance of the uneasiness and alarm in which Catalonia is living at the moment.

At the same time the Council of the Generalidad has taken the necessary measures to insure the strict fulfillment of its decisions." Embassy at Valencia, Ambassador Bowers and Admiral informed.

Perkins

Memorandum

By Consul L.W. Franklin

April 30, 1937 8 A.M.

In a conversation with two guards at the house this morning I was informed that 800 men of the FAI endeavored to take the airport at Prat, but that the officer in command of the airport, upon hearing of the intentions of the FAI, had time to order the planes to the air with orders to fire upon those on the ground in case a shot was fired. He so informed the leader of the 800 men and thus was able to prevent the airport from being taken;

That the exits from the city to Valencia, Lérida, etc., were controlled by FAI men, that even our guards would be of no service to us if we wanted to go out in that direction as they would have to deliver their arms or return and in the latter event we would have to proceed without them;

That two of their guards live near Torrassa (under control of FAI) and they could not go home the other night without delivery of their arms to the FAI and obtaining a permit from them;

That the Government warned citizens by radio last night not to be on the streets of Barcelona after ten o'clock as they could not give them the necessary protection. (Guard at Consulate and women serving meals to guards informed me they were listening to radio when this notice was given, 10 P.M.);

That a Government airplane flew over Hospitalet and the Cuartel at Pedralbes as a warning to the FAI people;

That five Civil Guards went to Hospitalet and had to return (Vile language used by FAI people);

That they received orders to capture two soldiers who had returned from the front and were taking a drink at a cafe on the Ramblas, with their hand bombs or grenades on the table; that they had to return without fulfilling their mission in order to avoid bloodshed as there were many people in the neighborhood who might have been injured or killed had they insisted on carrying out their orders.

852.00/5437

No. 309   Barcelona, April 30, 1937

Subject: Assassination of Roldan Cortada, Secretary to the Councillor of Labor

Sir:

I have the honor to refer to my despatch No. 296 of April 21, 1937, entitled "New Cabinet of Catalonia" and to state that developments since that date do not appear to warrant the hopes then felt for a more orderly administration of affairs in this area. In fact, the friction long existing between the two main groups of "socialists" and "anarchists" (PSUC-UGT) and (CNT-FAI) has become accentuated to the point of open clashes of a minor nature within the past week.

On April 25th, there occurred the assassination a short distance from Barcelona of Roldan Cortada, Secretary to the Councillor of Labor. He was proceeding with several friends in a motor car when the car was stopped by unknown assailants and Cortada assassinated. The other occupants of the car were not touched. It is understood that Cortada had previously been a member of the CNT, but had changed his allegiance some time ago to the UGT.

On April 27th, Cortada was given an imposing funeral, some 60,000 persons passing the Consulate-General over a period of three hours. President Companys, with other leading officials, walked at the head of the procession. Numerous standards were carried, bearing such slogans as:

"Fish with the gangsters of the rear-guard."

"Catalonia demands a Government that has the dignity to govern."

"Unified anti-fascism must serve to annihilate the Fascists at the front and in the rear."

The CNT groups did not take part generally in the procession, which seemed to develop into a communist demonstration as it gathered momentum. It is understood, however, that a CNT contingent was sent, inasmuch as all groups professed their indignation at the atrocity.

The real motive for the crime is apparently not known. It is possible that the purpose was to bring about an actual outbreak of local disturbances in Catalonia and that it may have been perpetrated by "fascists" who are seeking to undermine the "Revolution" in the rear. This is the view publicly expressed.

There is enclosed herewith the text of an article, with English translation, together with a photograph of Cortada and the funeral procession, as published in *La Vanguardia* of April 28, 1937.

Mahlon F. Perkins
American Consul General

852.00/5287

Telegram   Barcelona, May 1, 1937

Sec. of State

Very acute tension resulting in several minor clashes during past few days has now appreciably moderated. President of Catalonia has issued statement in part as follows: "I am glad that the threat from rifles so much needed at the front which has disturbed the decisions of the Council has disappeared and that it has been possible to return to more normal conditions without making use of all the resources within the hands of the Government. The Council will continue studying pending problems rejecting all coercion or the appearance thereof."

Perkins

852.00/5307

Telegram   Barcelona, May 4, 1937

Sec. of State

President Companys announces that he has done everything possible to control present lamentable situation but without success to date. He calls upon all forces faithful to Government to give proofs of patience and calmness before the attitude of "mad people."

Perkins

852.00/5321

Telegram   Barcelona, May 5, 1937

Sec. of State

Firing continued yesterday afternoon and throughout night in various parts of Barcelona. Catalan Government announces that agreement reached last night with labor organizations to cease hostilities but intermittent and heavy firing continues. Press reports heavy casualties.

So far as known all American citizens unharmed. Have not been able to communicate with Valencia. Please acknowledge receipt.

Perkins

852.00/5322

Telegram   Barcelona, May 5, 1937

Sec. of State

Persons named in Department's May 5, safe in the Majestic Hotel together with Vice President and Manager of the International Banking Corporation. Police authorities report that Government now in possession of telephone building. Heavy street fighting has continued all day.

Perkins

852.00/5333

Telegram   Barcelona, May 6, 1937

Sec. of State

The following telegram has been received from Ambassador at Paris: "May 5. Please report immediately concerning present condition your district."

I have replied as follows: "May 6. Your May 5, just received. For last three days certain labor factions have been fighting one another in Barcelona and outlying suburbs. It appears this morning that local authorities are in control of the situation which remains tense and uncertain. No Americans reported harmed. We have been able to keep Department, Ambassador at St. Jean de Luz and Admiral Fairfield fully informed."

Perkins

852.00/5337

Telegram   Barcelona, May 6, 1937

Sec. of State

Local Government authorities appear to be in control of most of the city but it is reported General Government at Valencia is assuming charge of public order in Catalonia. As yet no estimate of total casualties but probably about 200 killed and many more wounded to date.

New Government under President Companys formed yesterday consisting of four members representing Anarchists, Socialists, peasants and Left Republicans. New Socialist member killed shortly after appointment and replaced. Appeals through radio and press call all workers to withdraw from barricades and return immediately to their duties.

Embassy at Valencia contacted us this morning through courtesy French officials and Consulate General at Barcelona.

Perkins

852.00/5334

Telegram   Barcelona, May 6, 1937

Sec. of State

In my judgment danger of Barcelona situation is now such that it would be unsafe to evacuate Americans. British Consul General asked for war vessel against eventualities but not specifically for evacuation purposes and reports three British war vessels now standing by. He is waiting for situation to clarify. French Consul General reports three French war ships standing by with one transportation vessel and expects weekly passenger vessel tomorrow. French Consul General has some 3,000 citizens in Barcelona and does not intend leaving. Argentine Consul General not closing office.

Perkins

852.00/5339

Telegram   Barcelona, May 6, 1937

Sec. of State

CONFIDENTIAL

It has not been possible to state the precise alignment of all factions engaged in the fighting of the last three days. It may be said to be a struggle between the Socialist Communist groups supporting the Catalan Government and the Anarchists who fear that any increase of Government control will deprive them of powers seized by them and other "revolutionary" gains.

The Government is opposed to uncontrolled Anarchist elements but has not thrown in the weight of its own armed forces against them; thus the Government, possibly through weakness, seems endeavoring to maintain a quasi-neutral position which may be used to bring opposing factions to term or to take over complete control when an opportune moment arrives.

Perkins

852.00/5349

Telegram   Barcelona, May 7, 1937

Sec. of State

Hostilities have terminated at least for the time being. City gradually resuming its normal life, barricades have been opened, workers returning to their occupations, food supply trucks and passenger busses are beginning to function and streets are filling with people. Talked with Embassy at Paris this morning which will transmit resume of conversation.

Elements opposing Government state over the radio that authorities must not antagonize them further thus giving veiled threat of repetition of the outbreak.

Perkins

852.00/5352

Telegram   Barcelona, March 7, 1937

Sec. of State

Following broadcast yesterday afternoon by the President of Catalonia with the stated object of avoiding any misunderstanding that might handicap the legally authorized direction of affairs in these moments:

"President of the Generalidad makes known to all that, inasmuch as no Councilor of Defense was designated in the new Government, the President intended to preserve these functions to himself personally and that, in view of the designation of General Pozas by the Government of the Republic as Chief of the Fourth Division, there are assigned to General Pozas the functions of defense, and that he is given complete authority over the military forces of the Central Government in Catalonia and, where necessary, over those of the Government of Catalonia."

Perkins

852.00/5488

No. 314   Barcelona, May 7, 1937

Subject: Life of the Newly Dispossessed

Sir:

I have the honor to inform the Department that a short time ago this Consulate-General came in touch with a certain Spanish citizen, a school teacher by profession, who was induced to tell his personal experiences since the Revolution of last July. He sat down in the office and rapidly typed his story; there is enclosed herewith the English translation. I am pleased to have the opportunity to submit to the Department this first hand narrative, which, I am sure, will be impressive because of its truthfulness and simplicity. It is hardly necessary to add that this tale is but typical of the tragedies of uncounted thousands.

Mahlon F. Perkins
American Consul General

Life of the Newly Dispossessed

While the life of the worker during the regime existing previous to July 19th was unfortunate in certain aspects, it is much more terrible now as the life of the new poor, who are compelled by the tremendous circumstances of the present times to accommodate themselves in a very short period of time to sufferings of a physical moral character for which they were not prepared.

I know a lady who owned rural properties in Barcelona, more than 70 years old, who was living modestly from her rents and securities. As she is unable to get any money from interest on the securities she had deposited in the Banks, which she considered as something safe because they were Government bonds, she has been spending during the first months after July 19,

1937, the small savings she kept for current expenses of the house in a Savings Bank. These being exhausted and being unable to get any cent from the rent of her houses, which have been seized, she has to live at the expense of the savings of her old family servant. This case is very frequent and happy they can have it! In a very large number of cases the wealthy owners have been taken to the cemetery to be assassinated, the property passing thereby to new and unscrupulous hands. This has occurred in a village of the province of Castellón (Villafranca del Cid). This has taken place in another village of the province of Valencia (Carcagente). In this latter place the victims were chosen from among owners such as unmarried women, widows with no children or having no one who could protect them or take reprisals.

The rural owners who are obliged to work as simple laborers, endeavoring to humiliate and ridicule them, may consider themselves fortunate.

Among the small owners (trade and industry of a small size) there exists a great feeling of rancor on being dispossessed of what generally has been secured after hard work of many years. They regret to be treated as exploiters and hoarders of wealth when in reality they are former workers who have been able to place themselves a little over their comrades after much economy, savings, extra hours, help of relatives, etc. I know a man selling coal in a shop attended to by his wife and mother-in-law. He had, furthermore, a horse and cart permitting him to engage in the industry of transportation to a small extent. In this cart he transported the musical instruments of the municipal band, which was one of the regular clients he had for the development of his small industry, with which he was able to attend to the education of his children. Payment for his services of transportation of the instruments was delayed for eight months (and I do not know whether he has received payment up to now). His shop and small transportation industry were both socialized. He was converted from a small owner, with a right of initiative and relative autonomy, into a simple employee of a collectivized industry, with the aggravating fact of being obliged to feed a horse, which was no longer his property nor rendered any service to him.

A married man, after working hard and saving, had become the owner of a modest hotel, well known, capable for 60 clients. On being socialized, the cook and waiter became the arbiters, but they still had the condescendence of reserving for the former employer a post of confidence; he was appointed a delegate. The wife could not support the humiliation of seeing her husband as one more employee and decided to leave. The former owner has to witness the confusion and disorder existing in the establishment created with his work and converted at the present time into a chaos where everybody gives orders and no one obeys, and where since the first day of collectivization the disappearance of napkins and other things was noted without anybody being responsible for it.

I know the case of an exporter of oranges, who was put in jail at the beginning of the revolution, and released a few months later because of being one of the most important firms in the orange business, which firm was required by foreign importers who had little confidence in the collectivization committee. He was released from prison to make use of his signature. Upon seeing himself, formerly the wealthiest man of the village (and he was no usurer nor exploiter in the general opinion of the people), dressed at present like a beggar, confined to the former headquarters of the Civil Guards, his house collectivized, his family scattered, with no news between parents and sons, he asked himself to be killed in order not to survive such a misfortune. A discussion took place with different opinions; but, at last, he was killed.

The life of owners, industrialists and merchants has a certain standing and in their misfortune they find the compensation sometimes of a former servant who furnishes them periodically with a certain amount, someone who had received help from them and feels gratitude, a former fellow-worker who has sentiments of pity and humanity.

But there remain the modest employees, those retired, the orphans having a pension, who, on being charged with being fascists, only because of being Catholic, are suddenly deprived from their modest income which they considered safe and which was the base of support of a family living modestly, but honestly.

The orphan of a National Teacher, who received one peseta per day, which she heartily delivered to a religious community that gave her lodging and food, contemplates now her convent destroyed by fire, without her home (she was an orphan and her happiness was the new home), without the peseta per day and refused shelter by her cousins and other relatives for fear to compromise. How happy is the one that is able to find employment as a servant! I have learned of one, through a relative of mine, who spent some nights in the open air, in the public gardens, escaping from a militiaman she had encountered in a terrace and who was importuning her, offended in her dignity, with the fear of appearing as the refuse of society.

But the worst is not the inability to collect, but some times the lessees with impudence require the rents paid during the last years. The same happens with the owners of urban properties, who, not only do not receive a cent for the rent of their properties seized for the most futile reason, but are required to make at their expense important expenditures for improvements. In some villages they have been required to polish the front of all the houses, with wages excessively increased and without allowing the owner to select the workers, and so deficiently executed that I have seen myself to lose the color and become a calamity one of these houses painted no doubt with bad materials. The same may be said of water-closets and other improvements.

As regards rural properties I have seen young orange trees of the best quality being removed in order to plant potatoes, with great damage not only to the former owner but also to economy which is greatly damaged by cutting a source of income with which to balance trade, such as is the exportation of sour fruits. Examples are innumerable.

It should not be omitted in this brief statement of the situation of the new poor, the extremely serious situation of the fugitives, those persecuted, those in hiding. The moral suffering of these victims of the new situation may be judged from the number of sick persons attended to in the hospitals for nervous diseases, the enormous contingent of insane entered in the *Casas de Salud*, the growing and exorbitant number of deaths among children and old people. Very recently I have had the opportunity of seeing a wealthy *hereu* (the first born son) of a Catalan village, with pale face, who came to Barcelona where he has remained during six months in hiding. In his village he was the "father of the poor," and had influence and prestige among them. When the events of October 6 took place, when the separation of Cataluña was attempted, he used his influence to avoid the imprisonment of three of the leaders. On account of this fact and his activities in favor of working people, the Committee declared that he had nothing to fear. But the imposition of "strange" elements (as is usual in similar cases) on account of the pressure of a "single one" of the village who had lost a lawsuit with him, was of such a nature, that in spite of the assurance given by the committee and the reiterated requests that he should return to the village, he went to Barcelona remaining in hiding for several months. But when he learned that one man of his village knew he was hiding in a pension, he disappeared and went without any safe-conduct to another village where he would arrive at 10 at night, his intention being to pass it in the open air until the break of day.

The tragedy of catholic priests who have escaped requires the pen of a writer of records of martyrs.

I know of a village in Cataluña (and I am talking of what I know myself) where three of them met, dressed like beggars, going through forests and eating what they could. They were pursued by groups of hunters with dogs which discovered them with their barking when they were in hiding among the bush. I know one, 29 years old, with two careers, who after fifteen days of severe persecution, hidden under a pile of carob-beans, succeeded in leaving his place of birth (where his grandfather had been Secretary) hidden in the lower part of a cart loaded with carob-beans. Today he works in Barcelona and has not yet been discovered. This has not been the case as regards seven of his friends who had to be delivered, under the exigency of the Committee by members of their respective families, as otherwise one of each family was to be killed in case of not presenting the priest required. All seven were shot in the beach of Benicasim, near Castellón de la Plana.

I may not omit mentioning the martyrdom of one to whom myself and others owe gratitude. He was confined to bed with paralysis when some inhuman men went to take him. He reminded them of the times when he had furnished food to their own families. It was in vain: it was an order from the Committee. He was taken to the outskirts of the village, killed, covered with stones, "deprived from burial." Shall I dare to say it? It is a shame the point to which the sentiments so noble and generous of the Spanish people have been deformed. The entire village of Cinotorres, district of Morella, province of Castelló, has witnessed the fact that the dogs fed themselves with the bruised flesh of the Rev. Manuel Marin, the friend of children, the visitant of poor and sick people, who never intervened in politics nor frequented any casino.

What is the present situation of thousands and thousands of families of these victims? The use of mourning dresses are forbidden and the relatives threatened in case they should give visible evidence of sorrow. I have seen two women being shot because of having uttered words of affliction on account of the violent death of the husband and son, and having said veiled invocations to the Divine Justice. The entire village of Carcagente, province of Valencia, knows that in this manner were executed the widow of Mr. Escandell and the mother of the student of Law, José Viudes. Likewise everybody knows that Mrs. Talens was taken at her own request to the cemetery instead of being killed at the side of the road, and killed "before discovering the place where her husband was in hiding."

It is extremely painful for these poor families to see that besides the lack of income furnished by the head of the family there is the defaming note that it has been endeavored to put on the name of the victim. So it is not strange that in some cases the members of such families, through a comprehensible reaction, have manifested themselves many times, in a violent and illogical manner, against the ideology of the victim. This explains the number of nuns daubed with paint in order to avoid being recognized, priests who have become members of Committees of the FAI, many of them who have accepted works up to the present considered as not being very appropriate, such as sweepers, and those who have taken all exterior appearances of married life.

But it is sad that after a member of the spoliated classes has decided to adapt himself to the new state of affairs and subjects himself to the life of a worker, he meets with such difficulties not to be recognized in the present atmosphere of espionage and delation to the highest degree, that many are desperate and in their desperation either attempt to escape abroad (falling in traps of unscrupulous exploiters of fear) or they deliver themselves or allow themselves to be arrested thinking that with death they will terminate this life of suffering, inasmuch as their conscience does not permit them to take recourse to suicide.

The newcomer to a workshop is watched to see if his hands are not callous, his manner of sitting, his look. If he does not look at women with impudence he is suspected of being a monk or a priest. If in a pension wine is served in goblets instead of glasses the table companions wink, if in the manner of taking the goblet there is any reminiscence of acts of worship. Suspicion arouses on those who do not employ the "turbiloquio extremado" (extremist language). The number of accusers in a city like Barcelona is so large that it is very difficult that may escape from them those who come here in the hope that they are not personally known by anybody. Janitresses and servants (especially those that occupy flats of persons that have disappeared or escaped, who have little to do) make records of all those entering in the house and take note of the time the visit lasts and how often they are done.

I could mention, as a typical case, that of a janitress who keeps frightened all the people in the house and even presents herself with the greatest freedom whenever she wished during any visit. She constantly makes threats in which every tenant considers himself included. The terror that such a harpy has inspired in them is so great that, according to statements of the doctor living in the first floor, all must act as if they were in front of an Indian prince or a satrap when they meet the janitress' child, with its monstrous head and deficient health. At any hour they must ask how the child is getting on, and, alas to him who does not do so every day! The doctor assured me that he was worried thinking about the case, since he feared the maternal fury should the treatment prescribed not be satisfactory. Another doctor having an official position in Cataluña stated several days ago, when he learned about the mysterious disappearance of Dr. Vidal of Calle Provenza, that he would not be surprised if it was the vengeance of a janitress or servant since he himself had been told that he would be placed "with the face toward the wall" (revolutionary expression which means being killed) because he had refused to sign, falsely, a prescription for meat and eggs for a woman of the militia, bearing arms, and stating she was sick.

The regrettable fact of children of school age being corrupted in their most noble instincts is like the spreading of oil stain. A former acolyte, dismissed from a famous church in Barcelona on account of robberies, is now engaged in the profitable industry of denouncing people, for which he receives, as an average, one hundred pesetas for each verified case. Likewise, groups of boys dispute among themselves the honor of executing, in the place of hard-hearted men. It is something horrible to see this early cruelty in youthful hearts, which usually feel sympathy and pity for the downfallen even when guilty.

To finish this brief explanation of the situation of the new poor, let me describe slightly the moral torture of the sincerely religious persons who are lacking any religious assistance even during danger of death and for private matters. An old woman, eighty years old, who was being taken care of by a cousin of mine, feeling she was about to die, told my cousin that "she did not want to die like a dog" and asked her to suggest acts of contrition and help her to die a virtuous death. She did so. The charitable neighbor who assisted her spiritually, could observe that the dying woman with all Christian fervor, was doing what was proper, but after kissing the Crucifix, she was very careful to keep it hidden, and this she did repeatedly and intentionally, as she feared a profanation if after her death the image of the Redeemer should be discovered by those who had destroyed thousands of them.

In Barcelona a young married couple was arrested, and put in jail, and we do not know if they suffered even more because they were found *in flagrante* at the time of their canonical marriage in a private residence. The Priests arrested and shot on account of performing their duty privately have been numerous everywhere. It is a great torture for a soul sincerely catholic to be under this absolute prohibition of any spiritual help at the most solemn moments of life; I may state it because of having witnessed the immense sorrow of my poor wife when at her last hour she had to undergo terrible pains without relief, which may not be described here.

The state of mind on account of the afflictions undergone is such that it is even doubted whether this can have an end for spirits are losing their moral sensitiveness and the superior temper required. To suffer a national war is glorious; a civil war in which the fight is between brothers, and fathers with sons, is terrible; a civil war and a Revolution like the Spanish one, simultaneously, is Dantesque.

852.00/5349

Telegram   Barcelona, May 8, 1937

Sec. of State

Yesterday the arrival of some 5,000 troops of the Central Government was greeted by many with cheers. After an unparalleled example of suicidal madness in the face of a common enemy, Barcelona has now returned to normal abnormality. However, the situation should not be regarded as evidencing any assurance of stability; for the syndicates retain extensive supplies of arms and ammunition and the outcome will depend upon facts in the case at this moment not easily assessed.

Am in touch with Valencia and Paris by both telephone and telegraph.

                                                                    Perkins

---

[Excerpted below are portions of a diary kept by Perkins during the May Days. They serve as a summary of those events central to the fighting in Barcelona, ed. note.]

                                                         May 4, 1937 10 A.M.

Yesterday afternoon about 4 P.M. trouble broke out which had been pending for some days. Report came that Government was trying to get possession of the telephone building; pedestrians were stopped near the Consulate and diverted, not being allowed to approach telephone building. Some few armed men on the street; guards on top of police quarters opposite telephone building. Later firing on the Rambla. We went home early, taking the two cars. Bolard More came in, having been on the Rambla, where came across members of the 4th American Ambulance unit (3 men and 4 women), taking refuge in doorways from the firing. In charge of a Spanish woman, trying with a dictionary to show them the meaning of *peligro*. We had sherries and turned in early. Heard nothing during the night. Guards were not relieved as usual during the night, and may have to be with us some days.

Telephone report from Police Headquarters said *bastante malo* down town. We took the metro (Subway), few passengers. Crowd blocked the exit, but we pushed through and came across the street; found the door locked, but finally got inside. Remus there all night and said considerable firing during the night. Began preparing telegrams to the Department, reporting Companys announcement of last night and summing up the situation. My May 4: (9 and 10 A.M.). Top of Hotel Colon barricaded; rifle and machine gun fire going on intermittently. Streets almost deserted. Very fat woman crossing the street with basket of oranges. No taxis or tramways. Ambulances passing at times. No armed men in sight, but constantly sporadic fighting. Outside telephone service cut off. Difficult to tell how things are going, but I assume that there must be negotiations in progress—at present 10:30 A.M. is rather quiet. The big May 1 arch on the Rambla looks very pathetic with this civil strife in progress. Ambulance just passed, carrying wounded, I presume. A beautiful May day, but getting somewhat cloudy. I wonder just what news is appearing in the outside world, as at least some announcements of conditions have been made by radio.

May 5, 1937   11 A.M.

Yesterday proceeded home in motor car with Franklin, Jordain, Miss Haynes via Pelayo and Balmes. Barricades and soldiers ready for action, but not held up. Left More and Mrs. Ashdown at the Consulate. Reported heavy firing especially toward the P.O.U.M. building across the street. Jordain said that French Consulate still functioning. Yesterday P.M. was like a Fourth of July in the good old days. Gave orders for More to stay at Consulate over night. Radio reports about 9 P.M. of various speakers, of both organizations, all urging restoration of harmony and for brothers to stop killing each other and unite against Fascism and lend their help to the hard pressed Basques. It looks as if a definite effort were being made to stop hostilities.

Our two guards, both at house and Consulate, are not being changed. Came to office about 8:45 A.M. by the Metro. No firing at moment of arrival at the Plaza and crossed without difficulty to the office. Soon thereafter heavy and intermittent firing across the Plaza. Metro entrance crowded with curious people. A stretcher is carrying a wounded man into the Colon Hotel, headquarters of the P.S.U.C. Three men from there attempted to cross the street under fire and I guess they got one of them. Building opposite my office plastered with yesterday's bullets, but now seems dead. However, I notice firing from behind the closed blinds evidently at the Colon Hotel. This is an agency of the P.O.U.M. Decided better to move my typewriter desk to another part of the room, as usual place quite exposed to fire from the P.O.U.M. building. Heavy firing again. Dust flies from the mortar of building Royal

Bank of Canada; do not know who are in there; but several heads are visible from time to time. I dare say they are CNT-FAI, as they seem to be firing at the Colon Hotel. Occasional woman goes along the street. Ambulances passing from time to time, carrying large Red Cross flags.

Cerezuela said that in his street Guardias de Asalto had entered the CNT Telephone office and were stopping people on the street for documentation. If they had CNT cards, they were torn up on the spot and people told that they were to be free from now on. Guards took down CNT flag and sign and burned them in the street. I wonder whether this was under orders or just a bit of pleasure on their part. Does not seem to accord with harmony which was the theme of radio talks last night.

3:15 P.M.

Just had lunch at office with More and Mrs. Ashdown. Ham was bad apparently. Firing has died down for past two hours. Word that Valencia Government will take over public order in Catalonia in view of persistence of the situation. Between 12 and 1 P.M. radio announced that a new Government had been formed and that would take over at 1 P.M.. Directed all workers to return to their jobs in 4 hours. Then put on "Old Black Joe" (this was the Generalidad radio). Opposite in P.O.U.M. place five girls had the nerve to come to the balcony and waved to us. Then a shot and they all rushed back indoors. It is turning out a beautiful sunny afternoon. 3:25 P.M. CNT speaker who came last night from Valencia speaking over radio calls on the CNT to lay down their arms within one hour, as they are committing collective suicide by what they are doing. If that is their desire, let them kill themselves and be done with it.

10:15 P.M.

Have just had a fine dinner: baked beans, asparagus, soda biscuits, canned peaches, sardines, and tinned coffee. The smell of the ham at noon has permeated everything, but evidently not poisonous as none of us are sick at all.

German radio says that the Bolshevik Companys is trying to surrender the city to the Nationalists. That is ridiculous. *La Noche* reports that the UGT man who entered the New Government at 1 P.M. was killed while crossing the Rambla. Probably has been assassinated by the FAI. Also reports that the Valencia Government is taking charge and that a force of soldiers are on their way here from Valencia by sea. Now is perfectly quiet; apparently all have lain off for the time being; for dinner. Before dinner, we opened a bottle of Old Nick Rum, part of the Consulate "medicinal" stores. Courage is the difference of a couple of drinks. I don't wonder they serve out grog in the German Navy.

May 6, 1937   11 A.M.

Spent night at the Consulate radio room. Franklin came in about 7:30 A.M. having made a tour of barricades in central part of the city, reported all but one held by Government people. More people in the streets, but no normal resumption of street cars, busses, etc. It appears that they are simply holding their positions. A rather warm day.

5:15 P.M.

So far very quiet afternoon. Only occasional shots. Got off all telegrams to the Department.

May 7, 1937   9:15 A.M.

Yesterday, about 6:30, started to cross to the Metro when a rifle shot from the Colon Hotel at the P.O.U.M. building sped over head. Either thought we were a group, or else did it in sport. Crowd at the entrance jumped inside and one pointed out where the bullet struck. Bolard More remained on duty at the Consulate General. Quiet during the night with only occasional shot. Other night French Consul General kept 17 people in his office the time when I let Bolard More cross the street to return home. This A.M. people moving about to market; few busses in sight; barricades open; beer truck moving; garbage piled high in street being collected; and the whole appearance of the city like that of a ship after the storm. Papers announce that General Pozas took office yesterday afternoon. Appearance is that the thing is over with for the present, though it may be a lull. Last night about 9, Palery phoned the report that FAI and Juventudes Libertarias would cut off the light and water during the night; and so I filled the two bath tubs with water. Streets are becoming more filled with people as the morning wears on. Consular building appears to have been struck only twice, one hitting the mortar of a cornice and the other going through a window. As the chauffeur said, it had been "*un poco intranquilo.*" All employees are turning up this morning.

May 8, 1937   11 A.M.

Yesterday about noon, tramways began to function again. Most of the day in getting off wires to the Department. Walked down in the morning and back about 6:30 P.M.. No interruptions. Word that troops from Valencia were arriving. Franklin and others came, and reported seeing numbers of them with 20 trucks on the Diagonal; as passed were cheered by the people.

Came down in the tram this morning. Everything at work again. Papers say "*La Lucha ha Terminado.*" "*La Concordia Renace con la Paz.*" All the morning the streets as seen from the window are full of roaming squads of new soldiers, who are patrolling the streets. Many say, however, that all is only temporary; that the hatreds cannot be forgotten, that the syndicates are full of arms, etc. The streets are full of people. How soon they disappear at the first sign of trouble; they are really sheep in the hands of the wolves with guns.

Barcelona's finest hotel as political headquarters for the PSUC

Anarchist banner in downtown Barcelona

War-time scene near the Ramblas

Bombed-out apartment buildings, 1938

Typical scene after a bombing raid, 1938

A Barcelona street after bombing

4

AFTER MAY DAYS AND
WAR FROM THE AIR
(MAY 1937–DECEMBER 1938)

IN THE AFTERMATH of the fighting in May, life changed throughout the Catalan section of the Republican zone. Payne has outlined the consequences: "The result of the 'May Days' was a partial victory for the Communists and the state; it was a defeat for the extreme left and also for Catalan autonomy." He argued that these facts were realized in the following weeks when the large number of Republican police consolidated their control over the Catalan capital. The move to strengthen Republican authority spread out of Barcelona to every community in northeastern Spain because fighting and resistance to the central government had not been limited to the Catalan capital. Catalan autonomy quickly ended as the Republican government assumed power to make decisions affecting local economics, education, public administration, police protection, transportation, and utilities. Arms were confiscated, the news media subjected to censorship, and many radicals arrested. Government policy shifted and clearly began directing Catalan energy toward anti-Nationalist ends, instead of the internal political squabbles that too often had led to economic malpractice and deadly violence. In line with the government's objectives, many agencies of the Generalidad were either disbanded, taken over, or reorganized. Thus, the General Councils of Industry were created in August 1937 in order to coordinate better industrial and public policies geared toward the manufacture of war-related goods. Banking agencies were consolidated, and negotiations for a more coordinated effort between the Generalidad and the Republican government regarding financial matters ended when Franco's forces overran the rest of Spain. On June 16, 1937, a new Catalan government came to power without any Anarchist member. The cabinet was now dominated by members of the Esquerra and the PSUC. In the streets the Anarchists were disarmed, their militias broken up, and their leaders arrested, while propagandists for the Republic blamed the militants for the hardship recently experienced in Cataluña.[1]

---

[1]Payne, *The Spanish Revolution*, p. 298; Cattell, *Communism and the Spanish Civil War*, p. 150; Broué and Témime, *La révolution et la guerre d'Espagne*, pp. 288–89; the important issue of Catalan nationalism is treated well in Cruells, *El seperatisme català durant la guerra civil*.

One of the issues that generated debate among residents of Barcelona, especially within the middle and upper classes which had always provided the main source of leadership for Catalan aspirations, concerned the evolving role of autonomy after the May Days. With the Anarchists now rapidly disappearing from the political scene and the Republican government inclined to use local members of the Esquerra and other republican parties in the Generalidad, a more traditional form of concern for local rights that was less tainted by the rhetoric of various worker parties became evident. The Catalanists quarreled with the Communists over economics and politics while the central government continued to whittle away at the power they had won for the Generalidad throughout the 1930s. The Communists, through the vehicle of the Republic, wanted the central government to take over the duties of the Generalidad; the local regionalists wished to protect their rights. Thus the two groups clashed in government chambers and conducted a war of words as Republican forces and Communists consolidated their control over Cataluña. Companys, for example, thought that the Communists were killing too many of their enemies after May and said so in public. For weeks the Communist NKVD secret police continued to leave dead people along the sides of the roads all over Cataluña, especially in and around Barcelona. The Catalans sought to seize upon the graphic nature of these events to protest increased Communist influence but to no avail.

In fact, Catalan rights were rapidly diminishing. Then in November, the Republic moved its government to the Catalan city and thus destroyed, for all intents and purposes, the last vestiges of local autonomy. Along with the move came more stringent orders controlling the economy and centralizing police powers in the hands of the Republican bureaucracy. The Generalidad, once the seat of considerable power in Cataluña, hardly exerted any influence on events anymore.

A second important indicator of the changing way of life in Barcelona was the changing role of the Communists. They wanted the Republican government to suppress extremists on the political far left after May and therefore supported any efforts of the regime to destroy the power of the Anarchists. Thus, Communist forces cooperated in hunting down Anarchist leaders and helped police forces disarm them. The Communists used their political influence to have Anarchist organizations outlawed in the months that followed May. The Communists wanted to destroy the last vestiges of non-Communist opposition within Cataluña; however, confusion remained for many months among various political groups because the Communists failed—narrowly—to gain complete dominance. Cedric Salter, writing for the London *Daily Telegraph*, observed that during the fall in Barcelona "nowhere was there any kind of direction or authority. Different shades of anti-Fascist belief were busy killing one another over trivial divergences of political theory with a complete disregard for essentials."[2]

---

[2]Material for the previous two paragraphs came from Payne, *The Spanish Revolution*, pp. 309–10; on the Communists see Dolores Ibarruri, "The Heroic Struggle of the Spanish People"

The economic situation also changed in the fall of 1937. In this period of transition the government reorganized the economy to direct industrial output in support of the war effort. Arms production became a primary concern of the regime; considerable attention was paid to its increase throughout Cataluña and especially in the factory towns around Barcelona. Friction developed between plant managers and Catalan nationalists, on the one side, and the government, on the other, over the amount of centralized control to be asserted and the contributions to be made. All of this activity took place in a highly charged political environment marked by increasing suspicion and mistrust. A brief examination of industrial production cycles in Cataluña during the war suggests the degree of governmental concern. Between January 1936 and October 1937, production declined between 60 and 75 percent. While accurate figures for inventory levels are not available, one could conclude that they fell off proportionately, at the least.

Concern for industrial strength never ended during the war because so many problems remained. From October 1937 to March 1938 industrial production oscillated between index factors of 55 and 60 (with 100 the base period using January 1936). This was the period when Cataluña's economy was paramountly directed to feeding the war effort. These months were characterized by such activities and conditions as the production of weapons and ammunition, the establishment of credit facilities to support such production, the purchase and confiscation of food supplies for use by the military, and by the almost total elimination of consumer goods. After April 1938, the local economy completely collapsed as Cataluña then became a war zone.[3]

Barcelona and Cataluña also changed socially during 1937 and early 1938. By December, the city was grimly dedicated to fighting the war and working to meet the army's need for supplies. Citizens lived with shortages of everything. Crowded with soldiers and refugees, Barcelona experienced many problems in providing sufficient supplies of food to local inhabitants. Alexander Werth, then in Cataluña reporting for the *Manchester Guardian*, wrote on 21 December that "everywhere the food shortage was apparent." He told a story about how "in one small town we tried to buy some green apples we had noticed in a window, but in vain. Not only was food scarce, but its delivery was most irregular; on some days a great deal could be bought, on others nothing at all." He believed this vacillation crippled the rationing system yet recalled that clothing and soap were still plentiful.[4] Obviously the discontinuity of supply and demand had momentarily made these two items available.

in her *Speeches and Articles* (London, 1938), pp. 248–49; Juan Comorera, *El camino del Frente Popular anti-fascista es el camino de la victoria, Informe presentado en el Primera Conferencia Nacional del Partido Socialista Unificado de Catalunya I.C.*, 24 julio de 1937 (Barcelona, n.d.), pp. 15–16; Salter, *Try-Out in Spain*, p. 87.

    [3]Cattell, *Communism and the Spanish Civil War*, pp. 242–43; see Voltes Bou, *Historia de la economía española*, 2, pp. 780–95; Bricall, *Política económica de la Generalitat*, passim.

    [4]Salter, *Try-Out in Spain*, p. 163; Alexander Werth in Sperber, *And I Remember Spain*, p. 91.

Werth left us other impressions. In Barcelona he learned quickly about the availability of certain necessities of life:

> The wide avenue in front of the Basque Legation is crowded from morning till night by pitiful Basque refugees. Food is, generally, scarce; and yet by paying exorbitant prices—fifty pesetas—one can still dine luxuriously in one or two Barcelona restaurants. And round the corner from the Basque Legation with its refugees you hear at night while the streets are pitch dark the shrieking and bellowing of a jazz band. For the night life of Barcelona goes on. The hall is crowded with young officers in suspiciously spotless uniforms and well groomed young men with perfectly creased trouser legs, and good looking women with bare backs and shoulders.[5]

The excitement of a small bit of entertainment in a nightclub, however, could not long defer the realization that Barcelona had become a city made drab by war. On Christmas Eve, Werth wrote that "Barcelona is not a pleasant city. Unlike Madrid, with its wonderful unity of spirit, it seems tormented by doubts and contradictions." He reported further that

> in the wide luxurious ramblas of Barcelona walls and windows are riddled with bullet holes, and although by moving to Barcelona the Negrín government has made Barcelona more "war conscious" than it was before, there is still much political tension below the surface.

Werth thought that the contrasts in attitudes between classes were still pronounced: "In Madrid, an Anarchist remarked to me, 'one says comrade'; here one still says 'señor.' Barcelona is still dreadfully bourgeois."[6]

Prior to 1936, a tradition of anticlericalism existed particularly in the working class already politicized by left-wing parties. As recently as 1909 these groups had burned churches and attacked priests and nuns. Leftist parties in control of Barcelona after the start of the Civil War worked hard to destroy the grip of the Catholic Church on the lives of Catalan citizens. They closed churches, while the government took over control of education throughout the Republican zone. One commentator noted in December 1937 that "except for the Cathedral and one or two other churches of artistic value all the churches in Barcelona have been destroyed." Priests could say mass only in private homes. In short, religious activities sharply declined in comparison to past years.[7]

Werth provides a general impression of Barcelona in December 1937:

---

[5]Werth in Sperber, *And I Remember Spain*, pp. 93–94.
[6]Werth in Sperber, *And I Remember Spain*, p. 93.
[7]Werth in Sperber, *And I Remember Spain*, p. 93.

Just outside Barcelona we saw the first double-decker bus, almost exactly
like a London bus, but painted in the Anarchist colours of black and red
with "CNT" painted in white on the radiator. The buses and trams, and
many other things besides, are still run by the Anarchists in Barcelona.
We entered Barcelona from the east, through a grimy working-class
district. The tobacco shops had notices pasted on their windows saying
that there was no tobacco. Outside the food shops there were long queues
of women, some of them looking distinctly bad-tempered. The tram-cars
were overcrowded, with human "bunches of grapes" clinging on to the
footboards and buffers—a sight strangely reminiscent of St. Petersburg
in 1917.

He went directly to the Hotel Majestic, "near the Plaza de Catalonia, one of
the few big hotels commandeered by the Government, the rest having been
turned into hospitals or trade union headquarters." He could not help but
notice that the windows of his hotel "were pasted over with zigzags of brown
paper, and there were many bullet holes in the walls and shop windows along
the street—a memory of the Anarchist rising of last May."[8]

Life in Barcelona changed more dramatically during 1938 than at any
time during the Civil War. The war's effects were seen in the increasing
numbers of refugees, the soldiers billeted in homes and public buildings, and
the Nationalist air attacks. Bombardments and food shortages lasted from
early 1938 to the end of the war, and the growing depression of Barcelona's
citizens made life in the great Catalan capital difficult and sad throughout the
last year of the war. Various witnesses in Barcelona agreed that the city
virtually died as its citizens seemed to exist in a constant state of numbness.

Perhaps no series of events had a greater impact on the life of the
average resident than the bombings experienced in the course of 1938. As
the Francoists pushed forward into the eastern war zone toward Cataluña,
driving the shrinking Republican forces before them, the need to weaken the
morale of the Catalan people became an immediate military objective. Moreover, the requirement to destroy sources of supply and manpower for the
Republic also dictated that Barcelona become a military target for attack. The
terror bombings of Barcelona came at a time when strategists knew little about
the effects of such bombings on civilian populations. There had been some
limited experience with such tactics in the Basque country and in central
Spain, but not until Barcelona was continuously hit would either side appreciate what the impact could be. On paper and in theory, it made sense that
such bombardments should weaken the enemy. As the economic data cited
above suggests, the local economy was already in trouble and the destruction
of factories simply accentuated the economic difficulties in northern Spain.
The bombings clearly scared the population, but the Nationalists did not know

[8]Werth in Sperber, *And I Remember Spain*, p. 92.

what impact such events had on the will of the Catalans to continue fighting. History shows us that the average citizen could do little but somehow survive both the Nationalists and the Republicans.

The Nationalists had other motives besides morale for such bombings. First, the German Condor Legion had new technologies and tactics to test; there was a considerable body of pre-Civil War thinking in European military circles which held that such bombings would demoralize a civilian population. Second, there were actual military targets to hit (military installations and factories, for example). Third, the local economy and sources of supply could be disrupted by bombing the port of Barcelona and all the warehouses in that part of the city. Consequently, many of the air raids were conducted on the harbor area of the city. To the Nationalists, this last objective seemed the one that could best be measured, since their planes photographed the damage caused by bombs.[9]

The first major attack came soon after the start of 1938. It was the subject of much writing by foreign observers in the city. Yet the earliest of these bombings of the city to have profound consequences came in mid-March, when a big offensive took place to separate Barcelona from Valencia. On 16 March there began a period of several days of bombardments. Every three hours for three days bombers flying over from Mallorca let loose their lethal cargos over Barcelona. Cedric Salter recalled that

> after the first twenty-four hours it became a kind of sleepless nightmare in which incidents, times, and people became a shapeless blur. Huge loads of high-explosive bombs were tipped out indiscriminately into the center of town, each raid claiming hundreds of victims, and sending scores of houses crashing into ruins.

He noted that one raid, lasting only one minute and a half, caused about twelve hundred casualties. If they had time, residents rushed into the tunnels of Barcelona's subways. Salter reported that the metro lines under the Plaza de Cataluña were always dark and crowded with three to four thousand frightened Catalans.[10]

The damage was extensive. The very face of the city was altered north of the Gothic quarter and all along the harbor, and hundreds of families lost their businesses, homes, and kin. Reading Cedric Salter, one can sense the horror of those days:

> I hurried out toward a rising pillar of dust and smoke in the Calle Cortes.

---

[9]John Coverdale in his study of Italian intervention examined the question of the bombings of Barcelona, since in large part they were carried out by Italian pilots. He concluded that they "served no real military purpose and failed to weaken the morale of the Catalans." The bombings were done to hasten the end of the war, *Italian Intervention in the Spanish Civil War* (Princeton, 1975), p. 347 (quote from p. 349).

[10]Salter, *Try-Out in Spain*, pp. 166, 169–70.

Whole streets of houses had been wiped out, others had been carved neatly down the center like slices of cake. Cross sections of rooms, pathetically domestic, were suddenly revealed to the public gaze. A dining room on the third floor of a house was still neatly set for lunch, with table mats, glasses, spoons and forks, though only half of the room remained. A lavatory perched incongruously on the very brink of a sixty-foot abyss, the toilet roll flapping like a banner in the breeze of the open air.

He later found out that a 250-pound bomb hit the street just as a munitions truck was driving on it, causing the magnitude of damage he described.[11]

An American correspondent in Barcelona, Herbert L. Matthews, recalled that there were eighteen raids in forty-four hours, starting in the evening. Antiaircraft guns failed to protect the city and so the population stayed up that night in fear of its safety. He remembered that the damage and death were extensive and horrid: "One bomb dropped in a square at the foot of the Paralelo, a busy cross-section in the lower part of the city not far from the port. The trees around had been snapped off a few inches from the ground; one would have thought they had been sawn off but for the roughness of the break." He saw a blown-up street car with all its passengers dead, trucks on fire, and houses collapsed or burning. Since the bombs were dropped haphazardly over the city, no one felt safe. Even the owners of the large homes on the fashionable Paseo de Gracias were hard hit. Matthews would later remind his readers that every window in each house from the Plaza de Cataluña to the Calle Majorca was broken. Bombs twisted lamp posts and felled trees. "I never saw so many weeping women," he wrote, and added:

it was all a nightmare—the dead piled in trucks, gangs of salvage men digging in the ruins, stretchers stained red, street-cleaners sweeping up human fragments, a cock crowing lustily from atop a wrecked building, smoke, dust, powder—and blood everywhere, thick, sticky pools of blood, splotches and drops of it; wherever one looked there was something stained with blood.[12]

The hospitals and makeshift first aid centers all over the city were frantic centers of overcrowded activity where the city's patients competed for medical attention with the wounded soldiers from the Aragon front. To quote Matthews again, "Barcelona was not only terrorized but paralyzed."

Another resident of the city, Constancia de la Mora, reported a similar pattern of horror. The crowded residential areas suffered much damage; and for hours after the bombs stopped falling, "the sirens screamed, the fire engines

[11]Salter, *Try-Out in Spain*, pp. 166, 169–70 (quote from pp. 176–77).
[12]Herbert L. Matthews, *The Education of a Correspondent* (New York, 1946), pp. 126–27.

tore out of their stations" and people were carried off to hospitals. She estimated that over a thousand people died on 17 March and at least two thousand the next day. She recalled that "the days were bad. The nights were hell on earth." Barcelona's residents were exhausted due to their lack of sleep. "After the first day, we stopped speaking of the bombings. It was a serious breach of good manners to refer to the Fascist planes at all." Factories and offices attempted to function as normal, but it was impossible. Stores, hotels, and large buildings had been badly damaged. On the third day, Nationalist bombers destroyed gas tanks and the harbor. By the fourth and final day of the bombings, many buildings were on fire and the people were emotionally shaken.[13]

The sufferings of the Catalans continued to increase. During 1938, the almost total disappearance of currency, material shortages caused by blockade and lack of raw materials, halting of trade, and the unwillingness of other nations to aid the Republic substantially affected the available consumer items and foods in Barcelona. Industrial production declined by more than half when compared to its prewar levels. The two most important influences on this decline, in addition to the war itself, were the lack of raw materials and the loss of electrical power. Warfare damaged transportation and destroyed markets. The lack of manpower and good communications also meant that agricultural production dropped, causing Barcelona's food supplies to shrink seriously by summer. Theodore Dreiser reported that "there is no meat, no sugar, no butter, no milk. They serve a sort of pap, made out of vegetable matter . . . and fried with sauce, vaguely resembles meat." He also observed that "in the whole of Barcelona, you cannot buy a piece of soap." Besides being hungry and dirty, the city's residents were now poorly dressed: "The clothes of the middle class people are now as miserable as those of the poor. . . . Their shoes are worn out, broken open, tied with strings."

Dreiser also noted that with no electricity the streetcars did not run, forcing everyone to walk. On occasion, government officials would go by in one of the few remaining automobiles.

> Most horses and donkeys have disappeared. In the morning, you see little groups of people setting out on foot with sacks. They go out to forage in the country around Barcelona. They come back in the evening with a few sticks of fire wood, a cabbage, or a few turnips or with nothing at all. There are 12 million Loyalists in [a] territory which before held about two million. They are slowly starving.[14]

It did not take long for a black market to flourish under these conditions. Exchanges were made primarily by bartering, usually food for other types of food. Restaurants tried the best they could "frankly advertising five pesetas

[13]Matthews, *The Education of a Correspondent*, p. 128; Constancia de la Mora, *In Place of Splendor*, pp. 335–59.

[14]Quotes from both paragraphs are reprinted in Sperber, *And I Remember Spain*, p. 161.

for a cat, ten for a dog, and two for a rat. These delicacies were all served as 'rabbit' stew or as mincemeat balls better known as 'cojones de conejo'." Salter found alcoholic beverages extremely rare and cigars about equally so. No one seemed to make bread out of wheat anymore; it was now produced from ground nutshells and tasted terrible.[15]

The government in Barcelona unsuccessfully attempted to deal with the critical shortages. In November, it established a Food Supply Coordinating Committee that reported directly to the Minister of National Defense with the mission of coordinating all activities dealing with the production, distribution, and sale of food and clothing. By the time winter came, the war had ended, not allowing the committee enough time to implement any programs.

Bombings in Barcelona and in the surrounding countryside increased as the year went on and the battle lines came closer to the coast. Dreiser wrote about the bombings and offered a picture of how the people of Barcelona lived during the air raids. He quickly discovered that the maze of subway tunnels served as air raid shelters for a large percentage of the population:

> five miles of serpentine subways cut under the city. They have built them irregularly, with openings at all sorts of unexpected spots, with several entrances at all central places. They have built them like rabbits' burrows, so that if one entrance or exit is blocked, they can escape by another.

He went on to write that their "passages are very clever and very deep. There is room for benches, in some places. In others real shelters, with running water, lights, have been prepared. Some people spend half the day in these places, when an air raid has been announced." Most often, the air raid sirens gave people about five minutes' warning before the enemy began its deadly work of indiscriminate bombings.[16]

Terror bombings were known to other communities near Barcelona. Many of the refugees who poured into the city came from towns that had experienced similar bombardments. In August 1938, Dreiser visited just outside the city:

> As we near Barcelona, shell-shattered homes and villages grow more frequent. I saw one village cut literally in half by a shell. One part standing and with people going about their business. The other smashed, wiped out, dead. Then several villages I saw were completely shattered, annihilated. Little villages, without any possible military significance. In these, most of the people were gone. But there were usually a few old ones, sitting in the ruins of their homes, cooking, even between broken walls. In a certain village I saw only one old woman, sitting in a dream of misery.[17]

---

[15]Salter, *Try-Out in Spain*, pp. 212–13, 214–16.
[16]Quoted in Sperber, *And I Remember Spain*, pp. 160–61.
[17]Sperber, *And I Remember Spain*, p. 160.

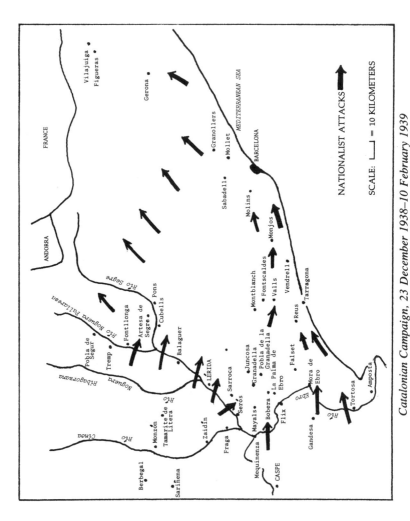

Catalonian Campaign, 23 December 1938–10 February 1939

Source: This map appeared in HITLER'S LUFTWAFFE IN THE SPANISH CIVIL WAR by Raymond L. Proctor, Westport © Greenwood Press, 1983.

The destruction increased almost daily. One resident of Barcelona estimated that by the end of the year over six thousand buildings had been destroyed in the city alone. Ships headed for Barcelona with food and medical supplies were also destroyed in an effort to bring the city to its knees.[18]

Despite the bombings and the shortage of food, Catalans remained politically active in the second half of 1938, although they lacked the enthusiasm of 1936 and 1937. In an attempt to gear up for the final defense against Franco's forces, the Republic in August militarized all factories, passed decrees to block the flight of capital out of Barcelona, and tightened police security throughout the Republican zone. Many Catalans saw these measures as a further reduction of their local autonomy. While the battle of the Ebro (July 24–August 1, 1938) raged, the Republican government destroyed what remained of Catalanist aspirations and political power by assuming responsibility and authority for all war-related economic and legal functions in northeastern Spain. There were still more complaints by Republican officials that the Catalan industrial community did not do as much as it might have for the war effort, and the military protested that Catalan military units did poorly in comparison to other elements in the army. Friction remained until the very end between the Catalans and the government. Catalan politicians on several occasions considered negotiating a separate peace and repeatedly walked out of Republican governments, as they did in August 1938, when the new decrees dismantled the last vestiges of Catalan autonomy.[19]

Morale dropped in Barcelona during the second half of the year as both the bombings and Franco's victories in the ground war continued. An increasing number of Catalans realized that the war was lost. Their economy and their lives lay shattered. Rumors of a pro-Franco fifth column made the end seem predictable.[20] The city grew quieter in anticipation of the final assault by Franco's forces. Except for sporadic shooting by a few terrorists, Salter wrote that "sickness, lost faith, starvation, and hopeless suffering was the only tale that there was to tell, and who cares for long to listen to such things?" He reported there was almost no food to be had by late fall. At the Hotel Continental, one could buy only a plate of gruel and half a roll of black bread per day. With supplies of gasoline exhausted, even official cars were not often seen on the streets, and the city suddenly lapsed into silence and inactivity.

---

[18]Constancia de la Mora, *In Place of Splendor*, pp. 373–75; Salter cited the case of Granollers, forty miles north of Barcelona where, during the summer of 1938, three thousand of the five thousand residents were either killed or wounded in one air raid. The village had neither defenses nor factories, *Try-Out in Spain*, p. 184.

[19]On the political history of this period see Cattell, *Communism and the Spanish Civil War*, p. 202; Payne, *The Spanish Revolution*, pp. 310, 359; on Catalan military contributions see Payne again for statistics, pp. 343–44, and José María Fontana, *Los Catalanes en la Guerra de España* (Madrid, 1956).

[20]Broué and Témime, *La révolution et la guerre d'Espagne*, p. 512; Carr, *Spain*, p. 668–69. How many Francoist agents were in Barcelona may never be fully determined. Most specialists agree that at least two dozen operated by 1938 along with an undetermined number of sympathizers among the middle and upper classes as a rule.

A Spanish doctor told Salter later that sixty-two thousand died in Barcelona alone between 1 September 1938 and 1 February 1939. Besides the loss of life caused by bombings, death came because of malnutrition, which also made people more susceptible to pneumonia. Diseases and infections became more serious. Conditions worsened without medicines. The lack of a laxative, for example, meant death by peritonitis, caused by the lack of fibrous foods. A cut on the hand might lead to gangrene or amputation without morphine. Both were common conditions. Yet Salter reminded readers that people tried to keep their sense of humor. He told the story of how Negrín called on the populace to resist the enemy. The next day in the Plaza de Cataluña someone placed a sign on a dead, emaciated donkey lying on a bomb rubble; the sign read: "Lo siento mucho, Señor Negrín, pero no puedo resistir mas [I am very sorry Mr. Negrín, but I can no longer resist]."[21]

It would be difficult to exaggerate the terrible living conditions in the city, particularly the state of mind at that time. On attitudes toward the end of 1938, Ricardo del Río, head of the Republican news agency Febus, wrote:

> For the spirit of resistance there had been substituted the idea of salvation. Everyone was afraid of being cut off. The soldiers knew the significance of the enemy's movement and were dominated above all else by the desire not to fall into his clutches. In fact, morale was only sustained in the leaders.

About the city of Barcelona itself he had strong feelings:

> Barcelona was a city of the dead. The cause of death was demoralization, caused by both those who fled . . . and those who stayed in hiding, without the courage to leave their houses. . . . It is no exaggeration to assert that Barcelona was lost purely because there was no will to resist either in the civilian population or in some of the troops who had become contaminated by its atmosphere. Morale was at rock bottom. With a few honorable exceptions, all those who used to give encouragement to the troops had disappeared. Though not exhausted by suffering and hunger, the people were tired of the war and, long before the enemy's arrival, had only hoped for a sudden end to it. Therefore, they remained shut up in their homes, which also served as a refuge for deserters fleeing from the front, who did not want to fight either, converting that urban concentration of a million souls into a wasteland spiritually deserted.[22]

---

[21]Salter, *Try-Out in Spain*, pp. 226–31. Some historian will eventually want to write a history of health conditions in Spain during the twentieth century, tempted, no doubt, by the voluminous records kept by the army of its recruits and by health agencies during and after the Franco years. The drop in general health caused by the Civil War will have to be measured as yet another indicator of the conflict's impact on Spain. As late as the early 1950s, residents of the city showed significant deficiencies in their health and bodily needs, making it understandable why visitors would see adults eating whole sticks of butter and abnormally large amounts of other dairy products and foods with high sugar content.

[22]Quoted in Payne, *The Spanish Revolution*, p. 360.

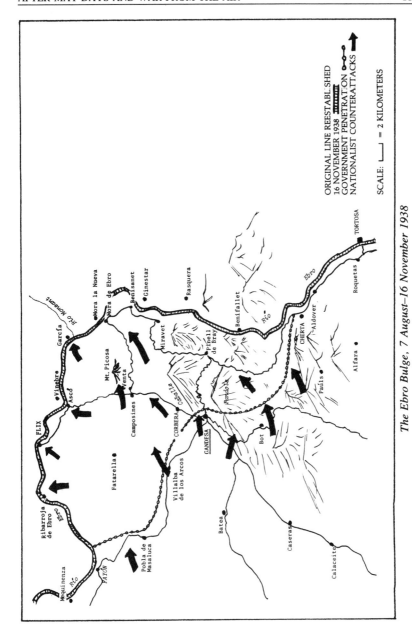

The Ebro Bulge, 7 August–16 November 1938

Source: This map appeared in HITLER'S LUFTWAFFE IN THE SPANISH CIVIL WAR by Raymond L. Proctor, Westport © Greenwood Press, 1983.

Professor Carr acknowledged the nutritional problems and military crisis, yet he emphasized a third cause for Catalonia's demise: after May 1937
(or certainly by early 1938), when the Republican government broke the
political power of the Catalanists, Catalan nationalists, both bourgeois and
proletarian, opted out of the war. While more research would have to be
conducted to evaluate the validity of this interpretation, it is true, as he
suggests, that "Companys, in his despair, surrounded himself with Catalanist
intellectuals. It was as if Catalan nationalism, in defeat, returned to the sources
of its strengths." An equally valid interpretation regarding why residents of
Barcelona lost heart in late 1938 was Victor Alba's observation that with the
defeat of the Republican forces in October during the final days of the Ebro
campaign, Cataluña stood exposed "at the mercy of the nationalist army,"
and everyone realized this.[23]

Thus from May 1937 to the end of 1938, the war came closer to
Barcelona and its effects on the city were felt more than before. The city
experienced bombings, fighting, an influx of refugees, the rapid decline in
standard of living, and the almost total loss of local autonomy. The city's
political role changed, and by the end of the year despair added an additional
mantle of grey over the lives of its citizens. With Christmas came the final
chapter of a city at war, the death of Republican Barcelona.

---

[23]Carr, *Spain*, pp. 671–72; Victor Alba, *Catalonia: A Profile* (New York, 1975), pp. 166–
67. A majority of this book deals with Catalonia in the twentieth century, providing many details
on life in Barcelona and a good basic bibliography on the area.

852.00/5360

Telegram   Barcelona, May 9, 1937

Rush May 9, noon

The arrival of the troops of the Central Government has, I am inclined to believe, minimized the danger of further serious outbreaks at the present moment. However, I am of the opinion that there is no assurance against an early or eventual recurrence of another situation in which it would be impossible with safety to attempt the evacuation of American nationals; and I am therefore reluctantly forced to the conviction that I must recommend a general suspension of consular functions and the evacuation of the American members of the staff with the exception of one officer. It is, therefore, recommended that Vice Consul Bolard More,[24] in whom I have come to have the greatest confidence, remain for the time being in charge of the archives, the performance of such services to American citizens as may be practicable, and as contact officer with myself and the Department. In this general relation, reference is respectfully made to my despatch 124 of November 25th.

I do not regard the immediate situation as calling for direct communication with Admiral Fairfield or for precipitate arrangements by the Department in this regard.

Perkins

852.00/5597

Telegram   Barcelona, June 1, 1937

Sec. of State

Spanish steamer *City of Barcelona* was sunk May 30 very near the coast thirty miles north of Barcelona en route this city. It is reported that the ship was attacked by a submarine presumably Italian and that fifty passengers were drowned.

Confidential

My private information is that the ship was bringing some 500 "foreign volunteers" from French port Vendres. That is circumstantially supported by the fact that first local press reports were heavily censored but contain among the injured several non-Spanish names. I am being constantly informed that

[24]James B. More was assigned to Barcelona 28 November 1936 and served until mid–1938. Prior to Barcelona, he had been in Madrid since 31 December 1934, Department of State, *Biographical Register, 1944*, p. 154.

small groups of volunteers still succeed in crossing the border from time to time and that war materials are being brought from France by truck and small coasting boats.

Perkins

Translation

The Bombardment

Appearance of Several Rebel Planes Over The Capital

At 3:20 A.M. the inhabitants of Barcelona perceived the motors of several planes approaching the capital.

A few minutes later after throwing some Bengal lights they formed two groups to carry out their purpose of bombarding the civil population of Barcelona.

Shortly thereafter grenades and incendiary bombs fell in several parts of the city. The alarm signals functioned to advise the people, who proceeded to the refuges.

The bombardment lasted approximately ten minutes and the rebel planes were first attacked by means of the anti-aerial batteries and later by loyal planes.

In view of the intensity of the bombardment, no doubt the most important of those suffered by our city, it was believed that the number of victims would be very large.

The Bombardment of the Barceloneta

The suburb of the Barceloneta was one of those suffering greater damages from the aerial attack of the fascists. One of the groups of rebel planes went to this suburb throwing a large quantity of bombs.

One of the bombs, of great power, fell on the Rebaix wharf, just at the side where the *S.S. Cabo Menor* was anchored. The bomb fell against the wall damaging it seriously.

Another bomb fell on the Paseo Nacional, destroying the inside of two cafe establishments and a dyer's shop.

Another fell in a house where a refuge had been provided, for which reason the number of victims in that place is about thirty. The bomb entered the house diagonally in the third floor and the explosion destroyed the third, second, first and ground floors, while the fourth floor was intact and the man living there suffered no injury. He had to be taken out from that floor by the firemen since the rest of the house was destroyed.

Other bombs fell on various other houses causing damages. A bomb falling on Calle Alegria destroyed two flats and killed four persons.

In the workshops of La Maquinista Terrestre y Marítima a bomb destroyed one of the sections and injured nine persons. Bombs fell on the gas factory but caused no damage.

The largest number of victims were assisted at the Barceloneta; a total of 47. One of the persons killed had in his pocket the sum of 18,000 pesetas.

The Bombardment of the Center of the Capital

Several bombs fell on Via Durruti where one of the houses was totally destroyed. The power of the explosion pulled out entirely the balconies. In the building of the Savings Bank the explosions broke all glasses. In all these buildings there were victims.

Two bombs fell on Calle Estruch and Calle Molas killing two persons and injuring others.

On Calle Bruch a bomb destroyed two flats killing a woman and injuring seriously another. On Calle Claris several bombs fell on the street but caused no damage or victims. The same occurred in other streets. On the Paseo de la República a bomb destroyed an apartment where there was a factory of knitted goods of Messrs. Balanzo y Font. The machinery was completely destroyed by the explosion.

Another bomb fell on the Cine Frégoli destroying the entrance of the Cine and killing the nightwatchman of that district.

A bomb fell on Calle Viladomat, on a lumber warehouse, causing some damage. Other bombs fell on the track of the railway passing through Calle Aragón, but caused no victims or damage.

As a consequence of the explosion of an incendiary bomb on the factory Hilaturas Barcelona, all the machinery and merchandise therein were destroyed. There were several victims. On the bridge on Calle Marina damage was caused by several bombs which injured a family which was under the same.

The Bombardment in Histafranchs

This suburb also suffered the consequences of the bombardment although it is one of the less damaged. Several bombs fell on Calle Cruz Cubierta; another on Calle Principe; another on Calle Viladomat, but none of these bombs caused any victims. A bomb fell on Calle Aragón partly destroying a warehouse.

The Bombardment in Pueblo Nuevo

Four bombs fell on Calle Curtidores causing some damage and killing and injuring several persons. In one of the houses a woman put a mattress on her little daughter to save her from damage. A bomb killed the mother and the child was unhurt.

On Calle Padilla a bomb destroyed almost completely a house, recently built, which fortunately was not yet occupied. A bomb caused damage and victims in a house on Calle Espronceda. On the Ribas road several bombs which fell in that place did not explode. The same occurred in the Monumental bullring.

The Bombardment in Other Places of the City

Besides the places referred to previously, other bombs fell in different parts of the city and its surroundings where no damage or victims were caused. One of the bombs fell on the recently built building of the Credit Lyonnais causing no damage or victims. Up to now the number of bombs thrown by the rebels cannot be determined but they are supposed to have been numerous.

852.00/5739

Telegram   Barcelona, June 16, 1937

Sec. of State

Strictly Confidential

Private information here is that steamer *Ciudad Barcelona* carried 104 American volunteers of whom over 50 lost their lives in the sinking of the ship; over 1000 foreign volunteers were aboard destined for international combat few of whose lives were saved.

Other, that ship was heavily laden with war material including 800 aeroplane motors of American make and that Government vessels are on the scene of the disaster with the intention of salvaging these motors at least. Insurgent radio broadcast that warships will prevent this if undertaken.

Perkins

852.00/5739

Telegram   Barcelona, June 18, 1937

American Consul Barcelona

From the information in possession of the Department, it would appear to be extremely unlikely that any airplane engines of American manufacture were on the ship and almost inconceivable that there could have been 800. Telegraph any further information which you may receive in regard to this matter.

Hull

852.00/5777

Telegram   Barcelona, June 19, 1937, 6 P.M.

In what appears to be a political move to crush the P.O.U.M. (Trotsky Communist Party) in Barcelona, police authorities have announced the arrest of numerous persons including "dangerous foreigners and personages of a certain political party." No names given and prisoners being held incommunicado pending investigation. Probable charge in most cases will be espionage.

Charles A. Orr, born at North Branch, Michigan and wife Lois Cutler Orr, American citizens, Jose Escuder, Spanish, representing North American Newspaper Alliance whose American wife is here, and possibly other Americans are among those held.

Upon attempting to interview Orr and his wife for the purpose of investigation, they were reported to have refused to see consulate representative. Will report further facts when available.

Flood

852.00/5847

Telegram   Barcelona, June 27, 1937

Sec. of State

Cabinet of the Generalidad resigned yesterday. Companys announced last night that not only would he remain as President but that he reserved to himself the executive functions of the new Government, that he would not permit a repetition of the movement of May 3rd, and that the armed forces and public order would remain under the control of Valencia. This appears to be an attempt to normalize the situation after the temporary small cabinet of the past seven weeks and to obtain further cooperation with Valencia. He began consultation with the political parties and syndicates today and expects a solution tomorrow.

Flood

852.00/5861

Telegram   Barcelona, June 29, 1937

Sec. of State

New government formed last night under the presidency of Companys is almost identical with previous. Esquerra, CNT and UGT (through Socialist

Party) each represented by three councilors. Peasants party and Catalan independents have one apiece.

Return of Tarradellas as Finance Councilor, decrease in CNT and increase in Esquerra representation (through assumption of first councilorship by Companys) as compared with last regular Cabinet are considered as indicating more conservative trend. Control of armed forces and public order retained by Valencia.

Flood

852.00/3882

Telegram   Barcelona, June 30, 1937

Sec. of State

CNT members of the Government formed day before yesterday have withdrawn before taking office. Reason stated was inclusion of Councilor without portfolio against their wishes. Real reason believed to be inability of CNT, by reason of decreased representation and loss of key positions in Cabinet, to play a controlling part.

Invitation to CNT to participate in the Government, on terms known to have been unacceptable, was undoubtedly deliberate maneuver, inspired by Valencia, to squeeze them out of the Catalan political affairs.

First official act of the Government was to issue statement pledging, *inter alia*, loyal cooperation with Valencia.

Flood

852.00/5972

No. 359   Barcelona, June 24, 1937

Subject: Possible Change in Catalan Government

Sir:

I . . . enclose a part of an article, with English translation, which appeared in the June 23 edition of *La Vanguardia* concerning the possibility of a resignation by Sr. Luis Companys of the Presidency of Catalonia. As of possible interest there is also enclosed a copy of my telegram to the Embassy at Valencia of June 22 regarding the same subject.

Juan Casanovas Maristany, President of the Catalan Parliament, was formerly a member of the Catalan Nationalist Party and a loyal friend and follower of Macia. Later he was First Councilor of the Catalan Government.

During the first months of the civil war it is said that the anarcho-syndicalists attempted to arrest Casanovas, but that he was able to escape into France through the help of Companys. His recent return to Barcelona is interpreted by some as indicating a weakening of the anarchist forces and as a move toward the practical suppression of the anarchist party as a major political force and their exclusion from the Catalan Government.

Douglas Flood
American Vice Consul

Translation of Article Published in La Vanguardia, June 23, 1937

The Attitude of President Companys

As to the attitude to be definitely adopted by the President of Catalonia, Mr. Luis Companys holds the secret. But on several occasions the President of Catalonia has made public that he could not remain with dignity in such high position unless he was supported by the full confidence of all the forces that had supported him up to the present. If in certain circles there exists an ambiance lacking this full and absolute confidence, it is logical that the President should open the doors for his substitution by a person enjoying this confidence, if it is denied to him. The Presidency of Catalonia being a post of honor, but also of sacrifice, should Luis Companys feel that his conscience requires it, he would abandon the post without any theatrical gestures, in simple manner, disposed to grant his support and advice, if requested, to the person taking his place, and his vote and adherence to the Government that should be formed. It would be a new proof of his patriotism and his love for Catalonia and the Republic, since for the purpose of winning the war he deems that all sacrifices should be made by the anti-fascists, from the most outstanding to the most modest.

If authority of the President of Catalonia should never be limited, now it should be less so than ever, because this limitation reflects lack of confidence. And only the men to whom public opinion grants absolute confidence are those called upon to unite together the will of all citizens to win the war.

True Reading of Telegram Sent

To: Embassy Valencia   Date: June 22, 1937

Rumor persists here that Companys will resign shortly and be replaced by Casanovas. Private information of disagreement between these two, causing split in Esquerra Party, lends credence to report.

Other information is that during eight days interval provided for in Article 44 of the Catalan constitution Valencia Government will take over.

Flood

852.00/6015

No. 366   Barcelona, July 1, 1937

Subject: New Government of the Generalidad de Cataluña

Sir:

The only really new member of the government, with the exception of Serra ámies, is Dr. Bosch Gimpera, the councilor without portfolio whose appointment caused the withdrawal of the C.N.T. members, all the others having served in previous governments within recent years, either here or at Valencia. Dr. Bosch Gimpera is rector (president) of the University of Barcelona, and a man of considerable prestige, both in Cataluña and abroad. His appointment is said to be in recognition of certain intellectual sectors of public opinion. While it is true that he was appointed in his individual capacity, rather than as the representative of any party, nevertheless he happens to be a member of *Acció Catalana*, a small independent party whose interests closely parallel those of Companys' *Esquerra Republicana*.

Douglas Flood
American Vice Consul

852.00/6058

Telegram   Barcelona, July 23, 1937

Sec. of State

Rebel warship fired twelve heavy calibre shells into the center of Barcelona last night. Unattained objective apparently airplane motor factory. Unofficial reports have 6 killed, 27 wounded. Considerable material damage. No American known to have been injured.

Flood

No. 388   Barcelona, July 23, 1937

Subject: Confiscation of Rural Properties by the Generalidad de Cataluña

Sir:

I have the honor to enclose a copy, with translation, of a decree published July 15, 1937, providing for the confiscation of rural properties belonging to persons considered to be rebel sympathizers. As in the case of collectivization of industry the present decree merely ratifies and gives a legal status to the actions of various groups during the first weeks of the war. It also appears to be regarded as one phase of the Catalan Government's social agrarian policy, but it is difficult to imagine what more could be done in this direction. The following is a summary of the principal provisions of the decree:

Article 1 provides for the confiscation by the Generalidad, without right to indemnity of any kind, of all rural properties within the Catalan territory belonging to persons and their husbands or wives, and entities, who participated either directly or indirectly in the rebellion.

Article 2 states that by "rural properties" shall be understood the lands for cultivation and annexed installations, forests and pastures. There shall be included in the confiscation all effects within said properties at the time the rebellion started: agricultural products, insecticides, fertilizers, seeds, forages, tools, machinery, vehicles, horses and animals of all kinds, and also the money and current accounts in the banks and savings banks of the owners in the proportion that shall be considered as having to do with the exploitation of the property.

Article 4 provides that the reports prepared by the Committee in charge of deciding on the properties to be subject to confiscation shall be transmitted to the Commission of Responsibilities, which will give a decision within a period of eight days. When it is found that no responsibility lies with the accused, the property will be returned to him in the same condition it was when originally confiscated. The interested party will be entitled to make claims for damages during the time of the provisional confiscation.

Article 6 provides that the non-rebel members of the families of persons who have been declared as compromised in the provisions of the Decree shall have right to continue working in the lands and enjoy the rights granted by the Decree to the beneficiaries of confiscated lands.

Article 8 provides that the cessions shall be usufruct and may be cancelled only because of improper use of the property ceded or non compliance with the obligations imposed by the Generalidad.

Article 10 states that as long as no definite cession is made, the Department of Agriculture will have control over the properties.

Douglas Flood
American Vice Consul

852.00/6103

Telegram   Barcelona, July 28, 1937

Sec. of State

Rebel airplanes bombarded Barcelona and environs twice last night with apparent military objectives. Airport and coast defense batteries not struck probably due to the poor visibility, but some damage in port section. All Americans believed safe.

Does the Department want telegraphic reports of all such incidents or only those of special significance or affecting American lives or property?

Flood

852.00/6116

Telegram   Barcelona, July 30, 1937

Sec. of State

Two small air raids early yesterday morning. Military objective. Slight damage.

Flood

852.00/6154

Telegram   Barcelona, August 4, 1937

Sec. of State

Light aerial bombardment last night industrial district of Barcelona causing slight damage.

Flood

No. 400   Barcelona, August 6, 1937

Subject: Local Reaction to Political and Military Situation

Sir:

I have the honor to report concerning the reaction of the people of Cataluña to the present political and military situation.

Following the events of the first week of May, and while the campaign for the conquest of Bilbao was reaching a critical point, there was a great deal of talk in this vicinity of carrying out a major offensive on the Aragon front to relieve pressure on Bilbao. After a great deal of parading through the streets of Barcelona, editorializing and speech-making, the offensive finally got under way a few weeks ago, and as far as I have been able to observe, the results have been unfortunate, both from a military and social standpoint. The proximate reasons for this seem to be the unpopularity among a great many Catalans, of the Popular Army, and the campaign of industrial sabotage being carried on by disaffected elements of the population.

In the early months of the war, troops sent to the front consisted entirely of volunteers, those of the laboring classes who had put down the revolution of the military in Barcelona and who were fighting for a political ideal, however vague. A large part of the troops who had borne the brunt of the fighting since the beginning, those belonging to the CNT-FAI, are said to be losing interest in fighting for a government in which they are no longer represented, a government which now is admittedly "bourgeois." To them, the "revolution" of the worker is definitely being betrayed and defeated. In order to maintain a supply of fresh troops, it was necessary to resort to conscription, and this, insofar as Cataluña is concerned, has proved unsuccessful. This is easily explained when it is realized that the greater part of the men drafted are those who did not respond even in the enthusiasm of the early days of the war, and those who had relatives and friends killed by the very people they are now asked to fight with. As a result, the authorities are having to fill the draft by a house to house search. Almost every day one may see squads of Assault Guards calling with large open trucks at the various restaurants, cafes and other public places to examine the papers of all male inmates of military age. Those whose documentation is not in order are taken forthwith and loaded into the trucks, and taken to military headquarters. It is interesting to note the reaction of the bystanders witnessing these incidents, which is either one of amusement or indifference, but never of hostility toward those who would have been known as "slackers" in the United States during the world war, and oddly enough, it appears that the penalty for any disinclination to comply with the draft is to be sent directly to the front. This attitude is the harder to understand in view of the fact that it was the Valencia government which restored public order in Cataluña, and saved the people from an impossible situation.

In the rearguard, this indisposition to cooperate with the Valencia government takes the form of the "huelga de los brazos cruzados" (folded arms strike). This has been the usual thing in orderly lines of business since the collectivization of industry, where the workers were secure in their employment and pay regardless of the manner in which they worked, and where their ranks included also the former owners and executives of the business. In these cases it has not been of any great significance, since most commercial business has been on a liquidation basis, and the commercial business workers have only injured themselves; but when it comes to the "war industries," the results are more far reaching. It has been several times reported to me that the syndicates have recently ordered their members not to deliver any finished war material to the representatives of the Valencia government.

The foregoing are what might be called the proximate causes of the present unrest and failure to cooperate in carrying on the war. (It has even been suggested that "Cataluña is the only country in Europe which has lived up to the non-intervention agreement.") In my opinion, the ultimate causes are more fundamental. In spite of what is written in the press, and spoken from the platform, the impression is inescapable that the average Catalan dislikes wars in general and this war in particular. This does not mean that he would not defend his territory against foreign invasion, as some people claim (history proves the contrary), but rather that he is not sufficiently interested in a "political" war to go away and fight for some other part of Spain. It might be argued that this does not seem compatible with the anarchist's love of violence, and with the fact that it has nowhere flourished so well as in Cataluña. But the fact is that the anarchists of the violent type, in Cataluña, constitute a small but noisy minority, and the percentage of them who are Catalans is still smaller. As a result of the fact that a large number of the radical extremists are still at the front, and that a proportionally large number of the capitalist class have been killed off in the rearguard, the largest (but least articulate) sector of the present civil population of Cataluña consists of the middle class, whose chief interest in life is to be let alone and allowed to get on with its business.

Respectfully yours,
Douglas Flood

852.00/6187

Telegram   Barcelona, August 9, 1937

Sec. of State

Various isolated disorders by extremists in Catalonia during the past week, including attempted assassinations of the President of the Catalan Supreme Court and General Pozas, have apparently caused uneasiness on the part of the authorities.

Probably of equal importance as the cause of apprehension is the widespread feeling of dissatisfaction and defeatism among the general public.

Flood

852.00/6288

No. 402   Barcelona, August 10, 1937

Subject: Establishment of a Frontier Zone on the Franco-Spanish Frontier in
    Cataluña

Sir:

    I have the honor to enclose a copy, with translation, of a notice published
by the Jefatura Superior de Policía on August 6, 1937, regarding the establishment of a frontier zone on the Franco-Spanish frontier in Cataluña.

    This measure has been found necessary in view of the fact that several
hundred Spaniards had been clandestinely leaving Spain during the past few
months to avoid military service, and all other precautions which had previously been taken, such as the frequent change of frontier guards, had proved
inadequate to prevent it.[25]

Douglas Flood
American Vice Consul

852.00/6208

Telegram   Barcelona, August 12, 1937

Sec. of State

    Valencia Government's abolition yesterday of Aragon council of defense
and taking possession of munitions factory and various minor transportation
units, all of them completely controlled by the CNT, has increased the tension
here. It is reported the Government also plans to forcibly dislodge CNT from
the control of tramways and other local transportation.

    On the basis of past performances this might lead to open hostilities
and extra precautions are being taken to preserve public order.

Flood

---

[25]Document omitted, see *Diario del Comercio*, 6 August 1937, p. 1, copy enclosed in
Dept. of State Records 852.00/6288.

852.00/6292

No. 403   Barcelona, August 12, 1937

Subject: Reaction to Proposed Transfer of Valencia Government to Barcelona

Sir:

Last week the head of the Valencia government, Sr. Juan Negrín, made a visit to Barcelona to confer with Sr. Companys, President of the Generalidad, and since no plausible explanation of this was given in the press, the usual number of ordinary rumors and *bulos* (propaganda rumors) attended his visit. The most persistent of these was that the Valencia government would sue for peace and the war would be over by the end of this month. Coincident with the arrival of Sr. Negrín, the principal C.N.T.-F.A.I. newspaper, *Solidaridad Obrera* (circulation about 200,000), was suppressed for five days, which also caused considerable speculation.

On the basis of information received from several sources, which are believed to be reliable, it appears that the purpose of Sr. Negrín's visit was to discuss: (1) The terms on which the Valencia government might move to Barcelona, (2) The attitude of the C.N.T.-F.A.I. in the event of a major insurgent offensive on the Aragon front, and (3) the reasons why the draft had failed so conspicuously in Cataluña, and that the motive for suppressing the *Solidaridad* was that [it] had attempted to publish an article to this effect. The paper appeared the following day under the name of *Catalunya*, which was a small, unimportant paper owned by the same organization, and nothing has been done about it yet.

Whatever may have been the matters discussed between Messrs. Negrín and Companys, the results were evidently not satisfactory, as the usual social amenities were not observed following their conference.

It is assumed the question of the C.N.T.-F.A.I. was taken up with Sr. Companys since he is a sort of president emeritus, or ex-officio head of that organization, although officially leader of the *Esquerra* party in Cataluña. This honorary position was conferred upon him in absentia, and, it is believed, to his considerable embarrassment; and it may have been in recognition of the fact that he was for many years the principal defender of C.N.T.-F.A.I. members in the law courts.

In the event the Valencia government decides to move into Barcelona, it may be expected that friction will result over the question of the Catalan autonomy statute. If it is not abrogated, or suspended, the national government would be in the position of a guest of Cataluña, which would be untenable from the standpoint of prestige. If it is done away with, it would probably put the Catalans in an even more unfortunate frame of mind as regards the war than now prevails.

One of the hardest things to understand in the present situation here is the attitude of the C.N.T.-F.A.I. Although not currently represented in either the Valencia or Catalan governments, this is still the most potentially powerful single organization (estimated 500,000 members in Cataluña) to be reckoned with. While it is true that they have been gradually but steadily persecuted and harassed in small ways by their opponents since the indecisive suppression of the May uprising, and have suffered confiscation of numerous small lots of arms, ammunition and syndicate properties, this process could go on at the present rate for several months without seriously affecting their power.

However, with the trend in this direction, and in view of their well known hostility toward the present government, it would seem that the sooner they made a bid for power the more chance of success there would be, yet they do nothing. (It is problematical how long the alliance between the C.N.T. and U.G.T., recently concluded at Valencia, would last in the event of renewed hostilities). It is reliably reported that the Assault Guards, and the more militant members of the P.S.U.C., are ready and anxious for them to "start something" so that they can be definitely and finally crushed.

Douglas Flood
American Vice Consul

852.00/2861

No. 328   Barcelona, August 14, 1937

Subject: Copy of Communication from American Consular Agent at Tarragona, Spain, dated August 13, 1937.

Sir:

I . . . enclose, in duplicate, a copy of a communication from Mr. Caesar F. Agostini, American Consular Agent at Tarragona, Spain, dated August 13, 1937, regarding conditions at Tarragona.

This exposé describes so accurately what is reported on reliable information as taking place in other towns within this consular district, as well as in Barcelona, that I am taking the liberty of transmitting it in this manner.

Lynn W. Franklin
American Consul

Tarragona, Spain, August 13, 1937

Sir:

I have the honor to give you the following information.

General conditions in this consular district continue in a trend of apparent normal rhythm. It however becomes daily more apparent that trade in all branches is steadily falling off and something tantamount to a general stoppage of work is foreseen for a not distant date owing to the lack of new orders and the curtailment of purchases in articles that can be done away with.

The establishment of the 40 hour work-week with each trade or industry having fixed the schedule of daily work hours to suit exclusively its own pleasure or convenience gives the towns in this province a curious aspect with many stores, offices or workshops totally closed at each hour of the day.

What principle of authority is to be sought in this province and especially so in the town of Tarragona gives the impression that the syndicalist, communist and anarchist organizations are steadily gaining ground in their apparent aim to substitute entirely the governments of the Republic and Generality of Catalonia by their own delegates. Such delegates are daily more numerous and are to be found in all sorts of public services and activities and most especially in the handling of the confiscated industries, buildings and valuables which are at once taken control of by the aforesaid labor organizations.

Houses are searched with unabating frequency, some of them having been searched as often as 7 or 8 times. In such operations religious signs or images, even those of great artistic or historic value, are with but rare exception torn to pieces on the spot. What money or objects of value are then found in excess of what the searchers consider should be sufficient to have at home are immediately seized and no receipt is given in exchange therefor. Although at the present time searches are prohibited unless by juridical writ, they continue being performed by patrols of the armed militias whose power seems to rest solely on the guns they carry.

Food is to be found in this district with but slight rise of prices in a very few instances. Information as to the near future is conflicting in that regard. The armed militias have accumulated great quantities of food in their respective headquarters, wherewith all their requirements can reportedly be met for a period of several weeks. Such mouth supplies have been requisitioned from the local stores or from shipments lying in the railway stations or local harbor and in exchange for them coupons (*vales*) have been given bearing the ink seal of the requisitioning organization.

For the preparation of daily meals for the militias a number of cooks and waiters have volunteered or been requisitioned and the meals are reported to be abundant and costly and of them partake officially the militiamen only but their families are reported to receive also a share of the delicacies always prepared in excess of actual official requirements. Daily expenses in that line are met either with coupons or in cash from confiscated funds or from funds originally destined to the field hospital of the Front Anti-fascist.

The Comisaria de la Generalidad in Tarragona meets promptly a daily bill for meals averaging 1,800 pesetas although when more guests than usual attend the bills run above the 2,000 peseta mark and one day topped 2,300 pesetas. Their meals are prepared by the best hotel in Tarragona.

Besides the usual meals cognac and champagne run freely, principally the former, reportedly to assuage the strain of hard work.

A subscription has been open for a couple of weeks to sustain the field hospital for the anti-fascist militias in Tarragona with a branch hospital just opened in Caspe, province of Saragossa. The subscription now amounts to 238,000 pesetas partly from voluntary contributions and mostly contributions in response to courteous threatening requests. As the need for money appears to be great, the information to hand at this time is that the courteous threatening requests will be extended and made to represent an amount in money proportionate to the real estate property and bank deposits of each eventual donor.

Propaganda activity by the communists, syndicalists and anarchists points to an early substitution of the present governments of the Republic and Generality by their own elements. They talk with scorn of the Left Republican Party of Catalonia (Companys), of the Socialists (UGT) and of the other republican parties accepting Mr. Azaña's leadership.

Of the armed militias now marching towards Saragossa it is stated that several incidents have occurred in those from this province owing to the opposition of their elements to be commanded by army officers even when the latter are known never to have been considered republican elements.

Citizens continue being executed by the armed militias of the radical organizations. In this town the sentencing tribunal is constituted by five men each from a different radical party, one of them being from *Estat Català* (separatist), the procedure being unknown but no appellation being given the sentenced man. They sit either on board the tied up steamer now used for a prison or in one of the labor organizations represented by its members. Executions are usually carried out between sunset and sunrise in the outskirts of this town but quite near to it as the reports of the guns are easily heard. The corpses are left on the ground until after sunrise when the motor truck fitted for the purpose picks them up and carries them to the morgue. In most cases the bodies are buried on autopsy without having been officially identified either because they are disfigured or because the relatives and acquaintances of the reported dead fear going to identify them, while in a few cases identification has been prevented by the armed militias stationed in the morgue. Six or seven men have been soaked in gasoline and kept burning alive for some time before being shot, this information having been obtained from one of the physicians attending the autopsies. In other cases the men have been killed with small shot and disfigured thus beyond identification.

Caesar F. Agostini
American Consular Agent

852.00/6246

Telegram   Barcelona, August 19, 1937

Sec. of State

Opening of Catalan Parliament yesterday marked by decisive defeat of PSUC on vote of non-confidence directed against Catalan elements and resolution postponing parliamentary elections until after termination of war.

Since PSUC is backed by Valencia Government and its armed forces, it is expected that the process of governing by decree will continue in Catalonia.

Question of legislative ratification of previous decrees has not yet been reached. This will undoubtedly be approved, but approval might be disregarded.

Flood

852.00/6435

No. 406   Barcelona, August 26, 1937

Subject: Reactionary Views Published in the Local Press

Sir:

I have the honor to refer to my despatch No. 400 of August 6, 1937 and telegram of August 9, 6 P.M., and to enclose a copy, with translation, of an editorial which appeared in today's edition of the *Diario del Comercio—Diario Federal*, organ of the Federal Republican Party. This party was founded at the time of the First Republic, under the leadership of Pi y Margall. Although not numerically large, and not represented in the present government, it has the distinction of being the oldest republican party in Catalonia. It does not advocate separatism, but a federation of autonomous states.

The views expressed in this article are indicative of the present feeling of dissatisfaction shared by a large part of the public. In fact, it begins to look as though the only people who have not been disillusioned, and who still privately believe in the infallibility of the proletariat, are to be found among the workers themselves and among the intellectuals. Of this latter group especially, there are many who support the government not because they are pro-communist or socialist, but because they are anti-fascist. The members of the Federal Republican Party come within this category.

The mere fact of publication of an article of this type is significant, since as little as three or four months ago such statements would have been considered political heresy and counter-revolutionary, and would have brought serious reprisals.

Douglas Flood
American Vice Consul

852.5018/8

No. 416 Barcelona, August 28, 1937

Subject: Food Situation in Barcelona

Sir:

I have the honor to refer to this office's despatches Nos. 227 and 339 of February 10 and May 26, 1937, regarding the difficulties in obtaining food in Barcelona and to report that the situation is fast becoming acute. Fresh milk has completely disappeared from the markets and the supply of tinned milk is running low. Fresh vegetables are occasionally found but fresh meat is practically unobtainable and fresh fish, when available, fetches fantastic prices. The restaurant syndicates have so far been powerful enough to keep the establishments under this control fairly well supplied, although the prices are far above the purse of the average citizen.

One reason for the food shortage is the blockade of the Loyalist coast by Insurgent naval vessels which has recently resulted in the sinking of several ships carrying foodstuffs. With the release of further naval vessels from the Cantabrian coast as a result of Insurgent victories in the North, the blockade may be expected to become even more effective.

For some time past the Consulate General has been obtaining daily rations of bread and eggs and occasional rations of oil, rice, beans and chick peas for the use of officers and employees from the Council of Supplies of the Generalidad. These rations have been an invaluable supplement to what could be found in the markets and more recently have made the lot of this office's personnel enviable in comparison to that of ordinary residents of the city. Nevertheless, this small supply of staples, even if it can be expected to continue, cannot furnish a balanced diet, and I have been considering for some time the advisability of importing food from France.

The French, British, Argentine and Cuban colonies have organized commissaries under the supervision of their respective Consulates, importing food from France by truck, and the staffs of the French and British Consulates General are plentifully supplied with necessities and canned food by their warships. In addition, the French Consulate General imports food on the S.S. *Imeréthie* for official use.

In view of the Department's well defined policy of discouraging the residence of American citizens in troubled sections of the world, the establishment of a Government agency for the importation of food for the use of American residents in Barcelona has never been contemplated. I have, however, approached the French Consul General on the subject of shipping supplies on the S.S. *Imeréthie* for the private use of American consular officers and employees. He informs me that the Austrian Consul here is now making arrangements through his Embassy in Paris for the carriage of supplies for the use of the Consulate on the S.S. *Imeréthie*, and I am planning to take similar steps.

Although it will be necessary to describe the supplies as official in order to obtain the authorization from the French authorities for their carriage on the S.S. *Imeréthie*, all transactions as to their purchase in France and their entry into Spain will of course be the private concern of the American consular officers and employees stationed in Barcelona, who are prepared to pay the prescribed duties.

Douglas Flood
American Vice Consul

852.00/6544

Telegram   Barcelona, September 24, 1937

Sec. of State

Port section of Barcelona bombarded from the air three times last night causing undetermined damage to warehouses and setting fire to one large gasoline storage tank.

Flood

852.00/6662

Telegram   Barcelona, October 11, 1937

Sec. of State

In a statement broadcast this afternoon President Companys declared that notwithstanding postponement of parliamentary election he will resign at what would have been the end of his term next month and that he will neither seek nor accept reelection.

It seems probable that this decision has been prompted by the progressive eclipse of Catalan autonomy by the Valencia Government since the events of May and by his own lack of control over the various Catalan factions plus the fact that end of mandate gives him lone chance to retire gracefully.

Flood

852.00/6695

Telegram   Barcelona, October 16, 1937

Sec. of State

Various sections of Barcelona and suburbs were bombarded from the air intermittently for an hour and a half last night causing undetermined damage and officially eight deaths.

Flood

No. 426   Barcelona, October 14, 1937

Subject: Revocation of Order Requiring Approval of Syndical Organizations for Municipalization of Public Services

Sir:

I have the honor to enclose a copy, with translation, of an order of the Generalidad de Cataluña, published on October 6, 1937, which revokes a former order dated March 3, 1937, requiring the approval of the syndical organizations in order to municipalize public services. This is obviously a first step toward the removal of Syndicates from the control of local transportation and other public services. The Generalidad itself is powerless to bring this about by any legislative means, since it no longer has at its disposal the necessary force to back it up. The order will, however, remove any possible legal objection to the taking over of these services on the part of the Valencia Government if and when it is attempted.

Respectfully yours,

Douglas Flood
American Vice Consul

852.00/6875

No. 436   Barcelona, October 30, 1937

Subject: Order Providing for Requisition of Household Equipment

Sir:

I have the honor to enclose a copy, with translation, of an order published in the *Diari Oficial de la Generalitat de Catalunya*, of October 19, 1937, providing for the delivery by residents of Barcelona of mattresses, sheets, blankets and pillows for the use of military forces and war refugees.

This will give an idea of the steps taken to provide for military forces and for the thousands of refugees which have been crowding into the city since the beginning of the war, and continue to arrive, via France, from Asturias, as a result of recent insurgent victories in the north.

The settling in Cataluña of large numbers of refugees, mostly of the lowest class, has given rise to a feeling of mutual dislike and distrust. House-holders and surviving property owners, live in constant fear of having their houses and apartments taken over for this purpose. As one long-suffering Catalan remarked to me, "It's bad enough for them to keep their chickens and ducks in the parlor and their goats on the balconies. But when they start chopping down the doors for firewood, I think something ought to be done."

Douglas Flood
American Vice Consul

852.00/6824

Telegram   Valencia, November 2, 1937

Sec. of State

The Permanent Committee of the Cortes has resolved to remove that body to Barcelona.

With the exception of President Azaña, Indalecio Prieto and Irujo[26] (who will soon leave) all heads of the Government are now in Barcelona.

The Ministry of State continues to function in Valencia, in the charge of the Secretary General, but will complete its transfer within the period mentioned in my 814, October 30.

Thurston

852.00/6872

Telegram   Barcelona, November 9, 1937

Sec. of State

Owing to censorship there has been no serious press comment regarding National Government's removal to Barcelona. General reaction to this move has been one of resentment or indifference as expected but in addition

---

[26]Indalecio Prieto was the Socialist minister of the navy while Manuel Irujo was a minister without portfolio in the same Republican cabinet representing the Basque section of Spain.

Government's vacillation and the coincidence of its removal with the fall of Gijon regarded as evidence of weakness and disorganization.

As a conciliatory gesture Generalidad is so far being permitted to carry on with Companys expected to remain in office but it is believed that the Government will not tolerate any interference with its apparent determination to bring Catalonia into line in order to coordinate the conduct of the war.

Flood

852.00/6885

Telegram   Barcelona, November 10, 1937

Sec. of State

Catalan Parliament has passed a resolution calling upon Companys to continue in office and he has agreed to do so. This apparently consummates deal made with National Government referred to in my telegram October 20.

Flood

852.00/7144

Telegram   Barcelona, December 31, 1937

Sec. of State

Today's communique states that rebel forces which with heavy reinforcements of men, artillery, and tanks are counter-attacking Teruel yesterday captured serious positions in government left flank.[27] The communique asserts, however, that this does not endanger the city which is still defended by strong lines. It adds that a simultaneous attack on right flank also resulted in relinquishment of Government positions but that they were later retaken. Within the city the Government claims to have occupied the seminary and to have blown up the Bank of Spain, thus presumably reducing rebel defenses to the civil government building and the Convent of Santa Clara, the water supply of which has been cut off.

Thurston

---

[27] The battle of Teruel was fought in southern Aragon next to the region of Catalonia between December 1937 and February 1938. The Nationalists were able to move closer to Catalonia and the end of the Civil War by defeating Republican forces in the area. Each side lost between fourteen thousand and fifteen thousand dead; the Republic, in addition, had to give up an additional five hundred square miles of territory. For details see José Manuel Martínez Bande, *La batalla de Teruel* (Madrid, 1974); R. Casas de la Vega, *Teruel* (Madrid, 1975); Carlos Llorens Castillo, *La Guerra en Valencia y en el frente de Teruel* (Valencia, 1978).

852.00/7145

Telegram   Barcelona, January 1, 1938

Sec. of State

    Government communique today concedes further rebel advances on its left flank including recapture of the Muela de Teruel which when taken by government forces was described as the city's most important defensive position. The communique likewise states that rebel efforts to enter the city itself had been repulsed presumably indicating that attacking forces have established contact with it. Rebel positions within the city are still held.

    An editorial presumably officially inspired seems designed to prepare public for loss of Teruel. It emphasizes viewpoint that the most important objective of the drive on Teruel was to break up the major offensive about to be launched by the rebels and that regardless of the outcome of the struggle for possession of the city, this end has been achieved. It concludes that the rebels will now require several months to reorganize during which period the government will carry out its own plans.

Thurston

852.00/7169

Telegram   Barcelona, January 8, 1938

Sec. of State

    Aerial bombardment by one plane at 6 P.M. yesterday afternoon caused damage to two factories in Pueblo Nuevo District. Two buildings including a school in the Barceloneta destroyed by incendiary bombs. Tentative official figures give seven killed and seven wounded.

Flood

852.00/7173

Telegram   Barcelona, January 9, 1938

Sec. of State

    Air raid six o'clock yesterday north section of the city and in Pueblo Nuevo District caused slight damage. Officers estimate twenty deaths.

Flood

852.00/7188

Telegram   Barcelona, January 12, 1938

Sec. of State

Air raid 7 o'clock yesterday afternoon in San Andres and Casa Antunez sections of the city caused slight damage and few casualties.

Flood

852.00/7202

Telegram   Barcelona, January 16, 1938

Sec. of State

Three rebel army planes bombarded Pueblo industrial district yesterday noon and afternoon causing moderate damage. Attacks repeated at midnight and again this morning with results as yet undetermined. Anti-aircraft defense active.

Flood

852.00/7208

Telegram   Barcelona, January 19, 1938

Sec. of State

Bombardment of the city by six planes this noon, the most destructive of life and property that has yet occurred, demolished or damaged several residential buildings in the Paseo de la República district and warehouses and dock buildings in the port section. While first official reports place deaths at over 100, unofficial and unconfirmed estimates place deaths at 500 and wounded at 1500.

Flood

852.00/7234

Telegram   Barcelona, January 21, 1938

Sec. of State

Air raid early this morning southwest of city officially reported to have been unsuccessful in destroying gasoline depots and to have caused no casualties.

Flood

852.00/7242

Telegram   Barcelona, January 22, 1938

Sec. of State

Bombardment early this morning officially to have been by three planes over port area causing little damage and no casualties. Anti-aircraft defense very active.

Flood

852.00/7246

Telegram   Barcelona, January 23, 1938

Sec. of State

Air attack by six planes early this morning reported to have been driven off by anti-aircraft firing, bombs dropped in western suburbs doing little damage.

Flood

No. 311   Barcelona, February 14, 1938

Subject: The Spanish Civil War: Aerial Bombardments

Confidential

Sir:

In the course of a conversation this morning the Minister of State expressed satisfaction over the fact that Barcelona has not been subjected to an aerial bombardment since January 30th., and stated that he felt inclined to believe that such attacks will not be resumed. I inquired whether, if his expectation should be realized, such a development could be attributed to the adverse public opinion that is developing with respect to that type of warfare, or to the specific activities of Great Britain and France. Sr. Giral replied that neither of these agencies could claim the credit, as it would be due simply to the realization on the part of the rebels that any further attacks on Barcelona would be followed by reprisals on a large scale. He added that the Government's reports from rebel territory indicate that the retaliatory raids last month on Salamanca and Sevilla were very destructive and created a condition of panic—followed by the exodus of thousands of civilians from both cities. In Salamanca, he said, one of the bombs fell within the barracks of the Condor Battalion (German) causing more than a hundred casualties, while another fell immediately in front of General Franco's place of residence.

The bombs employed during the two raids on Barcelona January 30th., were very destructive, apparently not only because of their size but because they penetrated very deeply before exploding—thus bringing down, as a rule, the entire building, whereas bombs designed to explode upon contact have heretofore merely demolished the upper floors of the building struck.

Respectfully yours,
Walter C. Thurston

852.00/7380

Telegram   Barcelona, February 22, 1938

Sec. of State

Air raids on Barcelona were resumed last night. Two attacks were made, at 1:30 and 5:30 with but slight damage and few wounded reported in the southern port district, there the Campsa gasoline depots may have been the objective.

Thurston

852.00/7516

Telegram   Barcelona, March 17, 1938

Sec. of State

A series of air raids on Barcelona between 10 and 2 o'clock last night, followed by another this morning at 8 and one a few minutes ago caused much destruction and apparent heavy loss of life. While obvious objectives such as railway stations were struck the bombardments were general in nature and affected business and residential districts in central portions of city.

Thurston

852.00/7533

Telegram   Barcelona, March 18, 1938

Sec. of State

Further air raids took place throughout night at 10, 1, 3 and 7 o'clock and again a few moments ago. Bombing again was general extending to residential districts in northwestern part of city.

Death toll up to last night said to be 400, and wounded 600. Population of city is demoralized and many are seeking safety outside.

Thurston

852.00/7538

Telegram   Barcelona, March 18, 1938

Sec. of State

The Nationalists have taken Caspe extending front to the Guadalope River, destroying Government resistance near Alcorisa and advanced the South Column east of Alcaniz to the Mossa road.

Barcelona population nervous and panic stricken many moving to the country owing to severe bombing of city yesterday and again four times last night and this morning. Faith in Government waning and disorders may be expected unless military situation changes.

Thurston

No. 366   Barcelona, March 26, 1938

Subject: The Spanish Civil War: Results of air raids on Barcelona

Sir:

It is now officially reported that the bombardments caused 875 deaths (512 men, 245 women, 118 children) and that at least 1,500 persons were treated for wounds. Forty-eight buildings were completely destroyed and 75 damaged.

Respectfully yours,
Walter C. Thurston

No. 371   Barcelona, April 12, 1938

Subject: The Spanish Civil War: Military Operations Affecting Barcelona

Sir:

In connection with recent references in my reports to impaired light and power services in Barcelona, I have the honor to transmit herewith a copy of a memorandum on that subject prepared by the Military Attaché:

Barcelona, April 7, 1938

Memorandum

Mr. Walter Thurston
Chargé d'Affaires
American Embassy

Subject: Electric light, power and water supply of Barcelona

Sir:

The undersigned has just had a conference on the subject matter of this memorandum with a civil engineer of the Department of Public Works upon which are based the notes below.

1. (a) Barcelona is normally supplied by hydraulic power stations situated on the river Noguera-Pallaresa, between Balaguer and Sort, 44 kms. north of Tremp at which latter place is perhaps the largest of the installations.

   The small automatic power plants on the river Ter (which passes through Ripoll via Gerona to the sea) are secondary.

   The stations already taken by the rebels on the river Esera and those near Serós assured an excess of supply of electric power for needed requirements.

(b) The enemy at present has reached the banks of the river Noguera-Ribagorzana, about 25 kms from the Noguera-Pallaresa on which are located the Tremp plants. Also the enemy has taken Balaguer which is only 12 kms south of Camarasa where is located one of the large hydroelectric plants contributing in large part to the electric supply of Barcelona.

In spite of the detours imposed by the intermediate mountains, the supply sources of hydro-electric power in Catalonia are closely menaced (in fact, are in immediate danger of being cut off or controlled by the rebels).

(c) The present needs of Barcelona are 100,000 kws (50% of normal), of which 40,000 kws is for lighting.

(d) The three central power and electric plants that control the city supply are located as follows: One in the city proper of Calle Mata, near the port, and two in the adjacent suburb Badalona.

(e) The emergency "thermic" plants in Barcelona have just been tested, after several years of laying idle. They are in working order, and in theory can supply the above mentioned consumption. However, their fuel requirement is coal and this product is not only scarce but most expensive, and of a quality not very suitable for this purpose. Again, it is believed that the available coal in reserve will have to be utilized in connection with the more important item of water.

(f) In any case, it is expected that, at least, some electricity for emergency uses will be available from some of the lesser installations.

2. (a) The water supply of Barcelona is obtained totally from two sources, viz., the Llobregat which furnishes 75% of the water consumed in the city, and the Rio Besos from which is obtained the remaining 25%.

(b) The installations which control the water supply of the city, are located at Cornellá, about 10 kms south of the city, and Santa Coloma, about 3 kms north of the city. Both of these installations require lifting power to raise the water to the level of distribution. For this purpose, they are normally equipped for electricity obtained from the sources noted above. However, these plants for emergency purposes can be operated with coal fuel, but the remark on the subject above is equally applicable to these installations. In this connection, it might be stated that the engineer who furnished the undersigned with the information contained in this memorandum stated that during his service with the water works covering a period of 21 years coal as a fuel has been used but on one occasion and that was during a three day strike period in 1920. The coal requirement for furnishing Barcelona with its daily water supply is 70 tons.

(c) There are several reservoirs for the conservation of water for the city, but the capacity of these pools are sufficient only for furnishing the city with a half a day's water supply.

April 8th

Note: Since the preparation of the above memorandum, the Nationalists claim on their radio announcement this morning that they have taken Tremp and all electrical installations in that neighborhood as far north as Pobla de Segur. At this writing the undersigned is unable to determine whether the above claim is based upon the successful advance of the column operating towards Tremp from the west or from the column from the south which took Balaguer.

[Signed] Stephen O. Fuqua
Col. Inf.
Military Attaché

Respectfully yours,
Walter C. Thurston

No. 402   Barcelona, May 9, 1938

Subject: The Spanish Civil War: Miscellaneous Notes

Sir:

Profiteering, hoarding, defeatism, and treason, have for some time served as topics for discussions by the newspapers—but little effective action has heretofore been taken against those guilty of such offenses. Recently, however, various special tribunals have been established to deal with the problems of the rearguard, and it is apparent that they are functioning in a most drastic manner.

La Vanguardia for April 29, for instance, asserts that the Common Court of Responsibilities (Tribunal Popular de Responsibilidades) has imposed fines, apparently since March 1, 1938, aggregating 173,000,000 pesetas. Many of these fines were for 1, 2, 3 and even 5 million pesetas. The Permanent Court (Tribunal Permanente) is said in the same article to have imposed sentences of from six to ten years imprisonment in several cases of "defeatism," while executions pursuant to death sentences passed by the Court of Espionage and High Treason (Tribunal de Espionaje y Altra Traición) are a matter of daily occurrence and frequently are carried out in the case of women.

Respectfully yours,
Walter C. Thurston

No. 1567   Saint-Jean-de-Luz, France, August 19, 1938

Subject: Reasons for Government Changes in Barcelona

Sir:

The Government naturally is using every precaution to prevent treachery behind the lines, to eliminate spies, etc., and in Madrid recently 160 were arrested and tried. The trial appears to have been conducted fairly, as shown by the fact that almost half were acquitted, and but twenty received the death penalty. These trials and death sentences are quite as numerous in the rebel territory.

The action of the Catalan member who resigned is easy to understand in view of the background of the disagreements between the National Government and some of the Catalans. Until the Government moved to Barcelona the factories there were turning out very little war material. That, according to word I had from both Sr. Negrín and Sr. Del Vayo at the time, was the reason the Central Government moved to Barcelona to bring pressure to bear, as I reported at the time. The Catalan resigned because he disagreed with the policy of the Government toward war industries.

While Sr. Irujo, the Basque Minister without portfolio, made that resignation the pretext for his resignation on the unimpressive ground that the Catalans and Basques had left the Cortes together, I have reasons, based on at least a dozen conversations with the Basque Ministers who have called on me here, to believe that Irujo's resignation came because of his opposition to the death penalty for spying and treason. This is due to the fact that there are a great number of Basque prisoners held by Franco, including the brother of Irujo. Many of these, several hundred, have been shot, though they surrendered under terms of capitulation expressly protecting them against that fate. Fear for the fate of these men is the strongest feeling I have been able to detect in all these conversations. There is a fear that the execution of disloyalists on the Government side may lead to reprisals against the Basques, and with Irujo in the Government, standing for the death penalty there was grave danger that his brother, of whom he is very fond, might be tried and shot. By resigning because of the death penalty, I am convinced he feels that he has done something to protect his brother.

The reorganization of the Government with just these two changes does not alter its complexion and does not affect the situation.

Much is made of any change in the Government at Barcelona which is brought about through the usual constitutional methods, and little attention is given to changes on the part of the Dictator. There have been a number of other members of Franco's Grand Council—which is the Government—removed, but in each case there has been an arrest and an imprisonment.

Respectfully yours,
Claude G. Bowers

852.00/8462

Telegram   Mataro, September 18, 1938

Sec. of State

Military Attaché, after visiting Barcelona harbor including all piers and docks, and scene of yesterday's air raids, reports:

That bombing was most severe ever registered in this area; that fifteen bombers with pursuit plane protection flying from west to east, height twelve thousand feet, dropping some one hundred bombs in harbor region from Barceloneta to the Moll de Contradique; that large Barceloneta market place was wrecked—accounting for half casualties being women; that six lighters with coal cargoes loaded and unloading were damaged, 3 British, *Bobie, Stanlakes,* and *Hollwill,* and 3 Spanish; that official figures give 31 dead and 124 wounded; that observations and talks with seamen, dock men and guards indicate panic existed along waterfront and activities crippled, and that examination of craters, fragments and wreckage point to bombs of unusual destructive power.

Thurston

No. 1616   Saint-Jean-de-Luz, France, November 16, 1938

Subject: Observations on Political Gossip in Barcelona

Sir:

Apropos of the reports from Barcelona on speculation regarding a reorganization of the Government, and on the fears of foreign intervention, I have the honor to submit my own impressions based on conversations with Sr. Del Vayo, and, more impressive to me, with Sr. Azcarate, Spanish Ambassador to London, who is not a politician and who served for years with the League of Nations in Geneva.[28]

There is always a possibility of the change of some Ministers to meet passing political contingencies, but there have been fewer changes during the war, despite numerous crises than during the two and a half years that the Rights were in power before the war began.

There unquestionably are some jealousies and resentments among some of the politicians of Catalonia because the Government has forced the Catalans to march in step with the Republic—something they distinctly did not do until

---

[28]Julio Alvarez del Vayo, a Republican diplomat, in the later period of the Civil War was a commissar-general who strongly supported the Communist cause within the Republic. Pablo de Azcaraté was a highly respected diplomat. Both wrote their memoirs of the Civil War: Alvarez del Vayo, *Freedom's Battle* (New York, 1940) and *Give Me Combat* (New York, 1973); Azcaraté, *Mi embajada en Londres durante la guerra civil española* (Madrid, 1976).

the Government moved to Barcelona for the purpose of compelling them so to march. All this I reported before the move was made when an emissary from Sr. Negrín came to see me to explain why the Government was moving to Barcelona.

The exigencies of war have necessitated the curtailment of some of the autonomous rights of the Catalans, but these curtailments are war measures imposed by necessity. The Catalan and Basque politicians are critical of these curtailments. This is important only to the extent that they may denote a disposition to break away from the common defense of the Republic. And this seems highly improbable for two reasons:

1. The autonomous rights were granted the Catalans and the Basques by the republican parties defending the Republic now and over the bitter protests of the elements that are seeking to destroy it.

2. The Government certainly has not withdrawn all autonomous rights and has made it quite clear that all rights are to be restored after the war; and General Franco has announced the withdrawal of all autonomous rights in the event he wins.

Since these rights mean more to the Catalans and the Basques than anything else, it is not reasonable to believe that they will ever join forces with the elements that are traditionally enemies of their claims and who have reiterated their opposition in most extravagant terms during the war, to defeat the elements that have been their traditional friends, who have merely curtailed these rights in the midst of war, and who announce their intention to restore these rights as soon as the war is won.

In conversations with Basque leaders, members of the Government of Aguirre, I find nothing to indicate any such foolish thought.[29] There is an uneasiness, however, lest in the centralizing process imposed by the necessities of the war the autonomous rights of the Catalans and the Basques may be lost or compromised. I get the impression that these leaders feel it their duty to assume a critical attitude toward the Government lest their claims be overlooked now and it be more difficult to recover them after the war is over.

There is a grim determination among the war leaders of the Government that no intervention by outside nations to impose a "peace of Munich" on Spain will be tolerated. The Government is quite frank, or its representatives have been in such conversations as I have had with them and in such letters as I have received from them, in its utter lack of faith in the political integrity or the personal honesty of Mr. Chamberlain. They have a feeling of contempt for the weakness of the French Government in constantly yielding to Chamberlain until he has deprived the French of all their allies and reduced France to a second-rate Power. Should the Four Powers, two Fascist, one, in its present Government, pro-Fascist, and the other in the vest pocket of the third,

---

[29]José Antonio Aguirre was the president of the Basque autonomous government during the Civil War, called Euzkadi. He lived in Barcelona after the fall of the Basque country to Franco. For a good study of him and the Basques see Payne, *Basque Nationalism*.

propose mediation, it would be rejected. The Government is thoroughly cognizant of the fact that even before he became Prime Minister and took over the Foreign Ministry in fact, if not in name, Mr. Chamberlain has exerted himself to the utmost in the interest of the Fascist cause in Spain.

It has been feared that belligerent rights would be granted on the insistence of Chamberlain, but Mr. Azcarate tells me that this is not thought probable. He adds that it is scarcely necessary since Franco is permitted to act as though these rights have been granted anyway. In brief, the position of the Government is that if the Four Powers attempt to impose a "peace of Munich," the two Democracies will have to assist the Fascist Powers in doing so by force. "There is no place in Spain for a Lord Runciman," Del Vayo recently wrote me. "Spain is not Austria or Czechoslovakia," he also writes; and two years and four months of fighting have indicated that much.

It seems to me that too much importance is being attached to the gossip about Julio Besteiro and the possibility of his entering the Government. He is an able intellectual, a professor of philosophy, and without any of the qualities of robust leadership. He may properly be described as an academic evolutionary socialist. He is opposed to doing anything by force—even to defending himself by force. He is a theorist who, despite what is going on throughout the world, still has faith that moral right must prevail regardless of planes, tanks and artillery. The result is that while he is respected for his fine moral and intellectual qualities he has never been a leader and cannot be.

I know that President Azaña has a very high regard for him as an intellectual and a man of moral worth, and I have no doubt he would like to see him in the Government, though I cannot think he would like to see him at the head of the Government. To believe that would be to believe that Azaña himself wishes to surrender Spain into the hands of the Fascists.

While impossible to know what is going on beneath the surface, I am quite positive in my own mind that the gossip about Besteiro is inspired by the enemies of the Government or regime and by the defeatists, who have never been militantly in favor of resisting the Fascist aggression from the beginning.

It is necessary to bear in mind in this connection that Spain is at war, that vast numbers have died in the fight against fascism, that the army is absolutely loyal to the Government, and that it is highly improbable that it would ever stand for a substitution of Besteiro for Negrín.

Respectfully yours,
Claude G. Bowers

5

FALL OF CATALONIA AND BARCELONA
(DECEMBER 1938–MARCH 1939)

THE FINAL NATIONALIST offensive of the fall of 1938 was designed to conquer the remaining Republican territory in northeastern Spain and thereby bring the Civil War to a close. For Barcelona it meant anxiety, more bombings, a virtual halt of all normal activity, and finally occupation by Franco's army. Considerable evidence from eyewitnesses exists for the historian interested in the fall of Barcelona, adding light on the last days of the city as the capital of the Republic. Not the least of this documentation are the unpublished papers of American diplomatic personnel.[1]

The offensive ultimately aimed at the fall of Barcelona began on 23 December 1938, when the Nationalists invaded Catalonia. The Republican army, composed of elements from the Army of the East and the Army of the Ebro, proved too weak and poorly supplied to mount any counteroffensive, let alone an effective defense. On 6 January, the Republican lines collapsed despite government efforts to mobilize the unarmed civilian population. Heavy bombing of key urban centers throughout northeast Spain, including Barcelona, took place all through January, while refugees and Republican soldiers streamed northward toward the French border. Ultimately over 300 thousand people would make this passage. The chronology of the defeat is a simple one. On 20 January, a six-day period of intensive bombing of Barcelona began. When Lérida and Tarragona, both provincial capitals, were overrun, refugees passed through Barcelona on their way north, telling tales of horror and tragedy and overcrowding the city's facilities and roads. The small town of Manresa fell on 24 January and, the next day, the Llobregat River was crossed by the Nationalists. On 26 January, Franco's forces began their occupation of Barcelona. Gerona surrendered on 5 February and within the next five days Nationalists arrived at the French border.

Up to the very end, the Republic called upon the confused citizens of Barcelona to resist the enemy. On 24 January, it put up posters all over the

---

[1]Most useful today on the Civil War in Catalonia is José Manuel Martínez Bande, *La compaña en Cataluña* (Barcelona, 1979).

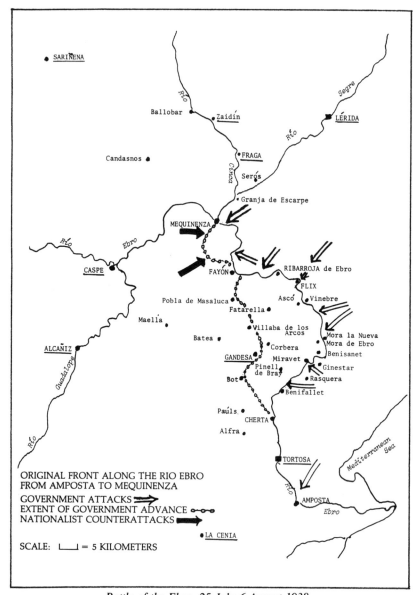

Battle of the Ebro, 25 July–6 August 1938

Source: This map appeared in HITLER'S LUFTWAFFE IN THE SPANISH CIVIL WAR by Raymond L. Proctor, Westport, © Greenwood Press, 1983.

city with such admonitions as "Catalonia is in danger. Everyone to arms!" and "Win this battle and we shall win the war!" However, the population, already convinced that the war was rapidly reaching a conclusion, had no energy for any further sacrifices. In fact, they were unarmed, too weak, and hardly organized to do anything anyway. The city, now so depleted of supplies, found that even its black market had just about ceased to exist by the end of January. Saccharine replaced sugar, and there was no electricity and little coal or oil. Up to 23 January, some bread could still be bought. All forms of entertainment ended as restaurants, bars, theaters, and dance halls closed. Residents recalled that the streets were empty and quiet, even the Rambla was deserted and unfriendly. During the thirty-eight hours before its final occupation, the city felt dead to one unidentified Catalan citizen. On 26 January, the Nationalists heavily bombed the port and overran all Republican defenses on the outskirts. By the end of the day, the Nationalist army began its occupation of the city after reportedly suffering only one casualty. By throwing several of them off the roofs of the buildings, the army quickly discouraged snipers from continuing their resistance.[2]

Recollections of the last six weeks in Barcelona uniformly refer to the city as dying and coming to a complete and silent halt after months of intense suffering. The city looked terrible by the end of January. Louis MacNeice, reporting for *The Spectator*, would later recall seeing:

> Near the cathedral a house six storeys high, its face and floor torn away; on the top storey a plate-rack fixed to the wall with all its plates unbroken and a shelf with two unbroken bottles. The district to the side of the port, Barceloneta, had been evacuated; all the streets are rubble, and all the houses like skulls.[3]

In the last month before its fall, he noticed that the population of the city had swollen to two and a half million because of the refugees; moreover, "money has lost its diversifying force." He wrote that "the shops are ghosts of shops, only open in the morning, the counters and shelves bare, one object every two yards. The cafes are ghosts of cafes—no coffee, beer, spirits, or wine, people making do with coloured water which is called lemonade or with terribly degraded vermouth." The mood was an odd one to him since he believed the city's residents had courage and a good sense of humor yet knew that "war is almost like a habit in Barcelona." He too commented that the food supply was declining and the restaurants were reduced to serving chickpeas when available, some horse, but no other meats or fish since November 1938. The lack of vitamin D, calcium, and phosphorus from dairy products resulted in a sharp increase in rickets among the children even though they

    [2]Broué and Témime, *La révolution et la guerre d'Espagne*, pp. 513–17; Coverdale, *Italian Intervention*, pp. 379–80; Carr, *Spain*, p. 693.
    [3]Quoted in Sperber, *And I Remember Spain*, p. 177.

were always fed first; furthermore, everyone seemed to have a skin disease.[4]

The bombings were of central concern to the people living in Barcelona. On New Year's Eve, bombs fell around the Plaza de Cataluña killing forty-four and wounding ninety-two. Negrín told Herbert L. Matthews on the next day that the bombings were cruel because of the date they came. Constancia de la Mora remembered that the attacks now arrived on a regular basis throughout January until the city fell. She later wrote:

> Day and night the sirens screamed, day and night the skies were lit with fires. Ambulances clanged through the streets at all hours; hearses collected the mangled bodies of the latest casualties. Hour after hour and day after day the fascists bombed Barcelona, destroying the children, maiming the women, shattering the nerves.

Although some women tried to organize themselves to man the defenses of Barcelona, it was hopeless because everyone knew Franco would come shortly.[5] Government agencies started to burn their files between bombings while other Spaniards left to join the thousands of others on the crowded roads north to France. Matthews recalled that with all the bombings and fires Barcelona "seemed to shrink into itself. People hardly dared to move out of their houses, while many, many thousands clung grimly to the refuges and subways, panting in the fetid air, without food, water, or light, but they were safe, at least." Even though rumors spread everywhere about what Franco would do to Barcelona and the Moorish soldiers to its women, Matthews thought "the city was amazingly calm and orderly, although the tension could almost be cut with a knife. The silence between raids was eerie and almost horrible."[6]

In the hours before the Nationalists came into the city, Barcelona's residents threw away their union cards, republican and communist posters and literature, and their newspapers, littering the streets rather than risking being arrested for having subversive materials. Then almost as if by signal, the city became deadly quiet while people waited for the end. At about 4:30 P.M. on Thursday, 26 January, unshaven Navarrese soldiers serving under Franco plodded down the Diagonal toward the center of town and the famous Plaza de Cataluña. Soon after, recalled Salter, "suddenly, dramatically, all the street lamps went on—the first lights in the Plaza de Cataluña for two

---

[4]Quoted in Sperber, *And I Remember Spain*, pp. 176–77.

[5]Matthews, *The Education of a Correspondent*, p. 147; Constancia de la Mora, *In Place of Splendor*, pp. 378–83 and on the evacuation along the northbound roads, pp. 386–400.

[6]Matthews, *The Education of a Correspondent*, pp. 159–61. Similar stories could be told about other Catalan cities as well. Salter passed through Tarragona in mid-January and reported it "was almost unrecognizable from the ruthless bombing that it had received, but was fiercely alive with the last frenzied preparations of the refugees. Mattresses were piled high on already overladen cars and wagons, everywhere the signs of urgent, desperate haste, for news of the breakthrough seemed to have traveled even faster than ourselves," *Try-Out in Spain*, p. 238. Salter had just come from the front when he made his comment.

and a half years."[7] What a symbolic event that must have been for Barcelona's survivors!

On the next day, the American consulate gave a similar account of the occupation and noted how peaceful the takeover had been. Municipal services were restored rapidly. A new mayor was appointed, Miguel Mateu Plá, a Catalan, who now faced a serious problem in finding enough food for the city's residents. The roundup of Republicans began immediately, and the new Nationalist bureaucracy organized seemingly hundreds of trials and conducted thousands of executions within the new few months. In fact, firing squads were still heard in the city as late as 1942. Yet despite continuing political arrests and the suppression of Catalan culture and language, the atmosphere in Barcelona began to change as some semblance of order and normalcy began to creep back into the lives and hopes of its residents.[8]

[7]Salter, *Try-Out in Spain*, pp. 242–50.
[8]Flood to Hull, Barcelona, January 27, 1939, 852.00/8903, U.S. National Archives, Washington, D.C.

852.00/8725

Telegram   Mataro, December 27, 1938

Sec. of State

On December 23rd the Nationalists started their announced offensive against Catalonia breaking the Loyalist front in the Seros Sector. During the last three days the Nationalist forces have made important advances and now hold the line Alfes-Granenabel-Llardecans-Almatret with Borjas Blancas as probable immediate objective.

Nationalist attacks in the Tremp and Balaguer-Lérida Sector claimed repulsed by the Loyalists.

Nationalist aviation controls air.

Thurston

852.00/8734

Telegram   Barcelona, December 30, 1938

Sec. of State

Nationalists continue strong offensive against Catalonia. Their penetration in the Lower Segre sector now reaches the line Alfes-Albages-Granadella-Detroit. Important advances have been made in the Tremp sector menacing the important strategical town of Artesa. Government first defense line facing Nationalist Balaguer bridgehead reported taken. Nationalist penetrations threaten remaining sectors of the first Government defense line in Catalonia still holding.

Other fronts quiet. Nationalist aviation controls the air.

Thurston

852.00/8745

Telegram   Barcelona, January 4, 1939

Sec. of State

One. Military. The initial momentum of the rebel offensive against Catalonia appears to have subsided although heavy fighting continues and ground is still being gained. The advance from Tremp has been south toward Baldoma; that from Balaguer north toward Cubells—the two advances converging on the strategically important objective Artesa de Segre. Most progress has been ordered to proceed south of Lérida where the line now runs approximately from Alfes, Albages, Juncosa, Cabaces, to Felix, and it appears probable that the Loyalist forces along the Ebro may soon be compelled to withdraw toward Tarragona.

The government's viewpoint is that its vital defense fortifications have not been affected, and that the rebel advances have been made only by prodigal and exhaustive expenditures of man-power and the employment of extraordinary quantities of artillery and aviation material supplied by Germany and Italy. It appears to be confident that it can check the advances, and it presumably will in due course launch a counter-offensive. Two additional classes will soon be called. The new recruits will be assigned to rear guard duty, releasing men of suitable age for active military service.

Two. International. Alvarez Del Vayo last night stated to me that he no longer looks for a favorable change of British or French policy nor does he expect any satisfactory development to follow Chamberlain's visit to Rome—with respect to which the Spanish Ambassador at London has been unable to obtain any information. It is taken for granted that Mussolini will press for the according of belligerent rights to Franco and assumed that this will be refused. In the meantime it is considered that the successful resistance opposed to the rebel offensive (planned to produce the downfall of the government before the Rome talks) will again defeat the Italian plans and perhaps threaten Franco's stability. In this connection Del Vayo said that the government has received reports indicating that fresh Italian forces are about to be embarked for Spain. He says the government forces now number approximately 1,000,000 men.

Thurston

852.00/8759

Telegram   Barcelona, January 9, 1939

Sec. of State

During the last few days the Nationalists have made great progress in Catalonia. The fall of key point of Borjas Blancas and subsequent advance in the strongly fortified sector of Mont Blanch and Fallset, the latter already outflanked on the north seriously threaten southwest coastal salient including important towns of Reus and Tarragona. Capture of Lérida salient appears imminent resulting in Nationalist advance Balaguer zone spearhead of which has reached some 12 kilometers northwest of Tarrega and parallels the Lérida-Fondarella Road at a distance of 3 kilometers.

Government defensive attack Fuente Ovejunte Sector (Córdoba) considered secondary importance only.

Thurston

852.00/8788

Telegram   Barcelona, January 15, 1939

Sec. of State

The rebel advance into Catalonia appears to be progressing relentlessly on all fronts, and if rebel claims are to be credited they have completed the initial stages of an enveloping movement which may result in the fall of Cervera—thus opening the direct road from Lérida to Barcelona. It is also claimed today but not confirmed that Tarragona has fallen.

The Government is making desperate efforts to meet the situation, and is attempting to establish new fortified lines and to assemble new reserves. Reports are in circulation regarding the receipt of fresh war material and the imminence of another Government offensive of diversion in the southern area. It is probable however that despite these measures the rebel offensive cannot be dominated in time to save Barcelona, and that (excluding the possibility of collapse) the Government must soon elect between capitulation and flight.

I respectfully recommend therefore that early consideration be given to policy with respect to the Barcelona Embassy and Consulate General regarding which my opinion is as follows.

(a) Under no circumstances short of personal danger should we run the risk of losing this important consulate (as in the case of Bilbao) by closing it. I have been assured by Nestor Vayo that if the government must succumb it will do so "with dignity," but should disorders occur or war operations envelop the city the consular personnel could go aboard a naval vessel until conditions improved.

In connection with the foregoing the Department may wish to authorize the Consulate General to warn the resident Americans that they remain here at their own risk and that no assurance can be given that an American naval vessel will be available to evacuate them in the emergency. Transportation to France is still available by highway, train and air. This would not of course preclude the evacuation of Americans (especially those of the bank, telephone company and correspondents whose work has held them here) if necessary.

(b) Should the Department regard the conquest of Catalonia as establishing Franco's paramountcy and desire to enter into de facto relationship with his regime the retention of this office would be indicated; should it desire to maintain its Embassy near the Government of Spain so long as the Government exists it would be feasible for me to proceed to the new residence of the Government on a naval vessel and I am of course ready to do so. I have informed you of the statement of the British Minister as to his intentions in this respect and I shall report as soon as possible the attitude of the representatives here.

Thurston

852.00/8804

Telegram   Barcelona, January 16, 1939

Sec. of State

Government troops appear unable to stop Nationalist drive on Barcelona. Capture of key strongholds of Tarragona, Valls, Montblanch, Tarrega appear to be making stand along Gaya River (east of Tarragona) although withdrawal to Vendrell-Igualada line appears imminent.

On the northerly sector, the Nationalist advance proceeds more slowly, axis of attack being the Artesa-Cervera road captured as far as Belver inclusive. Capture of Tarrega key road center on the Lérida-Cervera road together with penetration in Santa Coloma sector make fall of Cervera imminent. Present Nationalist line is as follows: just east of Belver, Tarrega Santa Coloma, Valls, Tarragona.

General mobilization ordered by government appears to indicate intention of fighting to the end although believed too late for stopping Nationalist advance against vital centers of Catalonia.

Thurston

852.00/8858

Telegram   Barcelona, January 25, 1939

Sec. of State

Following message received from Flood: No aerial bombardments today. Occasional artillery firing from the south sounds progressively closer. Government is apparently dynamiting those oil stocks at the CAMPSA which it has been unable to move. Otherwise city remains quiet with evacuation of citizens continuing. Water supply has failed but all tubs, etc., were filled yesterday so that we have sufficient reserve for a few days.

Thurston

852.00/8903

Telegram   Barcelona, January 27, 1939, 5 P.M.

Since the occupation of Barcelona yesterday the life of the city is gradually resuming normality. Despite sabotage of plants by fleeing workers the newspaper *La Vanguardia* appeared this morning as well as a newspaper the *Correo Catalan*. All municipal services are being reestablished, except telephone service, which has been temporarily suppressed. Popular enthusiasm over entry of troops continues and appears to be genuine.

A decree of General Franco published this morning appoints Brigadier General Eladio Alvarez Arenas in charge of military and civil order in Barcelona, placing under his direction all military and civil police forces as well as the press, propaganda and military judge of the mixed courts operating within the province of Barcelona.

Foreign correspondents arriving with troops report present drive has reached only to Badalona about 10 kilometers up the coast.

A few trivial incidents showing anti-American feeling among the troops have already occurred but it is not yet known whether this will be reflected in the official attitude toward this office. Repeated to Ambassador Bowers.

Flood

852.00/8885

Telegram   Perpignan, January 28, 1939

Sec. of State

The Nationalist drive culminated in the capture of Barcelona virtually without resistance on January 26. Columns entered from the south, northwest, and north. Troops were acclaimed by civilian population. Since that date progress has been made up the coast and in the center and north. At the present time the line is reported subsequently as follows: Arenys de Mar-Granollers-Caldas de Montbuy-25 kilometers east of Manresa-12 kilometers northeast of Solsona-Organa approaching Seo de Urgel. Three main drives are directed toward Ripoll up north, Vich in the center and up the coast in the south. This office is now located in Grand Hotel, Perpignan.

Thurston

852.00/8907

Telegram   Barcelona, January 28, 1939

Sec. of State

A proclamation of the Governor today assures the Catalans of their "moral autonomy" and the private use of their lands. It provides in part for the requisition of all vehicles (entirely American-owned cars have so far been respected) and commercial stocks over and above owner's consumption needs;

prohibition of all requisitions or seizures by any other authority; and the immediate resumption of all business and industrial activities.

This morning I called independently at the offices of the Military Governor, General Alvarez and the Mayor, Miguel Mateu Plá. A civil governor has not yet been appointed.

Flood

852.00/8884

Telegram   Barcelona, January 29, 1939

Sec. of State

Occupation of Barcelona this afternoon and evening has been carried out in orderly fashion. No aerial or artillery bombardments of city since Tuesday. Staff and all Americans believed safe.

Flood

852.00/8927

Telegram   Barcelona, February 7, 1939

Sec. of State

Today's papers claim capture of the important towns of Seo de Urgel, Bisbal and Palafrugell. A former employee of the Consulate General upon returning to Barcelona via Gerona and the coastal towns confirms the systematic destruction of factories by the retreating army and states he saw the bodies of numerous civilians along the road. The mails are not yet moving.

Two British warships have already visited Barcelona but no schedule has been arranged and no mail is being accepted at this end for transmission. The French have no plans to divulge.

Last night's radio announced that Franco would come to Barcelona and that any idea of a Catalan separatist movement would be squelched. Talk of the Nationalist Government's transfer to Barcelona persists.

The Consulate General was installed yesterday in the Plaza de Cataluña offices.

Flood

852.00/8913

Telegram   Barcelona, February 3, 1939, 6 P.M.

Today's *Parte* claims occupation up to Vich and Tordera.

I went to the Embassy yesterday and on the way back observed between three and four thousand Government prisoners of war returning to Barcelona practically none of whom wore any semblance of a uniform. The advancing coastal column is composed of the Italian Littorio and Blue Arrow divisions.

My January 31, 8 P.M., third paragraph, the worker's committees of the United Shoe Machinery Company and its affiliate, the Boston Blacking Company, have formally returned control to the owners reserving all questions of losses or damages sustained.

This afternoon I went with other members of the Consular Corps and the Governor on an officially conducted tour of inspection of the prison cells, and so called torture chambers of the former S.I.M. or Cheka. Only one of the four places visited showed any evidence of having been occupied and on the whole it was thoroughly unconvincing.

                                                                          Flood

---

852.00/8933

Telegram   Barcelona, February 8, 1939

Sec. of State

Occupation of the towns of Olot and Ripoll is officially claimed today. The following is a literal translation of the statements carried in today's press as having been made by Secretary Hull at a press conference yesterday, "The United States wish to await the development of events" and "as soon as the situation is consolidated the question of the opening of relations between the United States and National Spain will be arranged, with the consequent establishment of an Embassy near General Franco."

                                                                          Flood

---

852.00/8939

Telegram   Barcelona, February 9, 1939, 3 P.M.

Fall of Figueras the last important town in Cataluña is announced today.

London Times correspondent states that one division of 9,000 troops was embarked yesterday from Barcelona with destination unknown but believed to be Menorca. Another unconfirmed report is that the port of Mahon has again surrendered.

This morning I called on José María Mila y Camps the president of the Diputacion provincial of Barcelona and was cordially received. Principal officials of the new regime have so far been reasonably considerate toward us although some minor officials are being difficult.

Yesterday afternoon our residence was searched during our absence by agents of the secret police. Nothing was taken. They awaited our return and wanted to carry off a large wall map and office equipment belonging to the Military Attaché but were persuaded to leave them alone for the time being. We did not know of the search until after they had left. No protest has yet been made.

A Nationalist army officer informed Caragol that surplus captured war materials are sold to Japar. Repeated to Ambassador.

Flood

852.00/9189

No. X–2   Barcelona, February 13, 1939

Subject: Occupation of Barcelona and Vicinity

Sir:

I . . . enclose . . . a memorandum prepared by Vice Consul Jernegan concerning two trips to the former Embassy and Consulate General quarters at San Andrés de Llavaneras, following its occupation by nationalist troops.

As indicated in my telegram immediately preceding and following the occupation, there was slight resistance to the taking of the city proper. There had been considerable artillery fire directed at the outskirts of the city, and over the city, to impede the retreating troops, but this ceased when the city limits were reached. The only fighting within the city proper was a rearguard action between tanks, which took place on the way past our residence.

Within an hour after the occupation, the city, which had appeared deserted during the previous two days, was thronged with people, many of whom had not left their houses for over two years. Two or three days later store windows, which had been empty for weeks, were filled with merchandise. Public looting of food stores left behind by the Republican army, which continued during January 25 and 26, was immediately stopped upon the entry of the nationalist troops.

My telegrams of January 25 and 26, sent by courtesy of the French and British Consulates General, were necessarily brief, inasmuch as their sets were operating clandestinely; within half an hour after the occupation they were dismantled. The British Consul General had gone downtown for lunch the day the troops entered, and had considerable difficulty in returning to his office. I happened to be talking on the telephone to the British telegraphist at the moment the city was entered, and was in the awkward position of having "scooped" my British colleague with his own wireless set.

Douglas Flood
American Consul General

Memorandum

February 1, 1939

On Saturday, January 28, Mr. Caragol, Mr. Sacksteder of the Telephone Company, and I, accompanied by a chauffeur of the Telephone Company, attempted to reach Llavaneras in order, primarily, to bring back the cars which had been left there when the Embassy and Consulate General were evacuated on January 25. We found the highway full of motorized military equipment and troops, principally Italian, to judge by their flags and general appearance, and progress was slow, but we were not challenged by any control. The two highway bridges at Mongat had been blown up, evidently by the retreating troops, as well as the Badalona end of the railroad tunnel, and four of the eight spans of the big highway bridge between Vilassar de Mar and Mataró had been completely destroyed.

Immediately after passing this latter bridge, by means of a temporary road in the streambed, we were caught in a jam of trucks, and the appearance of our car aroused the suspicions of an officer in the car in front of us. He called up a higher officer, an Italian colonel, who spoke no Spanish. When I explained our errand, in French, this officer said that Llavaneras was still behind the enemy lines and that we could not possibly go there. A Spanish officer who came along a minute later said that we were in the vanguard of the army and could not be permitted to continue. He was very polite but firm, and insisted that we turn back, which we did as soon as the column of trucks moved on. As we recrossed the streambed we saw a battery of field artillery going into position with the guns trained in the direction of the hills back of Mataró, which dispelled our lingering doubts as to the advisability of returning without another try.

On the following day, Sunday, January 29, we obtained a pass valid to go to Caldetas and Llavaneras from the secretary of the military governor. The party was composed of the same members as on Saturday, with the addition of Mr. Homer Eddy of the Riegos y Fuerza del Ebro, who had just arrived in Barcelona. Mr. Eddy is the owner of the red Chevrolet, one of the cars which were believed to have been left at Llavaneras.

We had no difficulty in reaching Mataró, where we took the upper road which runs past Torre Gran into Llavaneras. Approaching the town we became suspicious of the lack of traffic and stopped twice to ask people walking on the road if it were possible to go to Llavaneras. They seemed a little dubious and reported that there had been fighting there earlier in the morning, but all agreed that we could reach Torre Gran, since it stands on the near side of the town. One party asked us to stop on our return and tell them whether it would be safe to go back to Llavaneras.

Arriving without incident at the driveway, we found some 40 or 50 Nationalist soldiers standing behind the wall along the road and the gate locked. Just as we stopped we heard, for the first time that day, the sound of a machine gun. The soldiers said that the "Reds" were down in the hollow below the house and on the hills on the other side of town, but that they would be cleared out in an hour or two. They advised us not to try to get the cars out immediately, as the sight of several automobiles might draw shell-fire.

Mr. Caragol reconnoitered and reported that the gardener and his family were in the lower floor of the porter's lodge and that the Clerk Miguel Remus and his family, together with the domestic staff of the torre, were in the basement floor of the main house. (It developed that earlier in the morning there had been a considerable artillery duel and two shells had burst in the garden not more than 50 yards from the house. We saw the craters.) The gardener warned us that a "Red" (Loyalist) machine gun had been firing through the garden between the porter's lodge and the torre a few minutes previously.

Taking our lunches, we scurried across the garden to the most sheltered corner of the main house, where we ate in picnic style. While we were there a machine gun sent several bursts past the other corner, apparently firing at random, as there were no troops that we could see in that direction and we took care to stay out of sight ourselves. Meanwhile Nationalist artillery, apparently some distance away, opened fire, and we could hear their shells passing overhead quite regularly. A Nationalist machine gun established itself on an upper floor of the porter's lodge. (Mr. Remus informs me that earlier in the day the troops had tried to install a machine gun in the house itself, but that with some difficulty he succeeded in persuading them to respect the Embassy.)

Individual rifle fire was almost continuously intermingled with the inter-mittent machine gun bursts, and at about 2 o'clock a light battery, probably of mountain artillery but possibly tanks, opened fire from somewhere just above us. All the artillery fire, fortunately, appeared to be in one direction, and no shells fell near Torre Gran while we were there.

After finishing our lunch we made a hurried entrance into the house, succeeding in our efforts to avoid drawing the fire of the machine gunner who had previously been spraying the garden. We found the house in perfect order except for broken glass from the windows in the Embassy office, dining room, kitchen, and some of the servants' rooms in the basement floor, all of which faced toward the valley or the sea and were thus in the line of fire of the Loyalist troops. One of the windows had been broken by concussion from bursting shells earlier in the day, and the others were perforated in a number of places by stray bullets, which were still entering occasionally.

It developed that the cars left at Llavaneras were Mr. Thurston's Renault, Mr. Gilbert's Vauxhall, and the Telephone Company's Ford. Mr. Eddy's car and the blue Chevrolet belonging to Mr. Rosalez had been left at Caldetas.

After a time the firing died away to occasional rifle shots, and as no more bullets were coming our way we proceeded to get the cars out. While this was in progress, two Loyalist airplanes flew over, drawing the fire of a number of machine guns and light cannon. They were apparently scout planes, however, and dropped no bombs.

After loading the cars with most of the typewriters and some other small articles from the offices, we returned to Barcelona, where we arrived without incident. Since the fighting appeared to be virtually over, Mr. Remus was left to take care of the house and prevent any troops being quartered in it.

The next day, Monday the 30th, Mr. Caragol, Mr. Jones of the British Consulate General and I went to Caldetas to recover the two cars left there. The highway was still crowded with troops, many of whom had evidently camped overnight between Mataró and Caldetas, but we had no difficulty along the way. Caldetas was quiet, but the personnel remaining in the British Embassy and Consulate there reported that fighting had been going on all day.

852.00/8974

Telegram   Barcelona, February 18, 1939, 4 P.M.

Sir:

Courts-martial of political prisoners (one of which I attended unofficially) continue. At least one well known person (Barriobero) has already been executed but correspondents were not permitted to report it.

All transfers of record of real and personal property made in Loyalist territory since beginning of the war declared null and void.

Food situation slightly improved but still grave due to the destruction of communications and to previous export of "surplus" crops by both sides.

During recent visits of English and French naval vessels the commanders paid formal visits to the governor without the question of recognition being raised.

My February 10, 11 A.M. Policy of the press regarding American news remains unchanged all recent articles being attributed to Fabra. One of these gives prominence to Mrs. Roosevelt's speech at Ithaca stating that her attacks on certain nations caused violent protests among the audience and reprinting alongside the critical comments of the *Giornale D'Italia*.

Flood

852.00/8979

Telegram   Barcelona, February 22, 1939

Sec. of State

Franco's first public appearance in Barcelona yesterday on the occasion of reviewing military parade comprising units of 40 divisions was marked by characteristic Catalan lack of enthusiasm (with the exception of organized cheering) for most things were not indigenous to the region, in contrast to first reaction following occupation of the city. It is believed one purpose of the demonstration was to show how many troops could be spared from the fronts. In a radio speech last night he affirmed his political ideology as based on the army.

                                                                    Flood

EPILOGUE

THE OCCUPATION of Barcelona started a new chapter in its history, a time of change with a new regime. Yet before reading a few despatches and telegrams on Barcelona after Franco won control over Catalonia, it would help to review events and draw some conclusions. Such a retrospective offers some tentative conclusions about life in urban centers during wartime, a lifestyle that existed in other Spanish cities during the Civil War and that would be reproduced in dozens of European communities during World War II.

The first observation concerns living standards. The city's economy was a delicate one relying on food and supplies of raw materials and consumer goods from outside of its vicinity. Thus the blockade of the port and the disruption of railroad and truck communications left the city virtually helpless and unable to maintain employment or respectable health conditions. The arrival of wounded from the Aragon front and of refugees from the south and west of Barcelona, swelling the city's population by about 150 percent, accentuated the problem. The inevitable gyrations of the economy, also caused by inflation, disjointed supply and demand patterns, and disregard for Republican currency brought living down to the basic level of physical survival.

Unquestionably, the density of population made bombings for psychological and military purposes too tempting to be resisted for long by the Nationalists and their Italian and German pilots. It seemed only natural that the Nationalists and their allies would try to cripple Barcelona's ability to contribute to the Republic's cause. The damage caused by such bombings was extensive, killing and wounding tens of thousands of people in the metropolitan area and destroying thousands of buildings. The population continued to support the Republic until the ground war went against them in the end. They reacted exactly like the Germans in urban centers when the Allies attempted to break their morale by fire bombings a few years later. However, this lesson was lost on most military strategists who worked during World War II. In the case of Madrid, Spain's other city of comparable importance to Barcelona, the populace remained enthusiastic about the war when their great moment of crisis remained an open issue.[1] By the time Franco launched

---

[1] Ronald Fraser, *Blood of Spain: An Oral History of the Spanish Civil War* (New York, 1979), pp. 264–65, 268; Kurzman, *Miracle of November*, pp. 241–61.

his offensive on Catalonia and Barcelona, most people firmly believed he would win the war fairly soon.

While the history of post–Civil War Barcelona awaits its historians and the few despatches below can only suggest some thoughts and experiences, it should be noted that the new government rebuilt the city with some speed over the next decade. This development was essentially repeated in other Spanish cities and towns badly damaged by the Civil War so that by the early 1950s most of the physical scars were gone. At least around Barcelona, moreover, it did not take many years for the local economy to match and then exceed prewar levels of production and activity. Not so quickly cured, however, were the emotional and ideological wounds caused by the Civil War, painful memories not forgotten even a generation later.

By the time Franco died in late 1975, Barcelona's population had more than doubled since the Civil War. The long-suppressed demand for Catalan autonomy resurfaced and the government of King Juan Carlos granted the region the right to establish the Generalidad once again. Catalan heroes of earlier years, such as Companys and Macía, had streets named after them, while the hard times of war were recalled.

At the outset of this book, it was proposed to contribute to our understanding of the human feelings and sufferings caused by the Spanish Civil War by looking at the effects of that conflict on Spain's second largest city. Clearly, Barcelona's role in the Civil War proved to be an important one, and its struggle a focal point during critical periods of the fighting. The city had been a staunch supporter of the Republic and a hotbed of local autonomist activity. At the start of the Civil War, it defeated a small yet potentially significant attempt by Franco's supporters to seize it and in May 1937 the city became the center of attention in the Republic's bid to control its own territory without competition from the hidden regime of labor groups. In the end, the fall of Barcelona signalled the conclusion of the Civil War. With its collapse, almost all resistance to Franco ended. For the citizens of Barcelona, the years 1936 through early 1939 were times of crisis and pain, ensuring the city's place of importance in contemporary Spanish and European history.

No. X–12   Barcelona, March 16, 1939

Subject: Nationalist Propaganda in Barcelona

Sir:

I have the honor to enclose a clipping and translation of an article published by *La Vanguardia Española*, Barcelona's morning newspaper, which is considered significant as an indication both of the attitude of the Nationalist Government toward Catalonia and of the importance which the Army appears to have in the political philosophy of the Nationalist movement.

The article represents far more than the personal opinion of its author, not only because all newspapers in Barcelona are rigidly controlled by the authorities, but also because it is typical of many other articles and "news" stories which have been published in the local press since the occupation of the city on January 26 and the tenor of speeches and statements made by General Franco and other government officials.

It will be noted that the article emphasizes the fundamental importance of the Army in Spain and points out the previous "shortcomings" of Barcelona in failing to recognize this importance. The note of warning to the city contained in the last paragraph typifies the tone of all such articles. The press, without exception, has taken the attitude that Catalonia has been the victim of a program of exploitation and separatism directed by a small minority of foreign-inspired communists and anarchists, but that it has now seen the error of its ways and should never return to the old ideology.

It is evident from the reiteration of this sort of propaganda and from the private statements of Nationalist supporters who have returned to Barcelona, that the authorities are far from confident that Catalonia will enter wholeheartedly into the new totalitarian framework of the state. In a recent interview with German correspondents, the Minister of Gobernación, Serrano Suñer,[2] said that Barcelona is a city "morally and mentally ill" and must be treated with the care given an invalid. An officer of the Falange,[3] a native of Barcelona, has told me that he believes the enthusiastic reception given the troops upon their arrival was due more to relief at the termination of the air raids and the expectation of abundant food than to real sympathy with the Nationalist cause. He fears that within a short time anarchist and socialist doctrines will again be popular among the workers of Barcelona.

---

[2]Ramón Serrano Suñer, brother-in-law of General Franco and at the end of the Civil War a leader of the Falange element in the new regime, was one of the major forces behind close diplomatic relations with Italy and Germany during the first half of World War II. For details on his role, see Charles R. Halstead, "Spanish Foreign Policy, 1936–1978," in James W. Cortada, *Spain in the Twentieth-Century World: Essays on Spanish Diplomacy, 1898–1978* (Westport, 1980), pp. 60, 64–65, 67, 69.

[3]Falange was the fascist party in Spain, and as part of a broader coalition called the *Movimiento Nacional* it was the only political institution resembling a formal party allowed in Franco's Spain after the Civil War. For details, see Stanley G. Payne, *Falange* (Stanford, 1961), passim.

In addition to propaganda in favor of the new organization of the state, the press has consistently used every possible means to discredit the former Governments of the Republic and of the Generalidad, giving publicity to alleged ill treatment of political prisoners, (as in the "chekas" of the secret police), anti-clerical acts such as the burning of churches and destruction of religious objects, exportation of works of art, reported banquets given by officials while the people were suffering from lack of food, etc.

Four daily newspapers, in addition to the *Boletin Oficial de la Provincia de Barcelona*, are now being published in the city. They are: *La Vanguardia Española, Solidaridad Nacional, El Correo Catalán*, (all morning papers) and *El Noticiero Universal* (published in the evening). Although each is independently managed, all carry virtually the same news and have identical editorial policies. *Solidaridad Nacional* is especially the organ of the Falange, but the other papers give only slightly less emphasis to Party news.

Most foreign news is credited to the agencies EFE (which is identical with Fabra) and FARO, and is obviously editorialized in accordance with Government policy. Recently the *Vanguardia* has begun to carry an occasional despatch credited to United Press. News from Germany, Italy and Japan is featured, always in a favorable manner, but French and English news is also given much space. The latter is usually presented in such a way as to imply popular enthusiasm for Spain in those countries and to discredit the elements considered hostile to the Nationalist movement. There has been much critical editorial comment on the conduct of France during the civil war, and, in a more moderate form, this has continued even after French recognition of the Franco Government. Criticism of England has been less severe.

News from the United States is confined chiefly to brief reports of speeches by the President on foreign affairs, developments in the armaments program, disasters of one kind and another, and speculations on the possibility of American recognition of the Nationalist Government. It is almost invariably presented in an unfavorable manner.

In general, both in printed material and in other media, every effort is made to create a friendly attitude toward Italy, Germany, Japan and Portugal, with Italy given first preference and Germany next. Immediately after the occupation, the civic authorities exchanged telegrams of felicitation with the mayors of Rome, Genoa and other Italian and German cities. Italian and German motion pictures are played up in the press reviews and are being shown in a number of theaters, although a majority of the pictures shown are old American productions which have probably been in stock here since the beginning of the civil war.

There is no evidence that the Catalans in general are affected by this campaign. In the grand review held on the occasion of General Franco's visit to Barcelona the Italian and German troops were given the place of honor and made up the bulk of the force participating, but there was no display of popular enthusiasm, not even perfunctory handclapping, while they passed. The Spanish units received mild applause.

Respectfully yours,
Douglas Flood
American Vice Consul[4]

No. 42   Barcelona, July 13, 1939

Subject: Interview with Serrano Suñer

Sir:

I . . . enclose . . . a translation of an interview with Mr. Serrano Suñer, which appeared in the *Solidaridad Nacional*, a local publication, on June 16, 1939. The Department will note that in this interview, Mr. Serrano Suñer indicated that while no policy of industrial reprisals would be followed in Catalonia, excessive industries in "certain zones" should be avoided, not only for economic reasons but also for "political and strategic reasons."

On the occasion of Mr. Serrano Suñer's recent visit to Barcelona upon his return from Italy, I was struck with the enthusiasm with which he was greeted and the preparations that had been made to welcome him. This can be explained in part by the office which he holds, but the comment of a prominent Spanish business man here was: "Naturally we welcome Serrano Suñer because after all he is a Catalan."

Respectfully yours,
Howard Bucknell, Jr.[5]
American Consul General

Translation

1. What changes has Your Excellency noticed in Barcelona since your previous visits?

---

[4]The lengthy article was omitted from this book since its contents were summarized in a despatch. The original is by Manuel Aznar, a leading Falange ideologue of the early Franco period, in an article called "Cataluña y el Ejército," *La Vanguardia Española*, 19 February 1939, p. 3, copy attached to despatch, Department of State Records, 852.00/9190.

[5]Howard Bucknell, Jr., joined the Foreign Service in 1921 and served in posts in the Far East before being appointed to various assignments in Europe and Latin America during the 1930s. He became consul in Barcelona effective 23 May 1939; first secretary at the embassy in Madrid in March 1940; then consul general at Madrid as well on 6 May 1940; counselor of embassy at Madrid at the same time on 27 September 1940. He finally left Spain the next month. Department of State, *Biographical Register, 1944*, p. 28.

I have noticed that Barcelona is making rapid progress towards normalcy. Outwardly, the care given to the streets and avenues, the cleanliness and increased traffic mean a considerable change from the conditions existing on the days just after the occupation of the city. There has also been an improvement—and a great improvement—in the aspect of the inhabitants, so distant from the sad and depauperated aspect they had five months ago.

2. Will the New State aim to the scattering all over Spain of the industrial activities now concentrated in Catalonia, in exchange for an intensification of agriculture in the four provinces? Or, will it respect the differentiation brought about by so many circumstances? Or, what is more interesting, will it foster that differentiation?

I believe it would be antieconomical to ruin without reason the Catalonian industry, or to follow an industrial reprisal policy which would be unfair because it would hurt many interests, mainly of modest people, without benefiting anybody. However, I also believe we must avoid excessive industry in certain zones, not only for economic reasons but also for political and strategic reasons.

3. When Paul Claris went to Louis XIII of France together with all his Council to offer him Catalonia, Richelieu, who was present at the interview, remarked to the king: "Majesty, Barcelona must always be a city of intellectuals and merchants." Does the New State reserve this role to Barcelona, or does it disapprove the idea of Richelieu?

I think the idea of Richelieu was all right, but I believe it too limited for the present day. Barcelona must also be a city of soldiers ready to serve for the greatness of the redeemed country.

4. What role is to be had especially by Catalonia—having in mind her history and peculiar characteristics—in a policy of empire?

I believe it is difficult to condense in one sentence, as you expect me to do, such a special role. The imperial policy is promoted by working, and still more than by working and by being a soldier, with the arms of culture, in the service of this unit that is Spain.

5. A well known French writer told me some years back that Barcelona was the only Mediterranean city where culture was something really native, really of the soil. Does your excellency believe that it would be very opportune to take advantage of this everlasting personality, which is of civilization, and of all Catalonia, for imperial purposes, to exert influence in zones where such influence existed in former times, zones which today naturally belong to foreign countries? To be more precise, does not your excellency think that it would be splendid to organize a great center of oceanic studies?

I have just spoken of the importance I attach to culture in the combination of minds which must bring about the greatness of Spain. Any endeavour with this end in view seems to me good. However, your question refers to something too specific—and too delicate—on which my words, no matter how clear they were, might be wrongly interpreted. Certainly they would be so interpreted by people who go about always trying to hunt ghosts, a sport which they alternate with that of sly and truculent inventions under which their presses groan.

As regards the organization of that great center of studies to which you refer, I am already busying myself with it. Within a short time you will hear positive and interesting statements on the matter. The basis of my work will be the labors of the *Institut d'Estudies Catalans*, raised to the rank of Great Center of Mediterranean culture.

No. 52   Barcelona, July 20, 1939

Subject: The Port of Barcelona

Sir:

I . . . enclose a translation of an article appearing in *La Vanguardia Española* of Barcelona, of July 17, 1939, concerning the present condition of the port of Barcelona.

A recent visit to the port has confirmed the statements in this article with regard to sunken shipping still lying in the port and the desolation and ruin to be seen about the wharves. It is interesting, however, to note that steps are being actively taken to repair the damage caused in the port and wharves mainly by aerial bombardment, and if this continues at its present tempo it is quite possible that the prediction, made in the last paragraph of the article, that Barcelonians will again be able to admire in the port that great traffic of ships, national and foreign, which had made so famous the commercial and industrial activity of Barcelona, will again become a reality in the reasonably near future.

Respectfully yours,
Howard Bucknell, Jr.
American Consul General

No. 58   Barcelona, July 27, 1939

Subject: Progress of Local Reorganization

Sir:

I have the honor to inform the Department that there have appeared recently in the local press a series of articles which are apparently designed to counter some local criticism with regard to the alleged slowness in attending to the cleaning up of Barcelona and the reorganization of the City Government.

As an example I have the honor to enclose a translation of an article appearing in the *Vanguardia Española*, of Barcelona, of July 12, 1939. The Department will note that the occasion chosen for self-congratulations is the celebration in honor of the visit of Count Ciano.[6]

Respectfully yours,
Howard Bucknell, Jr.
American Consul General

No. 79   Barcelona, August 4, 1939

Subject: Speculation in Foodstuffs

Sir:

I have the honor to inform the Department that the shortage in Catalonia of necessary foodstuffs has created a considerable illicit business in food speculation. As regards many essential commodities such as rice, sugar, olive oil, flour, etc., it is still almost impossible to purchase these commodities at the prices established by the authorities. A practice has been growing for holders of these commodities to insist to prospective buyers at the official rates set by the Government that their supply of these goods have been exhausted. At the same time they have been selling limited quantities of such commodities at much higher prices that those officially set. This practice has become so common in Barcelona that the authorities are making an effort to suppress speculation in foodstuffs.

As an example of the efforts to do away with this practice, I have the honor to enclose a copy of an article appearing in the *Vanguardia Española* of August 1, 1939, threatening several penalties against food speculators in the province of Barcelona.

Respectfully yours,
Howard Bucknell, Jr.
American Consul General

---

[6]Count Galeazzo Ciano was the Italian foreign minister throughout the period of the Spanish Civil War and most of World War II and thus was a major architect of his country's policy of intervention in the Spanish Civil War. For details see Coverdale, *Italian Intervention in the Spanish Civil War*.

Translation

Drive Against Foodstuff Speculators

The Delegation for Food Supplies and Transportation sends us for publication the following note:

"The Delegation for Food Supplies and Transportation finds itself in the necessity of applying to the public for their help to secure in the province of Barcelona the lowering of foodstuffs prices and the observance of the official standard prices. For this purpose it is necessary that the public discontinue being egoist and do not pay more than the official price for any article in order to secure it, whether it be foodstuffs, clothing or shoes. Instead, they should report to the competent authorities such individuals as propose or compel them to purchase an article in which they are not interested in order to get the particular goods really wanted. By so doing this Delegation will be able to punish the guilty merchants or individuals.

This Provincial Delegation, convinced that severity is necessary to secure these ends, has decided not only to punish infractors with the imposition of heavy fines but also to close down their shops if there is any cause for it, delivering, in addition, to the Military Authorities the unscrupulous people who with their machinations alter the normal prices of goods.

Last week two people were placed at the disposal of the Military Authorities, one of them for incurring in falsehood in the preparation of invoices which had been submitted for the approval of this Delegation and bore its seal but afterwards had been changed as regards the goods, their prices, and the buyer's name and the town of destination also stating that the goods thus sold came from the Textile Algodoners when in fact they came from the firm Martin Oliva, of this city, and neither of those firms had any knowledge of such falsehood.

Likewise it is believed advisable to publish that inspectors of this Delegation have today proceeded to search the places of grocery stores and others who, having withdrawn their stocks of potatoes from public view, had hid them in their private quarters and refused to sell them. Those who have been found guilty have been placed at the disposal of the Military Authorities for whatever punishment they may have incurred.

The foregoing will serve to warn infractors of the regulations that this Delegation is resolved to watch over the compliance of which has been disposed on this matter in order to stop abuses, and likewise for profiteers to know that they will be punished rigorously whatever may be their social condition."

No. 107   Barcelona, August 18, 1939

Subject: Local Political Situation

Sir:

I have the honor to inform the Department that as a result of renewed political tension in other parts of Europe, there have been continued reports regarding the fortification of the Spanish side of the Spanish-French frontier. It has up to the present been almost impossible to obtain sufficient confirmation of these reports with which to prepare any definite account for submission to the Department. Yesterday, however, I had a confidential conversation with a foreigner who has been resident in Spain for a considerable period and who is believed to be familiar with local conditions. In this conversation I was informed that it is definite that there has been continuing and considerable activity in the construction of defensive fortifications on the Spanish side of the French border, particularly around Puigcerdá and Cancfranc. My informant did not know exactly what fortifications were being and had been constructed, but said that according to his information they were strictly defensive in type and consisted largely of concrete pill boxes, concrete gun emplacements and a system of trenches and barbed wire entanglements. He was not informed, however, whether or not guns had been placed in the positions prepared for them, but stated that Italian vessels calling at Barcelona within the last few weeks had been unloading a number of howitzers and other war material at this port. He stated that the number and type of these howitzers was unknown, but that he personally knew of one shipment consisting of some twenty howitzers which had arrived from Italy only recently. He did not know to what point or points in Spain these guns had been sent. He added (and this has been confirmed from other sources) that when such material is being unloaded the docks are carefully guarded by Italian troops in uniform, thus preventing any unauthorized person from observing the proceedings.

My informant also stated that he had been informed on excellent authority that orders had been issued to the frontier authorities on July 27th that immediately upon a possible French mobilization all the civilian population, on the Catalan frontier at least, was to be immediately evacuated to a depth of thirty kilometers from the frontier. In this connection, I have the honor to inform the Department that I have received reports from Americans travelling to and from the frontier that they had noticed recently Italians and Germans who seemed to be attached to Guardia Civil posts and assisting in the interrogation of passing travellers. Furthermore, I have the honor to enclose a translation of an article appearing in *La Vanguardia Española* of August 15, 1939, which describes a dinner tendered by the Commander of the Fourth Military Region, Don Luis Orgaz, to "Italian Chiefs and officers attached to our Army and destined to be assigned to the Fourth Military Region." An observer in learning that there are Italian military officers attached to the Fourth Military Region is tempted to speculate whether or not this is not also the case for the other military commands in Spain. The substance of the above information was telegraphed to the American Embassy at San Sebastian on August 17, 1939.

With references to the international situation as seen locally, it is believed here by practically all well informed circles that in the event of a European explosion Spain would not enter the conflict unless she was actually attacked. For example, the mayor of Barcelona in a recent conversation with a foreign visitor expressed the opinion that in the event of a European war, Spain would remain neutral unless "certain countries made the mistake of attacking Menorca, Mallorca or Ceuta." There is a feeling in some local circles that this is probably just what an allied fleet would do in order to forestall a similar move on the part of the Axis powers. Others feel that even more drastic action would be taken, particularly from France, and that in the event of an outbreak of European war, France and Great Britain would deliver an ultimatum to Spain to the effect that she must either declare herself for the allies or take the consequences. It is thought locally that in such an event Spain might well refuse to make any commitments whereupon it is thought at least possible that France and Great Britain, and particularly France, might make an immediate attempt to invade Spanish territory. While it is difficult to assess the reliability or basis for these speculations, such preoccupations may serve to explain in some part the efforts which appear to have been made to construct defensive fortifications in the principal passes leading to Spain from the Pyrenees.

Respectfully yours,
Howard Bucknell, Jr.
American Consul General

No. 147   Barcelona, September 8, 1939

Subject: Local Political Situation

Sir:

As has been frequently reported to the Department, local opposition to the present Government in Spain, while at present completely under cover, still undoubtedly exists. As evidence of this, and of possible interest to the Department, I have the honor to enclose a translation of an unsigned communication received by the Consulate General on September 3, 1939. This letter is self-explanatory and requires no particular comment.

Respectfully yours,
Howard Bucknell, Jr.
American Consul General

Translation of an unsigned letter

September 2, 1939

British Consul, French
Consul, American Consul,
Barcelona

Gentlemen:

We request you to be good enough to transmit through diplomatic channels to the Ministries of Foreign Affairs of your respective countries the information we give below, which is of paramount importance to every country in the world.

The French Government is earnestly advised to take note that great preparations are being made at present in Spain to attack France at the Pyrenees. All the plans for invasion of Southern France are being looked after by Italy in accord with her servant, the traitor Franco. Every day greater quantities of war material is being accumulated at the frontier with France, and entire divisions of Italians, Moors and Spaniards are stationed there to await the proper time to attack France from the rear without notice, as is customarily done by the international fascism. At the moment this is being written, trucks are passing through Barcelona carrying war materials for the Pyrenees, disguised with tree branches.

The very small stocks of eatables we have in Spain are being shipped to Italy to be distributed with Germany. In this fight of treason, as always, Franco will assume the part of the neutral party so as to use the port of Barcelona mainly for the reception of the goods purchased in foreign countries by the totalitarian countries.

The cotton discharged here a week ago by the *SS Nishmaha* is all on the way to Italy/Germany, and as an excuse for not having been assigned any part of the cotton received, textile manufacturers have been told that the cotton had caught fire.

United States. The Consulate of the United States should immediately inform its Government that the purchases of cotton, about which there has been so much talk here, are a sham; that the real purchasers are Germany and Italy, as those countries want to make Spain serve as transshipment port for all their purchases from the United States and Argentina until France is attacked.

Civil Population. Here in Spain the civil population is starving to death. We are denied work, particularly in Catalonia, because 99% of the population is friendly to France, England and the United States and we hate fascism because it is antihuman. During the Italo-German war of invasion we have done everything we could in defense of European peace, but the democratic countries have been so shortsighted that they abandoned us in the midst of the fight and we now find ourselves in the dilemma of either starving to death or being violently exterminated, inasmuch as the number of republicans and democrats being killed by firing squads averages thirty daily. Arrests made are frightfully numerous, and it even seems impossible that the democratic countries should not have taken a hand in the matter to put an end to so tragic a situation.

Notice to France. We are perfectly informed of what is being planned against France, as we fill posts in the Government, and our remorse for the great treason perpetrated by Franco against Spaniards and for the crime we have committed in delivering Spain to the voracity and dirty play of international fascism, prompts us to write these lines to inform France so that she is not caught unawares.

Conclusion. In view of the foregoing, we suggest that you please inform your respective countries of the outrages Italy is preparing against Spain and Gibraltar. We are of the opinion that France, in accord with the countries of the Front of Peace, should suddenly attack Spain invading the country without declaring war, following fascist procedure. The trouble with democratic countries is that they act with too much fairness and this is the reason why fascism has grown so much. To commit its crimes fascism does not consult with anybody except the few pigs forming the government of those countries, as in Spain, where we have a government set up because it furthers the interests of Italy and Germany.

Final Notice. If France waits for things to happen she will have to fight at a disadvantage. If she attacks now she will throw Italy's plans out of kilter and will be able to fight with the certainty of success, as the whole people expects it.

BIBLIOGRAPHIC ESSAY

THE PURPOSE of the following pages is to suggest additional sources of material for the study of Barcelona during the Civil War, sources not already reviewed in the footnotes of this book. An appreciation of what other collections and publications exist will make the continued research on Barcelona's history and that of other urban centers in Spain more attractive. If there is one general comment to make, it is that an enormous amount of material is available on Barcelona and the Catalans. Proud of their past, sharing with other Iberians an inward-looking national trait that documents its efforts extensively, the Catalans have amassed large files on their history. Always noted for being a legalistically minded people, each agency of their governments and many organizations have always felt the need to record in considerable detail their various policies and actions.

Some documentary collections are worth noting for the period of the Civil War. The Biblioteca Central in Barcelona has a large collection of journals which are described in its *Guía* (Barcelona, 1959). The private collection of Josep María Figueras Bassols is now the nucleus of the Centre d'Estudis d'Història Contemporània. Well over one thousand titles for newspapers and correspondence, many dealing with the 1930s, can be found in this collection with primary emphasis on social and political history. The city's own historical society, Instituto Municipal de Historia, has thousands of items. Particularly useful for our period are its newspaper collection and over three thousand photographs on the Civil War. Propaganda posters and fliers constitute another one of its strengths. For details on this particular organization's holdings see its "Catálogo," in *Cuadernos de Historia Económica de Cataluña*, 11 (Barcelona, 1974). Socialist activities in Barcelona may be studied by examining the private papers of a rapidly expanding collection housed at the Fundación Pablo Iglesias, located in Madrid. An initial starting point for this collection is its *Cien años de socialismo en España (Bibliografía)* (Madrid, 1979). In addition, the library belonging to the Benedictine Abbey of Montserrat, outside of Barcelona, has one of the world's greatest collections of printed materials on the Spanish Civil War with particular emphasis on Catalan affairs and those of the city of Barcelona.

In other parts of Spain, additional archival holdings pertain to the Catalans. The Archivo General Militar in Segovia is a major repository of military records. This is not to be confused with the Servicio Histórico Militar and its Biblioteca Central Militar, located in Madrid and which has over the past fifteen years published numerous monographs on the military phase of the Civil War. This second institution has original documents, various transcriptions, plans, maps, other remains of the conflict, all dealing with Catalonia in part. The Servicio's Sección de Estudios Históricos has the mission to organize all the files dealing with both Republican and Nationalist armies, publications, reports, etc., and in this effort has acquired a major military archive on modern warfare. Its files on the Republican army, called the Documentación Roja, allow an historian to document recruiting and housing of troops in Barcelona itself.

Before leaving Spanish sources altogether, several others should be mentioned. Many of the municipal files of Barcelona for the period of the Civil War were not destroyed in the final weeks before the Nationalists overran Catalonia. These are increasingly being made available for historical research. The same applies to the records of the province of Barcelona, also headquartered in the city. A major new collection has recently come into the city from Geneva. The *Fondation Internationale d'Etudes Historiques et Sociales sur la Guerre Civile d'Espagne de 1936–1939*, known more commonly as FIEHS, moved to Barcelona in 1972 its growing collection of documents on the conflict along with its printed holdings. The research center was originally at Perpignan and now too is in Barcelona. In the years to come, this foundation will represent a major source of primary material on Barcelona, Catalonia, and the Civil War in general.

There are some sources on Barcelona outside of Spain that are helpful. Brandeis University Library in Waltham, Massachusetts, has a growing collection on the Civil War including a large number of items dealing with the POUM. Brandeis also has an impressive collection of posters and pamphlets commonly circulating in Barcelona at the time. A similar collection is now housed at the Bancroft Library at the University of California at Berkeley. While many libraries at universities within the United States have strong printed collections, manuscript holdings relating to Barcelona are as yet limited. Of some use, however, are the private papers of Claude Bowers, the U.S. envoy to Republican Spain, which have materials on the last several months of the Civil War, now at the Lilly Library at Indiana University at Bloomington. The Labadie Collection at the Michigan State University Library on anarchism and the Trotskyists has over forty thousand books, pamphlets, manuscripts, and posters covering the affairs of the FAI, CNT, POUM and other groups critical to the life of Barcelona during the first half of the Civil War.

As mentioned in the introduction to this book, the archives of the U.S. Department of State, housed in the National Archives in Washington, D.C., can be significant for the study of any major urban center in Spain. The papers presented in this book are reflective of the kind of consular material available. Embassy files also prove important sources for Barcelona. These records are exceptionally voluminous for the twentieth century, although those for the nineteenth century are stronger in regard to economic matters (ships calling at port, sale of cotton, etc.). Nearby at the Library of Congress are two collections that have considerable amounts of material on Barcelona. These are telegrams sent by the RCA Radiogram Communications and the Agence Espagne Informations Télégraphiques et Téléphoniques de Dernière Heure for the period May 1937–January 1939. These cover all aspects of life in Barcelona but with obvious concentration on war activities (decrees, bombings, invasions) and politics (Generalidad, Republic in Barcelona).

There are several other manuscript collections, these located in Europe, that should not be overlooked. The first two are diplomatic. The consular files for Barcelona housed in the Public Records Office in London, as part of the country file on Spain within the Foreign Office papers, offer the same kind of material as can be seen in the American collections. The quantity is also about the same. The French equivalents are less voluminous yet offer more interpretive analysis of events. The latter are housed in the archives of the Ministère des Affaires Étrangères in Paris. Since the Soviet consulate in Barcelona was a major focal point for many Russian activities in Spain, especially with regard to the politics of the Spanish Communist Party, the archives of that particular consular post would be extremely useful if they are ever made available to the historian. That does not appear to be as remote a possibility as it would at first seem because the Soviets have continued to show considerable interest in the Spanish Civil War by publishing useful monographs over the years based in part on primary materials found only within the USSR. As we approach the fiftieth anniversary of the Spanish Civil War, we might expect more such material. One other collection worth mentioning for Barcelona is that of the International Institute for Social History in Amsterdam. Its files on leftist groups are major, and that portion dealing with the Civil War includes manuscripts, letters, other documents, photographs, and various publications with particular strength in anarchism. Cipriano Mera, an active politico of the Republican side, is amply represented here with his personal papers. The Institute has also published a guide to its holdings, *Alfabetische Catalogus van de Boeken en Brochures van het Internationaal Instituut vor Sociale Geschiedenis, Amsterdam*, 12 vols. (Boston, 1970).

By now the list of published works on the Civil War is rapidly approaching twenty thousand titles. A survey of those dealing with Barcelona would in itself be a book-length manuscript. The situation is complicated by the fact that today there is an explosion of publications on all aspects of the Civil War. Therefore, a review of bibliographic material seems useful for those who would want to do additional research on Barcelona or on other Spanish cities. Fortunately some bibliographic aids exist. One guide covering a broad spectrum of material is the Instituto Nacional del Libro Español, *Catálogo general de la librería española, 1931–1950*, 4 vols. (Madrid, 1957–1965). To keep up with current publications appearing in Spain the most useful tool is *El libro español*, published monthly by the same organization since 1958; their *Libros español* are also useful. Two other current publications to consult would be the *Bulletin* of the Society for Spanish and Portuguese Historical Studies published in the United States. The second is the *Historical Abstracts, Part B: Twentieth-Century Abstracts 1914–* (Santa Barbara, 1971–).

There are a number of specific bibliographic aids on the Civil War as well. Ubaldo Bardi, *La Guerra civile in Spagna: saggio per una bibliografia italiana* (Urbino, 1974) covers all aspects of the subject with primary emphasis on contemporary publications; Ricardo de la Cierva y de Hoces' *Bibliografía general sobre la Guerra de España (1936–1939) y sus antecedentes históricos* (Madrid, 1968) is a massive collection of primary and published items by topic; it is cross-referenced. Another useful work is the series published by the Universidad de Madrid, *Cuadernos bibliográficos de la guerra de España, 1936–1939*, 6 vols. and never completed (Madrid, 1966–1969) covering serials, pamphlets, accounts by eyewitnesses and other memoirs. An older work, still useful, is by Juan García Durán, *Bibliography of the Spanish Civil War, 1936–1939* (Montevideo, 1964), which lists over 6,000 titles and is organized by subject matter. Also a major source for those interested in modern Spain is Fernando Gonzalez Olle, *Manual bibliográfico de estudios españoles*, prepared for the Universidad de Navarra (Pamplona, 1976). This massive guide (1,377 pages) provides material on each Catalan province and on Barcelona, along with discussions on archives. For a number of years there was published in Spain a guide to recent publications world-wide on Spain, with material broken down by period and area, called the *Indice histórico español*, 22 vols. (Barcelona, 1953–1976). Published four times a year in the format of a scholarly journal, it provides brief summaries of each entry and thus is one of the best sources for bibliographic material published during the years it appeared.

One final research tool should be mentioned in Barcelona: the one published by the Dirección General de Archivos y Bibliotecas, an agency of the Spanish government, *Los archivos de Barcelona* (Madrid, 1952), detailing somewhat holdings of various organizations on Barcelona during the Civil War. Peter T. Johnson, of the Princeton University Library, has prepared two broader surveys of materials on the Spanish Civil War, "A Select Compendium of Archives and Libraries on the Spanish Civil War," and "A Select Bibliography of Bibliographies on the Spanish Civil War," both in James W. Cortada, *An Historical Dictionary of the Spanish Civil War, 1936–1939* (Westport, Conn., 1982).

INDEX